TRANS(per)FORMING Nina Arsenault:
An Unreasonable Body of Work

TRANS(per)FORMING Nina Arsenault:
An Unreasonable Body of Work

Edited by Judith Rudakoff

intellect Bristol, UK / Chicago, USA

First published in the UK in 2012 by
Intellect, The Mill, Parnall Road, Fishponds, Bristol, BS16 3JG, UK

First published in the USA in 2012 by
Intellect, The University of Chicago Press, 1427 E. 60th Street,
Chicago, IL 60637, USA

A catalogue record for this book is available from the
British Library.

Cover designer: Holly Rose
Production manager: Jelena Stanovnik
Copy-editor: MPS Technologies
Typesetting: Planman Technologies
Front cover photo: Tony Fong
Back cover photo of Nina Arsenault: inkedKenny
Back cover photo of Judith Rudakoff: Christopher Gentile

Editor: Judith Rudakoff
Associate Editor: J. Paul Halferty
Editorial Assistant: Carina Gaspar

ISBN 978-1-84150-571-8

Printed and bound by Latimer Trend, UK.

Table of Contents

Acknowledgements

This book was made possible by the enthusiastic participation and support of Nina Arsenault. Associate Editor J. Paul Halferty offered perspective and insight and Editorial Assistant Carina Gaspar shared a keen eye for detail. I would further like to acknowledge and thank Myles Warren for his constructive comments and encouragement, and Serena Dessen, Brian Fawcett, and Hilary Sherman for their input. York University's Theatre Department Administrative Assistant Mary Pecchia and Undergraduate Program Assistant Rachel Katz provided administrative support with good humour and kindness.

I thank York University's Faculty of Graduate Studies and the Graduate Program in Theatre Studies for funding my graduate assistant, and the Social Sciences and Humanities Research Council for contributing to the project through their Small Grant program.

Introduction

Judith Rudakoff

After sixty surgeries at a cost of almost $200,000 to feminize and beautify her originally male body[1] (see Figure 22), transgendered Canadian artist Nina Arsenault has created a body of work emanating from her experiences that includes photographs, videos disseminated online, a website, a blog, several social networking presentation sites, stage plays, print media writing, and performance of the body in both celebrity appearances and daily public life.[2]

Arsenault was born in rural Ontario in 1974 and until the age of six lived as Rodney (see Figure 27) in a trailer park with her working-class family. Her father delivered bread for a large company, and her mother was a homemaker. In 1980, when her father's income increased, the family moved to a house. In high school, Arsenault came out to close friends as a gay man, and then declared her sexual orientation publicly on the first day of university at a freshman event.

All in all, Arsenault experienced a comfortable, *reasonable* beginning. But throughout her early years, Arsenault was also developing a need to externally manifest an internal yearning to express her feminine self and do so *unreasonably* by embodying extreme and even unreal representations of Western beauty.[3] By rejecting the binary of real versus fake and dedicating herself to exploring authenticity and beauty, Arsenault today continues to evolve in a process that began in childhood with an awareness of her transsexuality, continued in adulthood with surgical steps[4] towards Male-to-Female transition[5] and beautification, and now anticipates new challenges in midlife and beyond that will include physical and psychological responses to biological aging as well as unknown effects from the un-encased silicone that has been directly injected into the muscle tissue of her body.

Arsenault *is* her body of work. Whether in conventional performance situations—one of the aspects of Arsenault's practice that distinguishes her from many other transsexual performers is her commitment to telling her own stories[6]—or on view buying a coffee at the local corner store, she represents and interrogates the relationship between the female self and the constructed feminine body, as critics and scholars from a diversity of disciplines, spectators, fans, and curious bystanders observe and engage.[7]

Only some of Arsenault's surgeries were essential to her transition.[8] The rest were cosmetic procedures that addressed her yearning to be beautiful (see Figures 11 top and bottom, 19, and 25 top and bottom).

Arsenault's embodiment of the feminine form exceeds and defies heteronormative expectation while simultaneously emulating aspects of white, Western culture's most popular beauty models (see Figure 28). Arsenault's relationship to these icons is on the level of form: she embraces their aesthetics and representations of femininity and beauty, rather than enacting the role or persona of each physical model.

Arsenault asserts, "my work explores culturally constructed ideas of maleness and femaleness as well as notions of 'realness' and 'fakeness.' I see myself exploring femininity as an artistic form, a body that can be inhabited and performed. And most of all, I explore my body as an object, an art object."[9]

In her work, Arsenault confronts unanswerable questions emanating from the fake versus real conundrum. What is the relationship between a source that is true to nature and a heightened or modified representation of it? If a subject is real but modified, is the subject then fake? If a subject is unreal, is an accurate photographic image of it real? Does interpretation affect the authenticity of an image? How does interpretation differ from manipulation and artifice?

The only possible answer to all of these questions: Arsenault's enactment and interpretation of femaleness and femininity are simultaneously real *and* fake.

While Arsenault's surgically altered body represents an impressive feminine form (see Figure 17), and she has chosen to undergo an orchiectomy (surgical castration),[10] she has eschewed full gender reassignment surgery: she retains her penis (see Figures 16 and 30). This choice is, perhaps more than anything else, an embodiment of the subversive aesthetic she has adopted[11] and is part of her daily performance of an unorthodox, individualized concept of the feminine. Despite her current commitment to keeping her penis, she continues to examine the ramifications of this decision:

So much life force from inside me seems to come from my genitals. So much sensation. Sensation that is distinctly in male shape. This fucks up my ability to be in the moment but also feels like an enlivening force within me. Do I need to learn to accept my male genitals? To be comfortable with them?

I don't know if I should look to escape the sensation of being male to lose more inner life (how much more?) or risk it all? To be a doll? Would I objectify myself into an automaton? Would I be happier like that? Is that what I really want?[12]

Arsenault's radical choices go far beyond the decision to retain her penis. She has sculpted and altered her form to a degree that it has become a hyperfeminized interpretation of a human body (see Figure 12). In her photographic collaborations as well as in the multitudes of quasi-candid images of her—she is always aware of the lens—that populate social media sites such as Facebook, she is adept at posing and positioning her body to emphasize its proportions (see Figures 1 and 12).

Arsenault frankly evaluates her body modifications, "there's an avantgarde aesthetic to my body, because I have a body that's not like most."[13] She grapples daily with the reality of being part flesh and blood, part silicone and synthetic implants, and with viewers' reactions to and readings of her unnatural body:

[M]y body is not a human body, an animal body, anymore but a bunch of visual symbols, cues, like I'm a walking series of semiotics. I'm an image of a woman, a reflection of one in a Hall of Mirrors.

My body is part assemblage, part masquerade.[14]

As Arsenault delves further into performing the body and exploring the self as art object, investigation of the differences between her biological and manufactured body parts necessarily inform her ongoing acting and voice study.[15]

The deeper I go into my work I realize more profoundly how artificial I am. My body— not the external image of me, but my body—the sensations I feel, the sensations I am in dialogue with tell me with each breath what is human tissue and what is absent within me. I can feel it all the time. I feel these nothing spaces within me where I have no sensation.[16]

Arsenault continues to quest for beauty that pays homage but refuses to conform to conventional parameters. Choosing not to privilege natural beauty and instead to pursue what she describes as a "plastic, fake aesthetic" was a carefully considered decision:[17]

I wanted to find a self that I could live with, and I realized that I was going to have to do that in a way that was unusual … I found it so painful to look in the mirror before transitioning, and see male features, that I started to explore cosmetic surgery. That started my journey to alter my body and to try to erase the maleness in it. But in doing that I didn't create a female body, because in a way that's quite impossible. All I'm able to do is use the technological and medical tools that are available and as a result, I have a body that I would consider a cyborg body. It's a technologically enhanced cyborg body.[18]

Designing and constructing her body according to personal aesthetic—while acknowledging the influences of patriarchal culture on her notions of gender and femininity—has given Arsenault a degree of control over her image, but has also dissociated her inner self from her physical self.[19] Arguably, she has always experienced that schism:

In a certain way my being trans dissociated me from my body. Most people feel they *are* their bodies. But I never felt that, so in a way, even before transitioning, I was already objectifying myself because I thought of my body as the form that housed my spirit. I knew that the vessel itself was different from the core me.[20]

Her female identity—dissociated from the originally inaccurate form housing it—gradually became the external eye, relating to her body as a sculptor would to a work-in- progress. This split perspective on and relationship to the self has also informed the practice Arsenault calls "self-portraiture,"[21] a term that she applies—in an unconventional interpretation—to *all* her work, from photographic images that are sometimes autogenerated and on other occasions artistic collaborations with photographers, to video and theatre performances, to performing the self in daily life.[22]

Is Arsenault's quest to locate, develop, and perform a beautiful, feminine, self relevant to people outside her circle of experience? Taken as a metaphor for proclaiming identity, decidedly so. But on a level of simple, human need, Arsenault, for all her hyperbolic manifestations and the extremity of her life experience, also shares much with the public at large: humans need to locate home, whatever form or shape that personal anchor takes. Arsenault's search for home has led her to renovate a body to house her inner self.

Arsenault's body of work offers a strong advocacy message in its questioning of identity. Without overt political framing, her work, on stage and in performance of the self in daily life, underscores the need to identify voice, then enable and express it. Arsenault first acknowledged this aspect of her developing artistic mandate when she was a graduate student studying theatre at the University of Cape Town, South Africa, in July 1997. She explains:

> The most important thing that influenced me [in South Africa] was seeing a performance of storytelling. Someone that night (one of my university teachers) called it political autobiography. There was so much oppression there, that for a person of colour, a woman, a very poor woman, who had no voice in culture, for her to get up on a stage and tell her story … just that simple act meant that tonight she would be listened to. She would be heard.
>
> Tonight she would be important.
>
> I remember listening to her telling the story of how she had to wash an older, rich, white woman's body every day.
>
> She told this story in a simple, direct way to the audience. This storyteller was not a trained artist or an actor. She was a woman who was talking.
>
> I remember a timbre in her voice that spoke to me about hatred, obedience, service and also love.
>
> This paradox of emotions was political and not shameful. It was OK to speak of these things in the theatre.
>
> I wasn't interested in politics before this. As a young person and as a Canadian, I thought that politics happened on Capitol Hill [in Ottawa]. Politics seemed so abstracted, so out of my daily life, and at the time I understood feminism as this thing that women used to reassert their victimhood, or as something that was meant to brazenly assert women's power. I had never been confronted with any kind of feminism that acknowledged paradox.[23]

Arsenault's studies in South Africa[24] also coincided with the televising of the post-apartheid Truth and Reconciliation Committee hearings.[25] This public confessional process was meant to empower victims and attempt to reconcile them with their oppressors through direct contact, confrontation, and admission of guilt, and detailing of atrocities. In addition to the extraordinary impact felt by all who witnessed these proceedings, for Arsenault there was an unexpected ancillary effect.[26] Aspects of the hearings' presentational style—direct address, detailed descriptions, unflinching candidness—strongly influenced the style of her emerging performance practice and theatre writing.[27]

Arsenault's investigations of identity and empowerment are accessible and affective. Her subversive aesthetic, in theory and in practice, informs her artistic enactment and daily embodiment of authenticity and artifice, real *and* fake.

Anthologizing Difference

TRANS(per)FORMING Nina Arsenault is a collection of responses to one particular cultural object. The topics, themes, and ideas that the authors and photographers address, through their engagement with Arsenault as subject, object, and creative force speak to a broad range of issues. These issues are relevant to the practical and theoretical approaches to disciplines and perspectives that include but are not exclusive to Feminist Philosophy, Women and Gender Studies, Sexuality and Queer Studies, Theatre and Performance Studies and Practice, Religious Studies, Voice and Acting Studies and Practice, and Celebrity Studies: an *unreasonable* diversity of opinions for and from an *unacceptably* large variety of constituencies.

To reach as broad a spectrum of readers as possible, this anthology includes different forms of text (from theoretical analyses to anecdotal chronicles to performance text) and styles of photography (from stark documentary images to elaborately staged fantasies). This wide variety of forms and styles may challenge some readers, though for others this diversity will be appealing.

In this anthology, the texts are not, as might be expected, grouped by style or theme. Similarly, the photographs are not presented in chronological order. Instead, in consultation with Arsenault, the chapters and images have been ordered to offer contrast as well as complementarity.

Some writers in the collection know Arsenault personally or have worked with her, but others do not and have only recently learned of her work. As of 2011, Arsenault is primarily known in Canada,[28] through her live theatre performances, online presence, appearances on national television, and writing for national print media.[29]

This is the first book about Nina Arsenault. As such, one of its goals is to introduce her body of work to a multidisciplinary audience without any single preconception: without the limitation that can result from positioning an artist in a lineage of similarity. *TRANS(per)FORMING Nina Arsenault* therefore employs, in almost all of the chapters, a framework of exceptionalism, largely resisting the filter of comparative case studies, contextualizing figures, or shared practices as the basis for analysis. Future studies of Arsenault's body of work may choose to adopt other approaches.[30]

Further, while this anthology could be read as a type of tribute to Arsenault. given that she is the volume's sole focus, it offers greater value. The writing and images provide a cross disciplinary set of investigative and critical approaches to and documentation of Arsenault's body of work.

In this collection, you will find:

Veteran writer, director, and self-proclaimed drag queen extraordinaire Sky Gilbert reflects on his own experience of writing a monodrama for Arsenault to perform, titled *Ladylike*, as well as engages in a discussion of the politics of sex, sexuality, and gender in the here and now, and looking forward to the near future. With customary iconoclastic style, positioning Arsenault as his primary example, Gilbert contends that queers must embrace a potentially liberating artifice and cyborg hybridity.

Associate editor, theatre and performance scholar J. Paul Halferty analyzes Arsenault's unorthodox interpretation of "self-portraits," which atypically include body modifications, theatre writing and performance, as well as collaborations with photographers.

Acting teacher, performer, and scholar Cynthia Ashperger applies the Michael Chekhov Acting Technique to invoke the concept of the "Imaginary Body" to investigate Arsenault's "acting" and the identities that attend these performances both onstage and offstage.

Referencing a lengthy conversation with Arsenault, writer, club manager, producer of pornographic films, and former colleague in the sex trade Todd Klinck chronicles and analyzes her development as a transsexual woman working in various capacities within the sex trade, documenting the very real nature of her various sexual personae and their gradual evolution as facets of her personality. Further, he explores Arsenault's interaction with people as she enacted and embodied these facets/characters, designating this complex, lengthy process as the "evolution of a commodified sexual being."

Feminist social and political philosopher Frances J. Latchford locates Arsenault's body and her theatrical "body-works" in *The Silicone Diaries*, as a new response to the debate about the differences of queer versus transsexual subjects, particularly as this difference relates to embodiment and is discussed by queer and trans theorists such as Susan Stryker, Judith Butler, Jay Prosser, and Patricia Eliot.

Citing Arsenault's body modifications, and particularly her decision to not undertake full gender reassignment surgery, American black/trans/queer poet and educator J Mase III explores the transsexual conundrum of surgical and hormonal intervention as tools in transitioning and living.

Political and performance philosopher Shannon Bell suggests that Arsenault constitutes Jacques Lacan's ambiguous *object a*, a "given-to-be-seen," or, as Bell characterizes it, "a subject held in the gaze of the world."[31] Bell further situates Arsenault within her own empowering theory of "fast feminism,"[32] which she defines in her chapter as "fast because philosophy, pornography and politics mesh in action, feminist because action is grounded in female power."

Playwright, theatre and opera director, and journalist Alistair Newton briefly invokes the life and work of French "carnal artist" ORLAN and focuses on Susan Sontag's *Fascinating*

Fascism to investigate the moral implications of Arsenault's surgeries as integral components of her art practice. He suggests that the queerness of Arsenault's body allows her to negotiate a space between fascism and individualized liberation.

Arsenault contributes a creative response to the experience of traveling to the Yukon Territory, in Canada's far north, and performing her autobiographical stage plays there. This poetic rumination explores her understanding of herself as a woman, and her particular embodiment of femininity. Further, it examines the points at which her self-image intersects with or challenges the opinions of others, especially of those who embrace a more conventional reading of "woman."

Emerging performance scholar Benjamin Gillespie employs Jean Baudrillard's theory of the hyperreal, suggesting that Arsenault's acts of "dissimulation," in her feminine embodiment and in her stage plays, expose reality as simulacra.

Voice teacher, dialect designer and vocal coach for film, television and theatre Eric Armstrong investigates the largely uncharted landscape of Arsenault's voice. In doing so, he interrogates the concepts of "authentic" and "inauthentic" in voice training, and in the lives of Male-to-Female transsexuals.

In a series of thematically linked statements, eminent Israeli biblical scholar, dramaturg and translator Shimon Levy offers a personal response to Arsenault and *The Silicone Diaries*, riffing on how she and the play resonate with various religious texts, in particular several from the Old Testament.

Theatre practitioner and theorist David Fancy applies the theories of Gilles Deleuze and Felix Guattari to explore how Arsenault's life, onstage and offstage, can itself be understood as a work of art that challenges expectations around gender, performance, and identity. At the core of his argument is the idea that Arsenault's explorations and commitments lead her to verge on becoming a cosmic or mythological figure, a veritable secular saint.

The Silicone Diaries, Arsenault's autobiographical *tour de force* stage play, is published in its entirety in this volume. By way of introduction, Buddies in Bad Times Theatre's artistic director Brendan Healy, director of the premiere production, contributes a contextualizing note. The inclusion of *The Silicone Diaries* offers readers the opportunity to familiarize themselves with Arsenault's work and contextualize the many quotations that form a part of the scholarly texts in the anthology.

The thirty-five photographs that I have selected for inclusion (by seventeen photographers, including Arsenault and her father) are from different periods of Arsenault's life. Some images illustrate how real she is while others highlight how fake she is. Still others portray her as both real *and* fake. All are authentic.

Beyond reasonable in her aspiration to unnatural beauty, beyond acceptable in her choice to hyperfeminize yet resist full gender reassignment surgery, Arsenault's ongoing quest to re-make her body and assert her female self is explored in *TRANS(per)FORMING Nina Arsenault*. Through texts and images that are distinct and diverse in perspective, experience, form, and origin, this anthology aims to chart a course through Arsenault's *terra incognita*.

Dramaturg **Judith Rudakoff** has worked with emerging and established playwrights and artists throughout Canada and in Cuba, Denmark, South Africa, England, and the United States. She is the creator of "The Four Elements" and "Lomograms," transcultural dramaturgy methods for initiating live performance and visual art. Her work as dramaturg for *The Silicone Diaries* and "I W@s B*rbie" continues her long association with Nina Arsenault.

Her books include *Between the Lines: The Process of Dramaturgy* (2002) with co-editor Lynn M. Thomson; *Fair Play: Conversations with Canadian Women Playwrights* (1989) with co-editor Rita Much; and *Questionable Activities: Canadian Theatre Artists in Conversation with Canadian Theatre Students* (2000). Her articles on theatre and performance have appeared in *The Drama Review, TheatreForum*, and *Canadian Theatre Review*.

As leader of the *Common Plants: Cross Pollinations in Hybrid Reality* project (www.yorku.ca/gardens), Rudakoff initiated and facilitated a multidisciplinary transcultural web-based creative project funded by Canada's Social Sciences and Humanities Research Council involving professional artists, students, and community members from diverse cultural and geographical backgrounds, including Nunavut, South Africa, and India.

Her most recent play is *The River*, co-written with David Skelton and Joseph Tisiga, which premiered at Nakai Theatre in Whitehorse, Yukon Territory, in April 2011.

She is the recipient of several teaching awards including the inaugural Dean's Prize for Teaching Excellence (Faculty of Fine Arts) and the University-Wide Teaching Prize at York University, where she is a full professor of theatre, and three consecutive *NOW* magazine "Best of Toronto" awards. She was the first Canadian honoured with the Elliott Hayes Prize in Dramaturgy for her playwriting and dramaturgical work on the South Asian choreographer Lata Pada's multidisciplinary work, *Revealed by Fire*.[33]

Rudakoff is a member of the Playwrights Guild of Canada, and the Literary Managers and Dramaturgs of the Americas.

Bibliography

Arsenault, Nina. "Metaphysical Object." Speech given at ideaCity 10, Toronto, ON, June 16, 2010. http://www.ideacityonline.com/presenters/nina-arsenault.

Arsenault, Nina. *The Silicone Diaries*. In *TRANS(per)FORMING Nina Arsenault*, edited by Judith Rudakoff, 191–227. Bristol: Intellect Press, 2012.

Bell, Shannon. *Fast Feminism*. New York: Autonomedia, 2010.

Rudakoff, Judith. "Faux Arts or Beaux Arts: Nina Arsenault and the Possibilities of the New." "I W@s B*rbie," Toronto, ON, June 9–13, 2010. Playbill.

———. Untitled dramaturg's note. *The Silicone Diaries*, Toronto, ON, November 14–21, 2009. Playbill.

Notes

1. Judith Rudakoff, untitled dramaturg's note, *The Silicone Diaries*, Toronto, ON, November 14–21, 2009, Playbill.

2. For a multitude of links, articles, and online video work about and by Arsenault, see Nina Arsenault's official website, accessed June 1, 2011, www.ninaarsenault.com; Nina Arsenault's Facebook page, accessed June 1, 2011, http://www.facebook.com/nina.arsenault; Nina Arsenault's YouTube channel, accessed June 1, 2011, http://www.youtube.com/user/ninaarsenault.

3. Department store mannequins, nude centrefold models in so-called girlie magazines, for example. See Nina Arsenault, *The Silicone Diaries*, in *TRANS(per)FORMING Nina Arsenault*, ed. Judith Rudakoff (Bristol: Intellect Press, 2012), 206–207.

4. Arsenault temporarily left theatre and artistic pursuits when she started her surgical transformation. Practically, there was no time for creative work for eight years, as she was fully engaged in sex work to fund and then undertake the surgeries. In 2005, after most of her procedures were done (all were complete, except for her second breast augmentation), she returned to artistic practice, beginning with writing her autobiographical *T-Girl* column in *fab Magazine*. See Arsenault, e-mail, August 18, 2011.

5. Prior to starting a Master of Fine Arts (Theatre) at York University in Toronto, Canada in 1998, Arsenault announced her transsexuality via group e-mail to student peers and the academic community. She graduated in June1999. She had already decided to transition two years before, but waited to return to Canada to announce her choice as she was concerned that her transsexuality might complicate her studies in South Africa, where she undertook and completed an Honours Graduate degree in Theatre at University of Cape Town (December 1996 to January 1998). Nina Arsenault, e-mail to author, August 18, 2011.

6. Unlike some other transsexual performance artists, such as Americans Amanda Lepore and Allanah Starr, Arsenault maintains control over *all* aspects of her art. Further, Arsenault differs from American Kate Bornstein, who performs and presents stories of the self from the strong and focused perspective of gender politics: Arsenault's work emanates from and explores aesthetics and forms of feminine beauty, specifically as they relate to her own life.

7. I first came into contact with Rodney Arsenault in 1992, when I was his freshman year faculty advisor in the Bachelor of Fine Arts (Theatre) program at York University in Toronto, Canada. Arsenault also studied playwriting with me during this degree, which was completed in 1996. Between 1998 and 1999, as she was beginning her transition, I was Arsenault's thesis advisor and professor in the MFA (Theatre) at York University. When Arsenault returned to writing for the stage with her autobiographical play, *The Silicone Diaries*, she invited me to work with her professionally as dramaturg. I also worked with her as dramaturg for her play "I W@s B*rbie."

8. Arsenault's first surgeries were undertaken on January 3, 1998, in Cape Town, South Africa. She altered her nose, ears, and chin to feminize these features. Nina Arsenault, e-mail message to author, February 25, 2011.

9. Nina Arsenault, "Metaphysical Object" (speech given at ideaCity 10, Toronto, ON, June 16, 2010), http://www.ideacityonline.com/presenters/nina-arsenault.

10. Without testosterone being produced in the body, Arsenault does not have to take pharmaceutical testosterone blockers. Further, the surgical procedure is more effective in stopping testosterone production. Without testosterone, skin takes on a more feminine appearance and pharmaceutical estrogen works uninhibited. Arsenault still gets an

erection. She does not ejaculate, but feels a physical orgasm sensation. Arsenault, e-mail, August 15, 2011.

11. From a practical perspective, while working in the sex trade, there was a demand for so-called shemales and that helped Arsenault earn money for her many surgical procedures. Nina Arsenault, e-mail message to author, August 15, 2011.

12. Nina Arsenault, e-mail message to author, May 12, 2010.

13. Judith Rudakoff, "Faux Arts or Beaux Arts: Nina Arsenault and the Possibilities of the New", "I W@s B*rbie," Toronto, ON, June 9–13, 2010, Playbill.

14. Ibid.

15. This study depends on establishing, maintaining, and investigating connections and relationships between mind, memory, breath, and body.

16. Arsenault, e-mail, May 12, 2010.

17. Rudakoff, "Faux Arts or Beaux Arts."

18. Ibid.

19. See Todd Klinck's chapter and his exploration of Arsenault's personality facet named "Amber."

20. Rudakoff, "Faux Arts or Beaux Arts."

21. See J. Paul Halferty's chapter for a full discussion and definition of Arsenault's "self-portraiture."

22. With all her work, and when creating her body, Arsenault is undeniably located in and operating from within white, Western, largely patriarchal culture. Even when expressing her perspective on femininity that originates outside these spheres, she applies a filter that privileges art and aesthetics as objects.

23. Nina Arsenault, e-mail message to author, February 22, 2011.

24. She was in South Africa from November 1996 through to July 1998.

25. According to the official website:
"The South African Truth and Reconciliation Commission (TRC) was set up by the Government of National Unity to help deal with what happened under apartheid. The conflict during this period resulted in violence and human rights abuses from all sides. No section of society escaped these abuses.
The TRC was based on the Promotion of National Unity and Reconciliation Act, No 34 of 1995....
The TRC effected its mandate through 3 committees: the Amnesty Committee, Reparation and Rehabilitation (R&R) Committee and Human Rights Violations (HRV) Committee."
For more information and details on the process, see Truth and Reconciliation Commission, accessed June 1, 2011, http://www.justice.gov.za/trc/.

26. The extraordinary impact and intended goals of this set of hearings, as well as similarly configured processes in Canada and elsewhere in the world are, of course, of primary importance. What I am describing is a secondary, unanticipated, ancillary, personal effect that experiencing the South African hearings had on Arsenault.

27. This confessional style is evident in *The Silicone Diaries*.

28. Arsenault has difficulty crossing the border between Canada and the United States of America, for example, as she cannot offer Customs officials a traceable employment

record over the past decade. She is often perceived as either a flight risk or categorized as a prostitute and therefore deemed an unsuitable visitor. Nina Arsenault, e-mail message to author, August 17, 2011.

29. Her profile is consistently increasing, with a social media reach that is international (including a Facebook page, which long ago reached the imposed maximum of 5,000 'friends'). During Pride Week 2011 in Toronto, her website crashed repeatedly due to an overabundance of traffic.

30. For example, assessment of Arsenault and her work within the context of race/class discourse. This approach could offer enough material for an entire collection of essays.

31. This and other quotations in this introduction to the individual texts in the anthology, when not cited specifically, originate in the chapter being discussed.

32. Shannon Bell, *Fast Feminism* (New York: Autonomedia, 2010).

PART I

THE TEXTS

Chapter 1

Affirming Identity with Your Friendly Neighbourhood Cyborg

Sky Gilbert

It's over. The heady days of gay liberation that so intoxicated queer people in the late 1960s and early 1970s are gone. And the seeds of destruction were sown by queer academics themselves. In *The History of Sexuality*, Michel Foucault championed the notion that the homosexual identity was more constructed than real. And (soon after) Judith Butler expressed her ambivalent feelings about identity politics: "I'm permanently troubled by identity categories, consider them to be invariable stumbling-blocks, and understand them, even promote them as sites of necessary trouble."[1]

As the early queer theorists prepared us for a challenge to identity politics, AIDS was devastating the gay community and causing a tidal shift in gay sensibilities. The battles we had waged in the name of our identities, to allow bathhouses to remain open or to "keep the laws off our bodies,"[2] seemed selfish and indulgent in the shadow of AIDS. Conservative queers began coupling and moving to the suburbs. A plethora of gay pundits stepped forward to celebrate the decline of gay: Andrew Sullivan proudly proclaimed the queer potential to be just like everyone else,[3] Michaelangelo Signorile collected an entire book of interviews that confirmed the deurbanization of gay men,[4] and Bert Archer trumpeted "The End of Gay" in his book of the same title.[5] Queer academia provided a theoretical rejection of identity politics in the mid-1990s led by David Tuller, who claimed in *PoMoSexuals*, "sexuality is far more subtle than the rigid categories, the concrete bunkers that we create to describe it."[6] By the year 2000, the discussion of gay and lesbian identity was replaced by an exploration of the wider application of values inspired by same-sex attraction. The editors of *Queer Ecologies: Sex, Nature, Politics, Desire* say in their introduction:

> The essays included in this collection … share this fundamental supposition: scrutinizing and politicizing the intersections between sex and nature not only opens environmentalism to a wider understanding of justice, but also deploys the anti-heteronormative insistences of queer politics to potentially more biophilic ends than has been generally imagined.[7]

The editors of *Queer Ecologies* see their attitude as a harbinger of the future; on the one hand, there is a hope that environmentalism will be open to the contributions from queer culture (which of course implies there is a queer identity); on the other hand, the book wishes to make queer politics biophilic, which means nothing other than understanding how queer radical social notions (promiscuity, for instance) are, in fact, natural. So, however strange or outrageous our actions as queers may seem to some, we are part of an eons old, biological family.

My inclinations lie in a different direction. Not only am I sexually attracted to men, but I identify as effeminate and promiscuous. In addition, I was raised in a culture that trained me to view myself as a highly unnatural outcast. Like so many other queers born before gay liberation, I have learned to love my identity as a lone, effeminate, rebellious male and I cannot easily release myself from this romantic, tragic singularity. Thus, it's difficult for me to publish essays on the subject of gay politics. In 2009, I wrote a newspaper article in which I proclaimed that I was no longer gay, since gay, I proposed, now means being a normal, god-fearing, monogamous good citizen. I identified myself as an ESP (a category I invented for myself): an Effeminate Sexual Person. Ironically, the essay was rejected by the editors of Toronto's lesbian and gay biweekly newspaper *Xtra* because (as they told me in a telephone conversation in December 2009, and I'll paraphrase, "we're not into identity politics"). One of Canada's major national daily newspapers, *The Globe and Mail*, however, was not afraid to publish it.[8]

Not only am I proudly effeminate (and a proud drag queen!) but these days it makes more sense for me to focus on gender rather than sexuality. By writing about gender I am able to explore my queer agenda without dragging out the identity categories. This focus on femininity led me to write a stage play titled *Ladylike* for Nina Arsenault in 2007.

I first met Nina approximately ten years before, as Rodney, then a graduate student at York University, who asked me to have lunch with him. At lunch he inquired if I would be in interested in performing in a play he had written about three drag queens. I told him that I didn't much like acting; we discussed the state of queer theatre and queer politics. He then dropped out of my life.

I'm not sure when I first saw Nina after her transformation. It may very well have been on the Canadian television station OutTV's gay sports comedy show, *Locker Room*, where she played the role of a steroid-raging female bodybuilder. At any rate, I was a big fan. When I was casting my play, *Will the Real J. T. LeRoy Please Stand Up?*, I auditioned Nina for the part of "Tatum O'Neal." (The character was a beautiful, spaced-out female movie star.) Nina's audition was wonderful and though when the play was produced in 2007, I ended up casting Canadian actor Ellen-Ray Hennessy, I couldn't get Nina out of my mind. During the same time period, when I was working out the subject matter for a one-act play to produce in Hamilton, Ontario (where I now live), my partner Ian suggested that I write a play for Nina. At first I was intimidated by the idea. But I talked myself into writing a play for Nina by telling myself that the play would not be about identity, but instead about gender: *Ladylike*.

Ladylike is a one-act monologue with a few short scenes that take place between Nina's character and her boyfriend. The plot of the play is slim; Nina's character tries to explain to an audience (whom she obviously perceives as skeptical) why she has always loved femininity. She also tries to explain the relationship between femininity and masochism. The boyfriend character is not physically abusive, but it's clear that he has the potential for emotional abuse; for example, he takes drugs and occasionally disappears from her life. What Nina's character wishes her boyfriend to understand is that though she loves submitting to him (in and out of bed), she doesn't want, or deserve, to be physically or emotionally abused. In the final moments of the play, Nina's boyfriend seems to understand her arguments, and says that she is a "real woman," and there is a happy ending: they kiss.

When I sent the play to Nina for her consideration, I told her that this was not a play about what it means to be transsexual, but instead about what it means to be born a biological male who loves his femininity. Nina told me that she loved the script and identified with the heroine.

In proposing to work with Nina, I strove to take advantage of what I presumed we had in common. For instance, in Nina's play *The Silicone Diaries* she remembers how, as a child, she looked at naked pictures of women in magazines with the other boys, imagining that someday she would be a sexy lady: "This is exactly what I will be when I grow up."[9] Although I never wanted to be a woman, I, too, was an effeminate little boy and I dreamed of being a ballerina. Nina and I also share a love/hate relationship with masochism. I was inspired to write *Ladylike* partly because I had also seen Nina, on the Canadian Reality TV show *Kink*, struggling with her attraction to her hulking, ubermasculine, tattooed boyfriend (an ex-prison inmate): the type of man who is so wrapped up in his own problems that he has little time or energy to give a woman the attention she deserves. But though drag queens and transsexuals share some inclinations, they are also quite different. Nina lives as a woman (or perhaps more accurately, as an openly transgendered person). I dress up to perform—or occasionally to flirt. Also, I don't share Nina's passion for body modification through plastic surgery.

But although I can't identify with Nina's passion for body modification, it's what I love the most about her. She has chosen to become a highly unnatural-looking caricature of a woman; in fact, she likes to compare herself to the cartoon character Jessica Rabbit. There must have been a moment during Nina's plastic surgery when she looked enough like a woman to pass as one. She also could have had her penis removed. Why did she choose not to take advantage of these opportunities to make her less evidently a transsexual, and more seamlessly a woman? The answer can only be that Nina did not want to be an ordinary "real" woman, but instead to become the extraordinary creature she is. Nina is proud of her outsider status: she is quite open about being a shemale and having been a sex-trade worker. You can't look at Nina without thinking about sex and sexual difference; her transformation was less from man to woman than from man to a heterosexual man's porn star fantasy.

Nina's presentation of herself has huge theoretical implications; those implications are what make her (and her work) controversial. I would argue that Nina's brazen, hypersexual persona is a potent reminder that—postmodern theorizing to the contrary—our propensity for identity politics cannot be easily be dismissed. I certainly understand what might offend feminists about Nina. She has chosen the cosmetic sexist trappings that so many women have rejected as confining. Nina is the most fascist of body fascists: even as a child her fantasies about being a woman were more related to highly sexualized images of artificial-looking women (mannequins and men's magazine fold-outs) than to real women. The fact that Nina is thoroughly conscious of (and articulate about) the political implications of her choices is cold comfort to feminists who see her as someone who has chosen to wrap herself in the media images they feel consciously or unconsciously pressured to emulate.

But Nina's presentation of herself is anachronistic in another sense. She is a living, breathing reminder that identity is not fluid. Her approach to gender is in direct contrast to that of the hugely influential transsexual activist and trans theorist Kate Bornstein. As queer theorists began to reject identity politics in the mid-1990s, Bornstein proposed to abolish gender as an oppressive binary system. The introduction to her gender workbook says, "warning label: this workbook gets into the subject and area of something we can call for lack of a better (or any) term 'no gender.' That's how I see myself: I live pretty much without a gender, which paradoxically means I can do many genders."[10] Bornstein's argument is based on the notion of gender fluidity. Although she transformed herself from a man to a woman, she doesn't see herself as having chosen one over the other, but rather as a person who has shown her capability to do either. This notion of fluidity is shared by the anti-identity queers as well. For instance Bert Archer's decision to pronounce the death of homosexuality in his book *The End of Gay* was precipitated by his personal discovery that he is drawn to sleeping with women as well as men, and thus sees himself on an identity continuum.

In contrast, Nina's decision to become the "Pamela Anderson of Transsexuals" (to coin a phrase) is the opposite of fluid, and extremely identity specific (whether we agree with what we see as the political implications of her choice, or not.). Certainly, Nina's transformation has the possibility to empower us all to change our bodies in any way that we wish. But Nina has chosen a gender of her own creation: an artificial, super-sexual woman. And the very costly changes she has made to her body are not easy to undo.

Trans theorist Pat Califia has noted, "if Bornstein doesn't believe in gender, why has she gone to so much trouble to look like a woman?"[11] Ultimately, it's an improbable leap of logic to suggest that because someone like Nina or Bornstein has proved that anyone can conceivably change their gender through plastic surgery, this necessarily implies that everyone has the inclination (or dedication) to fiddle around with their identity willy-nilly. Similarly, just because some people are bisexual, or have lived as heterosexuals and then come out as gay or lesbian, doesn't mean that sexual identity is fluid. Most people are quite comfortable living with a single gender or sexual identity for most of their lives. What Nina's extraordinary journey suggests is the very opposite of fluidity: that people need to be extraordinarily committed and emotionally attached to their chosen—and very specific—gender identities and sexualities if they wish to go through the gut-wrenching emotional upheavals that are presently part and parcel of changing them.

The early gay liberationists imagined a world without sexual categories. Steven Epstein summarizes Dennis Altman's *Homosexual: Oppression and Liberation*[12] as a representational statement about the early politics of gay male sexual liberation, which "almost looks forward to not only the abolition of sexual categorization but also the elimination of 'masculinity' and 'femininity' along with the creation of a 'new human' for whom such distinctions would simply be irrelevant."[13] The paradox was that these early queer pioneers were using their queer identification in order to create a universe in which identities did not matter. But this early liberationist fantasy, along with the present day rejection of identity politics (and Bornstein's genderless vision of the world), are deeply flawed and wildly impractical. Those who would have us live in a genderless/identity free world are forgetting that humans seem—if not hardwired to identify as something—then at least in possession of an overpowering tendency to imagine who they are. And don't forget: sex thrives on the friction that is part and parcel of difference. Similarities are soothing, but difference is exciting.

There are also frankly pragmatic considerations. Personally, I would not like to live in a world without gender categories simply because, sexually, I am always on the lookout for persons with penises who like to have sex with other persons with penises! Foucault, though his constructionist writings may have paved the way for a critique of identity, famously came to understand gay liberation before he died. Bob Gallagher, a friend of mine who was close to Foucault in the early 1980s, claims that Foucault's change of heart was directly related to sex and the body. Foucault said of gay liberation (referring to Toronto's Gay Pride Parade) that "it all made sense when I saw those asses swaying in the sun!"[14]

It may very well be Nina's ass that makes all the difference. Her now famously modified body is both real and it is not; it is her own sexual fantasies made flesh. Nina cannot, will not, and does not, desire to pass. Some transsexuals modify their bodies in order that they may live as straight people. Some women who marry female-to-male transsexuals adopt children with their new husbands, move to the suburbs, and become heterosexual good citizens. I cannot imagine Nina doing this. (The church ladies would likely conspire to run her out of town!) Nina, because she is a self-admitted, living, breathing male-porn fantasy, has more in common with trans folk who do not pass (and do not wish to pass) or with trans people who proudly proclaim themselves queer, or with the feminine homosexual or the butch dyke who is a proud gender rebel. Nina quite simply doesn't fit in; she never will. She is a permanent freak of nature. Nina wears her sex and her sexuality on her sleeve (along with her heart).

It is my view that there are two possible paradigms for our future: one environmental and the other cyborgian. The environmental vision is profoundly heterosexual, since it focuses on families, children, and the optimistic notion that we can and will overturn the mistakes of the past and build an environmentally friendly world for our progeny. A more pessimistic, cyborgian outcome is, I would posit, much more likely. Our future may not turn out to be an overwhelmingly green one, the touching attempts to "get back to nature," and well-intentioned theories of queer ecology notwithstanding. Ecology may become a footnote along with our present notions of bodies and the material world. Bodies in the cyborgian future may well be significantly artificial. As we add everything from pacemakers and new knees to computer implants in the brain, we will all have the capacity to become unreasonable facsimiles—like Nina.

But this highly unnatural future will be, for queers, a return to our roots. Oscar Wilde's favorite book was Joris-Karl Huysmans's *Against Nature* (1884): both Wilde and Huysmans (a seminal late nineteenth century French aesthete) argued persuasively that objects that are artificial and imagined are more profound and beautiful than nature. A quotation from Huysmans, concerning the fictional aesthete/hero of his novel, provides an appropriate epilogue here. In this passage Des Esseintes compares a train locomotive (one that he describes later as an "adorable blonde with a shrill voice"[15]) to a natural woman. Of course, he finds the "natural" woman inadequate. Huysmans's vision of quintessential modern beauty as the epitome of all that is artificial (via Des Esseintes) could be a description of Nina Arsenault:

As a matter of fact, artifice was considered by Des Esseintes to be the distinctive mark of human genius. Nature, he used to say, has had her day; she has finally and utterly exhausted the patience of sensitive observers by the revolting uniformity of her landscapes and skyscapes … After all, to take what among all her works is considered to be the most exquisite, what among her creations is deemed to possess the most perfect and original beauty—to wit, woman—has not man for his part, by his own efforts, produced an animate yet artificial creature that is every bit as good from the point of view of plastic beauty?[16]

Sky Gilbert is a writer, director, and drag queen extraordinaire. He was co-founder and artistic director of Buddies in Bad Times Theatre (North America's largest gay and lesbian theatre) for eighteen years where he produced over twenty-five of his own plays, and he continues to produce new work there. His five novels have been critically acclaimed. He has received two Dora Mavor Moore Theatre Awards (Toronto) and the Pauline McGibbon Award for Theatre Directing, and he was the recipient of The Margo Bindhardt Award (from the Toronto Arts Foundation), The Silver Ticket Award (from the Toronto Alliance for the Performing Arts), and the ReLit Award (for his fourth novel *An English Gentleman*, 2004). In January, 2012, ECW Press published Sky's new novel *Come Back*, a fictional memoir by "Judy Garland" set in 2050. Dr. Gilbert holds a University Research Chair in Creative Writing and Theatre Studies in The School of English and Theatre Studies at the University of Guelph, Ontario, Canada.

Bibliography

Altman, Dennis. *Homosexual: Oppression and Liberation*. New York: Outerbridge & Dienstfrey, 1971.

Archer, Bert. *The End of Gay: And the Death of Heterosexuality*. Cambridge, MA: Da Capo Press, 2002.

Arsenault Nina. *The Silicone Diaries*. In *TRANS(per)FORMING Nina Arsenault*, edited by Judith Rudakoff, 191–227. Bristol: Intellect Press, 2012.

Bornstein, Kate. *My Gender Workbook: How to Become a Real Man, a Real Woman, the Real You or Something Else Entirely*. London: Routledge, 1997.

Butler, Judith. "Imitation and Gender Insubordination." In *The Lesbian and Gay Studies Reader*, edited by Abelove, Henry Michèle, Aina Barale, and David M. Halperin, 307–20. London: Routledge 1993.

Califia, Patrick. *Sex Changes*. Berkeley: Cleis Press, 2003.

Epstein, Steven. "Gay Politics, Ethnic Identity." In *Forms of Desire,* edited by Edward Stein, 239– 93. London: Routledge, 1992.

Gilbert, Sky. "If That's What It Means to Be Gay, I Quit." *The Globe and Mail*, December 1, 2009.

Huysmans, Joris-Karl. *Against Nature*. London: Penguin, 2003.

Mortimer-Sandilands, Catriona, and Bruce Erickson, eds. *Queer Ecologies: Sex, Nature, Politics, Desire.* Bloomington: Indiana University Press, 2010.

Signorile, Michaelangelo. *Life Outside: The Signorile Report on Gay Men; Sex, Drugs, Muscles, and the Passages of Life.* New York: Harper Collins, 1997.

Tuller, David. "Adventures of a Dacha Sex Spy." In *PoMoSexuals: Challenging Assumptions About Gender and Sexuality*, edited by Queen, Carol, and Lawrence Schimel, 174–88. Berkeley: Cleis Press, 1997.

Notes

1. Judith Butler, "Imitation and Gender Insubordination," in *The Lesbian and Gay Studies Reader*, eds. Henry Michèle Abelove, Aina Barale, and David M. Halperin (London: Routledge, 1993), 308.
2. "Keep your laws off our bodies!" is a chant long used in queer demonstrations.
3. Andrew Sullivan, *Virtually Normal* (New York: Vintage, 1996).
4. Michaelangelo Signorile, *Life Outside: The Signorile Report on Gay Men; Sex, Drugs, Muscles, and the Passages of Life* (New York: Harper Collins, 1997).
5. Bert Archer, *The End of Gay: And the Death of Heterosexuality* (Cambridge, MA: Da Capo Press, 2002).
6. David Tuller, "Adventures of a Dacha Sex Spy," in *PoMoSexuals: Challenging Assumptions About Gender and Sexuality*, eds. Carol Queen and Lawrence Schimel (Berkeley: Cleis Press, 1997), 188.
7. Catriona Mortimer-Sandilands and Bruce Erickson, eds., *Queer Ecologies: Sex, Nature, Politics, Desire* (Bloomington: Indiana University Press, 2010), 30.
8. Sky Gilbert, "If That's What It Means to Be Gay, I Quit," *The Globe and Mail*, December 1, 2009.
9. Nina Arsenault, *The Silicone Diaries*, in *TRANS(per)FORMING Nina Arsenault*, ed. Judith Rudakoff (Bristol: Intellect Press, 2012), 207.
10. Kate Bornstein, *My Gender Workbook: How to Become a Real Man, a Real Woman, the Real You or Something Else Entirely* (London: Routledge, 1997), 14.
11. Patrick Califia, *Sex Changes* (Berkeley: Cleis Press, 2003), 259.
12. Dennis Altman, *Homosexual: Oppression and Liberation* (New York: Outerbridge & Dienstfrey, 1971).
13. Steven Epstein, "Gay Politics, Ethnic Identity," in *Forms of Desire*, ed. Edward Stein (London: Routledge, 1992), 253.
14. This was a comment Foucault supposedly made many times, relayed to me by Bob Gallagher. It is cited in my book: Sky Gilbert, *Ejaculations from the Charm Factory* (Toronto: ECW Press, 2000), 105.
15. Joris-Karl Huysmans, *Against Nature* (London: Penguin, 2003), 12.
16. Ibid., 11–12.

Chapter 2

Unreal Beauty: Identification and Embodiment in Nina Arsenault's "Self-Portraits"

J. Paul Halferty

Nina Arsenault designates all her artistic work as "self-portraits,"[1] including her surgically altered and augmented body, her theatrical performances, and her photographic collaborations. She nominates these activities and their documentation in this unusual way because she views all of them as vehicles for the performative production of the various identities that she embodies and lives, on stage and off. While Arsenault's definition of self-portrait runs counter to its received meaning, her resignification of the term is a purposeful and powerful act that is meant to frame, convey, and foreground the uniqueness of her artistic practice.

> Traditionally, self-portraits are the artist making an image of themself, and this is what I do. I create images of how I see myself, and how I want to see myself, in the world, in the theatre, in photography, in writing … For me, the differences between my surgeries, the way I present myself on the street, a memoir or a visual self-portrait, are very blurry and actually not very helpful. I think of myself as a self-portrait I created—with the aid of some very good surgeons—and a memoir as a narrative self-portrait of the author. It's the medium that's different.[2]

By focusing on the production and reproduction of self in the manner that a traditional artist would create a conventional self-portrait, Arsenault takes her body as her medium, making the performativity of art and life inseparable.

In this chapter, I investigate Arsenault's "self-portraits"—her body modifications, and her theatrical and photographic collaboration—arguing that the common feature that exists among these works is the practice of identifying with and embodying what are commonly considered "unreal images of femininity." I argue that her identification with and personification of what are commonly considered imaginary figures are, like her gender transition, externalizations of her internal identifications and understandings of self. This is to say that, when working with a photographer or a surgeon to achieve her desired look, she does so to externalize somatically, and then disseminate discursively, the identities and images of the "self" that she desires to effect, to be, and to become, be it a mannequin, Jessica Rabbit, or a faery. To explore this practice, I employ Donna Haraway's "A Cyborg Manifesto: Science, Technology, and Socialist-Feminism in the Late Twentieth Century"[3] as theoretical framework and model for an unorthodox form of identification and embodiment. In the chapter's first section, I elucidate the connection between Haraway's theory of the cyborg and Arsenault's practice of embodying unreal images of femininity as forms of identification and ontology. In the manner of Haraway's theory of the cyborg, Arsenault's identifications and embodiments—that is, her self-portraits—are predicated upon the imbrication of imagination and material reality as they are conceived and lived within Arsenault's contemporary North American and Western context, making her the apotheosis of Haraway's "image of the cyborg."[4] In the second section, I turn to my reading of Arsenault's autobiographical play *The Silicone Diaries*,[5] which recalls and examines her transformation from a lanky young man to the embodiment of a hyperfeminine image of woman. Or, as she puts it, "an imitation of an imitation of an idea of a woman. An image which has never existed in nature."[6] In this section, my discussion concentrates on Arsenault's decision to forgo normative concepts of femininity, and how she came to understand her extreme surgical alterations as an artistic practice that she calls self-portraiture that follows in, but also departs from, this practice in Western art history. In the essay's final section, I build on both my discussion of Haraway and the evolution of Arsenault's artistic practice by examining a small selection of her collaborative photographic projects. Following Arsenault's own thinking, I approach her photographic collaborations as an extension of her practice of self-portraiture.[7] I take this perspective not to make the case that the photographers are not agents and/or authors of the work, but rather to posit all of her work as performative exercises of identification and embodiment, and to argue that these exercises are key to understanding her particular conflation of life and art. What emerges from this discussion of Arsenault's body modification, theatrical productions, and photographic works as a series of self-portraits are the many paradoxes that this Arsenault-specific practice brings to light. Furthermore, the discussion also reveals how her particular identifications and embodiments have made the process of living into a performative and plastic art whose subject *and* object is always Arsenault's desired self.

Ironic Embodiment: Haraway's Image of the Cyborg

In "A Cyborg Manifesto," Donna Haraway powerfully and famously argued that "by the late twentieth century, our time, a mythic time, we are all chimeras, theorized and fabricated, hybrids of machine and organism; in short, we are cyborgs."[8] Central to this argument is her analysis of three distinct "boundary breakdowns."[9] She contends that formerly distinct divisions between human and nonhuman animals, between organisms and machines, and between the "physical and non-physical"[10] have become "very imprecise for us."[11] For Haraway, the reconceptualization of man as another genus of "animal," the medical/technological interventions—from the extreme to the mundane—that we all now make to our bodies, and the ever-increasing number of technologies that mediate the ways we interface with and conceive of material reality, have created these ruptures and thus made the cyborg "our ontology."[12] Haraway argues that this does not place us in an apocalyptic scenario. On the contrary, the image of the cyborg presents us with an ironic image of embodiment, a technological, and perverse ontology, through which we can advocate and experience "*pleasure* in the confusion of boundaries and *responsibility* in their construction."[13] Furthermore, the cyborg is an ironic image of identification and embodiment that disrupts the binaries that structure so much of Western thought.

A product of science fiction, the cyborg emanates from these boundary breakdowns. A combination of machine and organic material, the cyborg is also, according to Haraway, a creature of our social reality.[14] In Haraway's theory, the cyborg presents us with an ironic and blasphemous image of identification through which we might understand our embodiment and our ontology. The cyborg is, as Haraway suggests, "a matter of fiction *and* lived experience that changes what counts as women's experience in the late twentieth century. This is a struggle over life and death, but the boundary between science fiction and social reality is an optical illusion."[15] I can think of no better analogy, no more apt framework for describing the ways that Arsenault performatively effects identity in her self-portraits, which she positions as her ontology, than Haraway's theorization of the cyborg.

Haraway makes two other important invocations about the image of the cyborg that directly relate to Arsenault's paradoxical position as artist and art object, and as her own self-portrait. First, following Chela Sandoval, and using the example of political appellation of "women of colour," she suggests that the cyborg can enable coalition through "affinity, not identity," for marginalized women who have been cut out of white, Western feminists' conceptions of "woman." Second, and again invoking the work of "women of colour," she suggests that "cyborg writing" offers the possibility of intervening into representational practices as a *means* of survival. Similarly, Arsenault's position as "trans" and "queer" creates the possibility of affinity among many diverse, non-heteronormative lived identities, criss-crossing lines of race, class, and sexual orientation. Furthermore, her dual position as art object and artist (one who literally writes her body through surgeries and the artistic representations that she creates) is a mode of identification, embodiment, empowerment, and survival. As Haraway argues:

> The poetry and stories of US women of colour are repeatedly about writing, about access to the power to signify; but this time that power must be neither phallic nor innocent. Cyborg writing must not be about the Fall, the imagination of a once-upon-a-time wholeness before language, before writing, before Man. Cyborg writing is about the power to survive, not on the basis of original innocence, but on the basis of seizing the tools to mark the world that marked them as other.[16]

As self-portraits, Arsenault's body and her other artistic endeavours are all self-consciously about creating/living her body as means not only to signify, but also to be recognized and acknowledged as existing within the social world, and to express the complexity of her experience. As a sex-worker and a marginalized transwoman, who never passed as a biological female, Arsenault decided to position her transition as an artistic practice, to take control and to create a place for herself in the world.

Like the cyborg, Arsenault's self-portraits sit at the blurry boundary of imagination and material reality, an idea that is most spectacularly expressed in her surgically altered body, and her practice of self-portraiture as a means of her survival. Arsenault has not adhered to the contemporary conventions of intelligibility that attend dominant conceptions of "sex" and "gender," nor other dominant (i.e. what is considered "real," "natural," "normal," or "healthy") paradigms of identity; rather, she has taken pleasure in the confusion of various imaginative and material boundaries, and has also taken responsibility for her construction of new modes of identification and being by framing her work as an artistic practice, and sharing it in the communal act of theatre. Overt and audacious, Arsenault has openly undertaken trauma and danger to (literally) incorporate hyperfeminine features discursively promulgated as fake.[17] She has consciously decided not to pass as a biological woman, but to position her body as an art object and its modification as a form of self-portraiture. Arsenault's hyperfeminine and ironic image of "woman," which she embodies onstage and offstage, is a self-consciously theatrical production comprising make-up, synthetic hair, plastic surgery, diet, exercise, and discipline, aided by the surgical integration of several pounds of medical-grade silicone. Like Haraway's image of the cyborg, and her conception of cyborg writing, Arsenault's body as self-portrait brings into striking relief the intractable interrelatedness of imagination and material reality in her and in all of our ontologies, as well as in the collective construction of our social realities.

For these and other reasons, Arsenault is a transgender heiress to Haraway's conception of a cyborg feminist: a self-conscious construction achieved through technological intervention and performative framing; a *living representation* of femininity, inspired by fantasy, and Barbie dolls, and achieved through surgical intervention and artistic practice. Arsenault's self-portraits are, in a sense, all "cyborg portraits" because they are rooted in the ironic and blasphemous iconography of her embodiment of unreal, imagined, and mutable femininities. Arsenault has *made* herself through the suturing of biology, technology, and imagination, and continues to find new ways of being through her art practice, which is to say, her life. By living her life conspicuously at the interface of imagination and material reality, which are, according to Haraway, "the two joined centres structuring any possibility of historical transformation,"[18] Arsenault's feminine embodiments, and her practice of effecting the self through self-portraiture, constitute new ways of being and making art.

Theatrical Self-Portrait: *The Silicone Diaries*

At the outset of *The Silicone Diaries*, Arsenault addresses the audience directly and recalls two scenes from her childhood. In the first, she recounts seeing a mannequin in the lingerie department of her local Zellers department store. She recalls being overwhelmed by the beauty of the figure; she asked her mother if the mannequin was real. In the second, Arsenault remembers spying on a group of boys in their forest clubhouse, as they surreptitiously consumed pictures of naked women from a pornographic magazine. At first the boys are reverent with these images, but they quickly become violent, ripping pages from the magazine, and then tearing apart these photographs of women's bodies. Considering the boys' actions but focusing on the images of the women they are violating, Arsenault has her first epiphany: "I don't know how I know it. Or why I know it. But I know that this is exactly what I will be when I grow up."[19]

At the opening of the performance, these two memories are situated as Arsenault's experience of the primal scene: at a tender age she is irrevocably touched by these representations of women, trauma, desire, and dismemberment, which come to characterize not only her conception of feminine beauty, but a driving, obsessive need to embody this beauty herself. The monologues also introduce the confessional form of the performance, as Arsenault recounts important moments in her transition, complete with photographs and videos, which document who she was and what she looked like at specific moments in her transition, projected on a screen behind her.[20] With each titled and dated monologue, Arsenault recovers and claims an aspect of her creation, the results of which we see on stage. The stories, however, do not just describe her physical transformation; rather, each conveys insight into Arsenault's changing relationship to silicone, plastic surgery, her body, and to beauty. In fact, because *The Silicone Diaries* is the story of Arsenault's surgical transformations, the performance is, more profoundly, an account of the inception, motivation, and evolution of her art practice, the primary medium of which is her body. *The Silicone Diaries* is, thus, the story of her body modifications not as solely necessary to her gender transition, but as a means for achieving extreme images of beauty, and as a performative practice of self-portraiture.

Beyond the scenes of primary identification in childhood that I have just glossed, Arsenault's gender transition began in earnest in 1996, when she was twenty-two years old and visited Toronto's Centre for Addiction and Mental (CAMH) Health Gender Identity Clinic. At the clinic, she was told by a doctor that while he recognized that she suffered from substantial gender dysphoria, he would not recommend her for their Gender Identity Clinic Program—the gateway to gender-reassignment in the province of Ontario—as he felt she was too masculine-looking, would not transition well or easily, and would be happier continuing life as an effeminate gay man.[21] At this time in Ontario the cost of gender reassignment surgery was covered by the province's public health insurance program, and therefore free to any Ontario resident who successfully completed CAMH's Gender Identity Clinic Program.[22] Arsenault neither fit well into the received narratives of gender reassignment surgery, nor was her *performance* of femininity, at the level of somatic signifiers and physical gestures, convincing within the normative structures of what "women" are, or what they can be. Because of this, and despite the doctor's assessment, Arsenault was forced to fund her transition herself. In order to pay for the hormones, and large amounts of plastic surgery that would be necessary for her to transform her body and pass as a female, she began to work in the sex trade, first as a webcam shemale, then as a stripper, and eventually as a prostitute, engaging in countless hours of labour to become the woman she wanted to be.

Sandy Stone speaks of these issues in "The Empire Strikes Back: A Posttranssexual Manifesto."[23] She suggests that transnarratives have been tremendously limited by a medical establishment that approaches gender dysphoria as a pathology, and, importantly, a case history, replete with particular narrative conventions. As a result, those who do transition under the aegis of a gender clinic, or under the supervision of a psychologist, usually disappear into their own "plausible histories."[24] That is, having recapitulated the medically received narrative of gender dysphoria as well as performing his/her gender with the proper amount of skill—two tasks Arsenault was unable to successfully complete at the age of twenty-two—a transsexual person is granted sex-reassignment and encouraged to "pass," and pass quietly, into heterosexual culture. According to Stone, for transsexuals,

> What is gained [by passing] is acceptability in society. What is lost is the ability to authentically represent the complexities and ambiguities of lived experience … Instead, authentic experience is replaced by a particular kind of story, one that supports the old constructed positions.[25]

In her theatrical and photographic self-portraits, Arsenault investigates the complexities and paradoxes that have attended her experiences of gender, sex, and identity. By rejecting the pathologizing and limiting diagnosis of her doctors, and by being open and truthful about her own transgender identity,[26] Arsenault takes *pleasure* in disrupting traditional boundaries, and *responsibility* for the performative construction of new identities. As Arsenault explains in an interview with Judith Rudakoff:

> [I] started my journey to alter my body and to try to erase the maleness in it. But in doing that I didn't create a female body, because in a way that's quite impossible. All I'm able to do is use the technological and medical tools that are available and as a result, I have a body that I would consider a cyborg body.[27]

At about mid-point in *The Silicone Diaries*, Arsenault delivers a stream-of-consciousness monologue titled "I am my own self-portrait (2004)," which recounts the moment she chose to forgo plastic surgery as a means to become a "natural-looking" woman, and decided instead "to get artistic with [her] body."[28] In the scene, she recalls sitting at her make-up table, looking at her reflection, observing what she had already achieved in her gender transition. "This is the most I will ever look like a normal, natural woman," she says. "It's not enough. It has to be enough. The quest has to end eventually. One has to be reasonable, right?"[29] Arsenault's "natural" feminine image, which, ironically, she had achieved by altering her body with hormones and plastic surgery, was only ever contingently passable: "I fool some people, some of the time. For a moment. In good lighting. A few parts look plastic. Tastefully plastic … But the jaw line, the brow bone, the nostril size, the cheek-to-chin ratio, the down-turned nose … It's not enough."[30] By the monologue's end, Arsenault has made a decision: to forego submission to normative conventions of natural feminine gender, and to embrace fakeness in order to achieve hyperfeminine beauty.

If you cannot look like a normal woman, sacrifice being normal. I will be plastic. I will think of geisha. Stylized abstractions of beauty. Shuffling through the world. I love them. Nina, give yourself permission to be fabulous instead of reasonable. Really fucking fabulous. Every fucking day.[31]

Citing what are considered "exotic" forms of beauty from a Western point-of-view, and the fakeness of plastic surgery, Arsenault's experience of her body modification evolves from a process of gender transition into a performative practice of embodiment, one that is not beholden to discourses of "naturalness," but intervenes into historical and contemporary discourses of beauty.[32] Arsenault is thus "her own self-portrait": through over sixty plastic surgeries, she has designed herself "with an eye to line, form and mass,"[33] producing and reproducing externally her internal and developing understandings of self.

By the end of *The Silicone Diaries*, Arsenault has resolved to approach her body modification as an artistic practice. She confronts the pains and pleasures that have attended her surgical alterations, and realizes herself as an artist, in the play's final monologue, "Venus/machine (2007–2009)." In order to reconcile the extent to which she had objectified her body, Arsenault buys an exercise bicycle. On the bike, which she names Beelzebub because "every day I will get up on it and ride out my demons,"[34] Arsenault learns to breathe again, to accept the trauma she has experienced in her transition, and to re-establish feeling in and with her. Riding the bicycle, moving and breathing, helps Arsenault to reconnect with her presence, to sensation, and to artistic inspiration. In the monologue she comes to understand that she must be reasonable, but not in the ways that society dictates:

> Underneath me, the shadow of the bike becomes a horned demon I am straddling. The demon's face is a glowing red face that stares back at me with changing computerized digits and schematics of moving dots that reconfigure into new formulations. ...
>
> I look into the mirror, and my body is the body of a giant serpent. I see the serpent in a spiral. I see the breath moving through the spiral. Glittering scales. The skin shedding off the snake.
> It unfolds. ...
>
> The next phase is to be reasonable.
>
> To be rational.
>
> To accept the moment as it is happening.
>
> To accept that my pleasure and my sublime privilege is to suffer.

And to live.

With. Beauty.[35]

For Arsenault, being *reasonable* does not mean following what medical authorities say, the narratives of what society deems normal, nor what are commonly understood as legitimate forms of identification or, for that matter, art. For her, being reasonable, in her personal definition of the term, refers to employing her own senses and consciousness to identify with and embody various images of femininity, be it a woman, a Barbie, or a snake. Arsenault accepts that it is her "sublime privilege"[36] to live and then represent, in as authentic a manner possible, the truth of her experience, and the paradoxes that attend her identifications and embodiments. In short, what Arsenault is saying at the end of *The Silicone Diaries* is that she will live the life of an artist whose canvass is her body, and whose product is her *self*: the rest of her life will be based on pursuing the pleasures and pains of living with beauty.

Haraway appealed to the image of the cyborg to "suggest a way out of the maze of dualisms in which we have explained our bodies and our tools to ourselves."[37] Similarly, Arsenault explicates her identification with and embodiment of unreal images of femininity as an approach to art and life through her conception of self-portraiture as a form of performative self-production and survival. Each monologue in *The Silicone Diaries* is a step in her journey to becoming an artist for whom life and art are inseparable because both are predicated on the production of the self through an unorthodox approach to and understanding of self-portraiture.

Photographic Self-Portraits: *Fey, Liminoid,* and *Transformation*

Referring to Arsenault's photographic work as self-portraits may seem a more grievous misnomer than using the term to refer to her body or her plays as she is the *subject* of these photographs that have been taken by professional photographers, each of whom brings his/her own particular aesthetic, style, and point-of-view. There are, however, two reasons to view Arsenault's *photographic collaborations* through the lens of her idea of self-portraiture. The first is ontological. Arsenault does not differentiate between the surgical transformation of her body and her more overtly performative/artistic projects: she sees all of these activities as external modes of feminine embodiment that express her internal, psychic identifications. By this logic, the photographs taken of her by others are akin to documentary representations of her creation, a kind of mediated self-portrait, which does not deny the importance of the photographic agent, but places equal artistic weight on its subject. The second is methodological. Each of the three examples that I discuss here, *Fey, Liminoid,* and *Transformation,* are collaborations between Arsenault and photographers who shot, and in some cases altered, the photographs. Arsenault's role in these works is not simply that of subject or model; she was also an active collaborator in their artistic conception and photographic production.[38]

In her creative partnerships with professional photographers, Arsenault elaborates her practice of self-consciously embodying iconic images of femininity. For example, in the series titled *Fey*, which she undertook with photographer Michael Chambers (see Figure 13), Arsenault embodies a faery, a magical creature that is part of the Western European mythic tradition. Arsenault suggests that her identification with the faery enables a new way of being that lies outside contemporary medical and scientific discourses.

[Transsexual] sounds so medical to me, knowing that the words and the identity boundaries were created in a medical context by a group of outside male authorities. The word "transgendered," on the other hand, I associate with theorists who were actively creating a more inclusive word that would and could identify anyone who challenged society's gender norms. That places my gender and its challenge to society at the heart of my identity. Do I want to carry that around with me all the time? Furthermore, why should my identity have to be so theoretical? It's lighter to be a faery. I don't think that it's the final word on my identity, but thousands of years of folklore, myth and esoteric—lost, forgotten—wisdom, has to be on to something.[39]

Her construction of self-portraits has thus become a performative practice of identification and of embodiment that calls upon the mythic, unreal, and fantastic examples of ontology, and epistemology. Arsenault's self-portraits (including those which document her surgical alterations) are exercises in constructing new ways of being in the world.

Arsenault directly explores her status as cyborg in a series called *Liminoid* (2008), a collaboration with photographer and pornographer inkedKenny (see Figures 6 and 15). The series title is a theoretical invocation that enables Arsenault to place it on a historical continuum of body modification and beautification that have been a part of all human cultures. "Liminoid" is a term coined by anthropologist Victor Turner, whose scholarship investigates ritual in various cultural contexts. Turner distinguishes liminoid from liminal, defining the latter as relating to transformative practices, such as rites of passage common to tribal and agrarian cultures, which are defined by obligation and usually concern the entire social group. He defines the liminoid as similar transformative experiences in complex, industrial societies, such as theatrical performances and sporting events, but which he notes are usually voluntary, and do not involve the entire community.[40] Arsenault's allusion to Turner in the title of this series resituates her body modification as a contemporary practice of beautification that is not dissimilar from those undertaken in the historical past, for example Chinese foot binding and European corseting, or from the present-day practices of agrarian and tribal societies such as the wearing of neck-rings and lip discs. The series title conveys the contemporary paradox of privileging some forms of beautification and degrading others, as well as highlighting the cultural silences and shaming that attend plastic surgery when used towards purely aesthetic ends. For Arsenault, *pace* Haraway, *Liminoid*'s correlation to the past and to the "strange" forms of beautification in "exotic" cultures is empowering because it allows her to take discursive responsibility for her self-portraits, her cyborgness.

Arsenault's complicated and paradoxical relationship with medical technologies is expressed in *Liminoid*.[41] For example, in Figure 15 she straddles the base of a medical chair from its front. In the image, she seems to be contemplating the chair as a sentient and living being. Her position is sexual, erotic, and loving, but might also connote birth: Arsenault could be seen as giving birth to the chair in the manner that ORLAN's[42] self-portrait, *ORLAN accouche d'elle-même* (ORLAN gives birth to her beloved self),[43] depicts the artist with her legs wrapped around the upper half (waist, torso, and head) of an armless mannequin. However, in the context of the *Liminoid* series, the chair and the medical procedures and technologies it represents can also be viewed as giving birth to Arsenault. The photograph, thus, presents the paradox of Arsenault as an empowered subject, changing her body to live a fulfilling life, and as a disempowered object of patriarchal discourse, bio-medical technologies, and oppressive fantasies of beauty. Indeed, *Liminoid*'s medicalized images directly relate to the film and photographic documentation that Arsenault has made of her surgical procedures, conveying the pleasure and pain inherent to her surgical transformations (see Figures 11, top and bottom; 25 top and bottom; 19 and 29).

Perhaps the most aggressive and stunning example of her photographic collaborations is an image titled *Transformation* (see Figure 30), shot as part of an unnamed series by Canadian film-maker, photographer, and pornographer Bruce LaBruce. Like Arsenault's other photographic self-portraits, *Transformation* continues to use her surgically altered body to inhabit unreal, and, in this case, mythic examples of femininity, and to present the paradoxes of her experience. Shot in 2006, the photograph shows Arsenault sitting on a chair in a room that is spattered with copious amounts of blood, pools of it so deep that they catch reflections. Her head is tilted back, and her face is not seen; one arm is clearly visible, and the other hidden. Unlike the room around her, her body is pristine, with blood barely discernible on the soles of her feet. Her penis lies between her legs, but is only apparent upon close inspection. Her right breast is large and spherical, while the left is small and deflated, because its silicone implant has been excised temporarily due to medical complications.

By self-consciously invoking classical myth and art-historical discourses, *Transformation* provocatively posits their patriarchal provenance as framework for viewing Arsenault's body. *Transformation* appeals most significantly to the classical feminine images of Aphrodite/ Venus, the goddess of love and beauty. According to Greek mythology, Chronos cut off the genitals of his father, Uranus, and cast them into the sea. Once in the water, sea foam arose around the bloody member and testicles, and they transformed into the goddess of love and beauty, Aphrodite/Venus. *Transformation*'s composition, which has Arsenault's body sitting on the chair in the sea of blood, references Botticelli's *Birth of Venus*, which depicts Venus on a shell, emerging from the sea. *Transformation* thus conflates the mythic story of Aphrodite/ Venus' creation with Arsenault's. The portrait links the classical images of violence, conflict, castration, and blood, which gave birth to the goddess of love and beauty, to the surgical procedures and traumas that gave birth to Arsenault's feminine form. In *Transformation*, Arsenault's penis is seen, suggesting that as she was born into a male body she is, at one level, like the Greek myth, classical/Renaissance sculpture and painting, and the other forms of femininity that she has emulated: the creation of white men within Western patriarchy. *Transformation* powerfully suggests that Arsenault's embodiment of these feminine ideals cannot be divided from the trauma she underwent to achieve them, nor the patriarchal, racist, and misogynistic discourses that produced them. Rather, this tense, violent image ironically posits violence, hatred, and pain as inseparable from beauty, love, and pleasure.

Similar to Haraway's invocation of science fiction as a means to offer an accurate—and strikingly prophetic—assessment of our ontology, Arsenault's public decision to be plastic, to align herself through self-portraiture with artistic, historical, exotic, and mythical discourses of femininity and beauty, offers radical new modes and positions for being in the contemporary world. Indeed, Arsenault's recognition of the subversive potential of medical technology and her blasphemous and ironic embodiments of hyperfeminine images, through plastic surgeries and performative/artistic practices, make her a contemporary paragon of Haraway's theory of the cyborg, and her practice of self-portraiture a form of cyborg writing. By being truthful about her motivations and traumatic realities she has experienced in her embodiments, she links empowerment, pleasure, and engagement, to objectification, pain, and superficiality. Arsenault's self-portraits, her body, her theatrical and photographic works place in arresting relief the mutually constitutive nature of imagination and material reality in art and life.

Before returning to graduate school, associate editor **J. Paul Halferty** taught acting at the Randolph Academy, and was assistant producer to Sherrie Johnson at da da kamera, as well as at the Six Stages Festival, all in Toronto. Currently, he is completing his PhD dissertation, a history of gay male theatre in Toronto from the late 1960s to the late 1990s, at the Graduate Centre for Study of Drama, University of Toronto. He has taught at York University, the University of Toronto, and at Brock University, mainly in the areas of theatre history, acting, and gender and sexual diversity studies. His work has been published in *Theatre Research in Canada, Canadian Theatre Review*, and in the anthology *Queer Theatre in Canada*, published by Playwrights Canada Press. Paul has served as president of Buddies in Bad Times Theatre's board of directors since 2007.

Bibliography

Arsenault, Nina. "Excerpts from My Artist Talk 'Self-Portraiture: Identity, Transformation and Performance.'" Lecture presented during *The Body: From Liminal to Virtual* series, York University, Toronto, ON, published Feb 7, 2011. http://ninaarsenault.com/2011/02/excerpts-from-self-portraiture-transformation-identity-and-performance-part-of-the-body-from-liminal-to-virtual/.

———. "'Fey': A Photo Portrait by Michael Chambers (2010)." NinaArsenault.com. Last modified March 5, 2011. http://ninaarsenault.com/2011/03/fey-a-photo-portrait-by-michael-chambers-2010/.

———. *The Silicone Diaries*. In *TRANS(per)FORMING Nina Arsenault*, edited by Judith Rudakoff, 191–227. Bristol: Intellect Press, 2012.

Haraway, Donna. "A Cyborg Manifesto: Science, Technology, and Socialist-Feminism in the Late Twentieth Century." In *The Transgender Studies Reader*, edited by Susan Stryker and Stephen Whittle, 103–18. New York: Routledge, 2006.

Muñoz, José Esteban. *Disidentifications: Queers of Color and the Performance of Politics*. Minneapolis: University of Minnesota Press, 1999.

ORLAN. *Body Sculpture 1964–1967*. On ORLAN's official website. Accessed May 13, 2011. http://www.ORLAN.net/works/photo/.

Rudakoff, Judith. *Faux Arts or Beaux Arts: Nina Arsenault and the Possibilities of the New*. "I W@s B*rbie," Toronto, ON, June 9–13, 2010. Playbill.

Stone, Sandy. "The Empire Strikes Back: A Posttranssexual Manifesto." In *The Transgender Studies Reader*, edited by Susan Stryker and Stephen Whittle, 221–35. New York: Routledge.

Turner, Victor. *From Ritual to Theatre: The Human Seriousness of Play*. New York: Performing Arts Journal Publications, 1982.

Notes

1. Nina Arsenault, personal interview with author, May 7, 2011.
2. Ibid.
3. Donna Haraway, "A Cyborg Manifesto: Science, Technology, and Socialist-Feminism in the Late Twentieth Century," in *The Transgender Studies Reader*, eds. Susan Stryker and Stephen Whittle (New York: Routledge, 2006), 103–18.
4. Ibid., 104.
5. Nina Arsenault, *The Silicone Diaries*, in *TRANS(per)FORMING Nina Arsenault*, ed. Judith Rudakoff (Bristol: Intellect Press, 2012).
6. Ibid., 219.
7. Nina Arsenault, "Excerpts from My Artist Talk 'Self-portraiture: Identity, Transformation and Performance,'" lecture presented during *The Body: From Liminal to Virtual* series, York University, Toronto, ON, http://ninaarsenault.com/2011/02/excerpts-from-self-portraiture-transformation-identity-and-performance-part-of-the-body-from-liminal-to-virtual/.
8. Haraway, "A Cyborg Manifesto," 104.
9. Ibid., 105.
10. Examples of each are: animal-to-human organ transplants, pacemakers, and the Internet as virtual space.
11. Haraway, "A Cyborg Manifesto," 106.
12. Ibid., 104.
13. Ibid.
14. Ibid.
15. Ibid.; emphasis mine.
16. Ibid., 111–12.

17. Arsenault's appearance as Barbie at Toronto Fashion Week, to celebrate the doll's fiftieth birthday, and the one-person show that she created based on the experience, "I W@s B*rbie," are salient examples of this practice of identification and embodiment.
18. Haraway, "A Cyborg Manifesto," 104.
19. Arsenault, *The Silicone Diaries*, 207.
20. In fact, the videos for *The Silicone Diaries*, designed by R. Kelly Clipperton for the November 2010 production at Buddies in Bad Times Theatre in Toronto, were a creative artistic project in their own right. They beautifully conveyed important information about Arsenault, and, underscored by music and sound designed by Richard Feren, also conveyed each monologues' atmosphere and tone.
21. Nina Arsenault, personal interview with author, November 20, 2010.
22. Gender reassignment surgery was delisted as an insured benefit covered by Ontario's public health insurance program under Premier Mike Harris' Conservative government in 1998. In June, 2008, under Premier Dalton McGuinty's Liberal government, it was re-listed; however, those who want to undertake the surgery must still complete the CAMH's Gender Identity Program.
23. Sandy Stone, "The Empire Strikes Back: A Posttranssexual Manifesto," in Stryker and Whittle, *The Transgender Studies Reader*, 221–35.
24. Ibid., 230.
25. Ibid.
26. It should be noted that Arsenault has not undertaken sex reassignment surgery.
27. Judith Rudakoff, *Faux Arts or Beaux Arts: Nina Arsenault and the Possibilities of the New*, "I W@s B*rbie," Toronto, ON, June 9–13, 2010, Playbill.
28. Arsenault, *The Silicone Diaries*, 217.
29. Ibid., 215.
30. Ibid., 215.
31. Ibid, 217.
32. It should be noted that as a white person within the Canadian context, Arsenault is afforded a certain and arguably privileged relationship to images of beauty with which she chooses to identify. It is likely easier for Arsenault to identify with the dominant images of femininity within Western culture than it would be for a racialized person, who might disidentify with images of whiteness. Furthermore, her ability to identity with *geisha* as images of femininity is no doubt connected to their status as racialized images of Asian femininity within Western culture. For more on dis/identifications across "race," see José Esteban Muñoz, *Disidentifications: Queers of Color and the Performance of Politics* (Minneapolis: University of Minnesota Press, 1999).
33. Arsenault, interview, November 20, 2010.
34. Arsenault, *The Silicone Diaries*, 225.
35. Ibid., 227.
36. Ibid.
37. Haraway, "A Cyborg Manifesto," 116.
38. Arsenault, interview, May 7, 2011.

39. Nina Arsenault, "*Fey*: A Photo Portrait by Michael Chambers (2010)," NinaArsenault.com, last modified March 5, 2011, http://ninaarsenault.com/2011/03/fey-a-photo-portrait-by-michael-chambers-2010/.

40. Victor Turner, *From Ritual to Theatre: The Human Seriousness of Play* (New York: Performing Arts Journal Publications, 1982), 52–5.

41. The series can be seen on NinaArsenault.com, http://ninaarsenault.com/?s=liminoid.

42. ORLAN spells her name in upper case letters.

43. *Body Sculpture 1964–1967* on ORLAN's official website, accessed April 4, 2011, http://www.ORLAN.net/works/photo/.

Chapter 3

Daughter of the Air: Three Acting Sessions and Nina Arsenault's Imaginary Body

Cynthia Ashperger

In October 2010, I conducted three private acting sessions at Ryerson Theatre School in Toronto with Nina Arsenault. I am an actor, director, and an acting teacher who specializes in Michael Chekhov's (1891–1955) acting technique. Chekhov developed Stanislavsky's system of acting by shifting the emphasis in training from the creation of a sense of truth and the achievement of verisimilitude to the development of body–mind connection through the use of imagination. In my work I am particularly interested in how the body affects psychology, working with the concept of the Imaginary Body, which I will be examining here. Before our sessions, I had only met Nina casually at theatre performances in Toronto. To begin our process, I sent her the following questions via e-mail, which we then discussed when we met in person: What does it then mean "to act" once a performer has physically transformed into a role permanently? Is this still acting? When she acts does she still play a part, or is the part playing her? When doesn't she play a part? How could she (and would she) want to step outside the role/s she has created for herself? Is one type of role enough to keep her interested? Does she want to play outside the type she has created? Has Nina's self-objectification possibly led to her subjectification?[1] Nina's initial responses were exceptionally candid:

> I would like to become unselfconscious: the line between performing and me is blurry. Do I take on a character? As an actor, I take on a character, but my body shapes are a big part of what I do. I always concentrate on the form first. If I had to cast me outside my type, I would play a monster: when you are not male or female, it is easy to think of yourself as a monster.

We agreed to meet a week later in a studio to engage in work outside the type she has created for herself, to seek experiences that are not self-conscious, and to explore the monstrous.

Session One: The Unintentional Voice

In our first session, on October 21, 2010, we focused on the uncomfortable and unintentional effects of Nina's transition from male to female, as well as the need to feel beautiful inside.[2] "If I am walking down the street and I feel beautiful, no one says anything. If I don't believe in my beauty, and I feel like a fraud, people sense that energy and then I am attacked." This statement echoed another moment in our initial meeting where Nina mentioned that she believes in her appearance but that she doesn't believe in her voice: she thinks that her voice doesn't match her body and that it betrays her as a fake. This unwanted voice was where I suspected a source was hidden.

At our first exercise I asked Nina to sing, and she chose *Amazing Grace*. Afterwards, we tried to identify any unwanted sounds that might have occurred. For example, was her voice softer than she wanted, did she lose breath, or did her voice quiver? Nina described her involuntary sound as "metallic." I then asked her to amplify that metallic sound, so that during her second attempt at *Amazing Grace*, her singing became more powerful both in volume and expressivity. Inspired by the sound she created, and from the sensation she experienced while singing, I asked Nina to imagine a fairy-tale creature who could sing in just that way. After some searching, Nina started working with an image of a courtier. This courtier spoke loudly and the most important part of his body was his expansive chest. When I asked her how she felt in the courtier's body she said, "I am proud. Very proud. Strong. Powerful." When I asked her to describe how the pride might manifest, she said, "I speak very loudly and decidedly in a large courtroom." These last words brought a smile to her face, and she was now speaking in a loud, staccato manner. It sounded like a giant train engine powering up: "It-makes-me-feel-very-strong-and-very-good!"

I then asked Nina to merge this strength with the courtier's pride and to sing again, but this time as Nina. She looked at the ground, despondent. When I asked her about this, she revealed, "I feel that power isn't feminine and I also feel that a puffy sternum is very unbecoming. It is unbecoming for a woman to have big breasts and push them forward." This was worth pursuing, so I asked Nina to walk around, as herself, but with the pride and power of the courtier, and she did so, though clearly not enjoying it. I commented:

> You don't want to cross the edge into being a man. But maybe if you cross that edge, you could start feeling real beauty. [As the courtier] you said, "I am proud!" But as a woman you don't want that feeling. Try to walk with the pride that the courtier had, but as Nina. Mix the two feelings. You have the artistic control over how you will synthesize them, as you are the creator.

Soon Nina was physically integrating the pride sensation, and we were simultaneously commenting on the effects it had on her walk. I saw more energy, but Nina corrected my observation by citing initiative rather than energy. She enjoyed this permission to take initiative more than she expected, and we were both surprised by what had been discovered. Nina surmised that while these discoveries weren't an end point in our exploration, she was a step closer to an ideal state. I suggested that the ideal state could better be called *wholeness*. And then she sang again, allowing the man and the woman inside her to sing together. There were beautiful moments in this third attempt at *Amazing Grace*, which Nina analyzed thus:

Yes, sometimes I fall into emotion, dropping my breath, and I feel like I collapse, but I was surprised that I could have pride through the pain and strength through what I thought was soft. The emotions became complicated. Not just one emotion, but the pride is moving with the breath, the pain, the sorrow. The pride can be one with pain and with dignity.

We focused further on one particular moment in the singing, which to me appeared to be a moment of true synthesis, an inspired moment. Nina shared that in that moment she was focusing on being a man. Quite paradoxically, at that very moment, to my eye, she became the least self-conscious and the most feminine she had been thus far in our exploration. Furthermore, she added that by not trying to be a woman, she felt a sense of wholeness and integration that she normally doesn't feel. I commented, "Who would have thought when you were going through your sixty operations that embodying the man within, as you did today, would help you to be more of the woman you are now?" My question prompted a long discussion about self-doubt, and we agreed to look further into this in our second session. Nina concluded, "There have been many surprises along the way."

Session Two: The Inner Critic

Our second session took place a day later, on October 22, 2010, at the same location. We began this session with Nina recalling the integration of the courtier and walking with pride: "[T]he best way to walk with pride is to have pride sensations. I have had difficulty with that. There are a lot of voices saying, 'you are not that special. This is all fake.' It is really hard to get those voices out of my head." I was very glad that Nina brought up critical voices because my plan for this session was to work with Amy Mindell's powerful Critic's Fuel Exercise. I have used this exercise in conjunction with elements of Michael Chekhov's Acting Technique with excellent results. The Critic's Fuel Exercise helps use trapped energy from a blocked creative impulse.

In the original exercise, a person remembers a time s/he was blocked, and imagines a figure that has some form of a supernatural power that "is against [his/her] creativity."[3] For example, this power could be invisibility, clairvoyance, or omnipresence. Next, s/he sketches an image of this Supernatural Figure, and then steps into or embodies the imagined figure. Finally, s/he attempts to "imagine its essence in terms of a piece of nature: a river, a cave, a rock,"[4] and is instructed to "assume a position that expresses that essence."[5] This can then be unfolded further in an artistic manner by "let[ting] the essence express itself in a short poem, writing or in a relationship."[6] Role playing and switching roles are also often used. To this sequence, I have added some of the major elements of Chekhov's psycho-physical acting to help the actor personify "that which is against one's creativity,"[7] so that I work with atmospheres, qualities of movement, Imaginary Centres, and an independent image of the character through the Imaginary Body and the Psychological-Gesture (PG). The theoretical explanation of each one of these tools goes beyond the scope of this work; however, it will suffice to say that the goal of all of these tools is to enhance the body–mind connection externally, then internally. First the actor moves in accordance with an imaginary impulse, and, once the movement has sufficiently changed the actor's psychology, s/he internalizes this process.[8]

To begin, Nina chose a situation where she felt blocked, and after some time was spent in the atmosphere of that situation, she drew her Supernatural Figure. Nina's described the figure as a "man who emanates vapour spirals with a dark cloud over him and a lightning bolt coming out of the cloud." This creature was part real, part imagined, and was critical of every aspect of Nina's personality. I then asked Nina to embody this evil figure, and while doing so she found it enjoyable being in his skin, as he was "totally unapologetic." The creature's aim was to convince her that she was despised by her entire community, which she referred to as "Church Street."[9] Then it was time to switch the roles, so that I played the part of her creature, but only to mediocre success as I couldn't achieve the proper tone or offer the right insult. We decided to switch again, so that I could learn more about him. The critic/creature had a very campy, exaggerated voice, and the physical movement of an older person. Nina described him as "someone who has power, an omnipresent psychic. A vampire. Always on drugs so there is no way of hurting him. An impenetrable person that plays games."

Nina embodied the creature even more, which is to say, she physicalized (moved with and from) the supernatural, impenetrable part of him. As we worked on the PG, the creature grew tentacles, and Nina started to move in a very intricate dance of angles. We sped the movement up, and connected it to her breathing, at which point the Critic's Fuel started to energize Nina, who was like a moving Egyptian sculpture. Beautiful.

CA: What is the energy of that?

NA: It is direct. Across the room. Very sharp. A lot of pointedness, quick changes. You can't even keep up with it. Like an active whip, sharp, quickness.

CA: How does Nina feel in this body?

NA: In this body? I feel sharp and quick.

CA: And how else?

NA: EVIL!

We continued with the sharpness and the quickness of the movement, but now with the aim of finding something comparable in nature that has a distinct kind of movement: an animal, a natural phenomenon, or a natural space. Nina began with an animal. There was a lot of turning of the head in a sharp way, and angled, sharp arm movements. Finally she named it, "It's an octopus. A robot-octopus!" The octopus came with the feeling of a new sensation in her pelvic area, one that she normally doesn't have, and it also freed some aspect of Nina's personality: "It feels great! I am allowed to be just me. I like that. I like that a lot." Then, I noticed a marked change in the quality of her movement: "You are always *legato* aren't you? But now you are *staccato*." She responded, "and I feel that as a performer. I am always playing smooth, but I am not smooth." And there it was: the insight that we had been searching for. Nina articulated:

> NA: My experience is fragmented. I am fragmented. You are not supposed to be fragmented when you are a performer. You are supposed to be integrated and have a smooth, solid, grounded flow.

> CA: But through fragmentation, you *were* integrated. Your performance was integrated. Your movement had different lines, and you kept going with it. You weren't running out of ideas. You were playing with the image of the octopus.

> NA: It morphed. It was sometimes a praying mantis, and sometimes a spider, and a woman made of sticks.

> CA: These are similar images of many legged creatures, of broken joints, of something fragmented. You don't want to be the integrated actor who is able to play every part.

> NA: I don't. I don't want to be Everywoman. [I will be a woman] in my own shattered, unique way and create from that place.

Nina's Inner Critic led us back to what Nina already knew: hers is an aesthetic discourse. Hers is a kind of *l'art pour l'art*, and it is essential for her, as she clarified, to "walk around as a rarefied artistic discourse." She performs herself. In her performance of self, a sense of form, composure, and beauty is crucial. Yet the critic she discovered also morphed into a praying mantis, a robot-spider, an octopus, and a woman made of sticks. Because these characters had a strong natural component, the impulses born out of these roles were easily integrated into the experience of her body. Thus integrated, they helped Nina tap into her natural beauty, which is a completely inner quality. The external movement that came out of these images was also quite original.

Session Three: Imagine!

Our third and final session took place at the same Toronto location, two weeks later, on November 5, 2010. Nina was now in rehearsal for the remount of *The Silicone Diaries* at Buddies in Bad Times Theatre, and we chose to focus on integrating our work into her upcoming performance. To explore new ways of moving we began by working with a number of images, a model who had impressed Nina at an avant-garde fashion show, a spider, and a cobra. Nina wanted "to find physical shapes that the audience wouldn't think would be typical of [her]."

We then proceeded to work with the "Me 'n' Tommy Lee" section of *The Silicone Diaries* in order to integrate an image/Imaginary Body into the text. The main task was to break the speech down into the consonants and the vowels and leave the meaning of the text aside. As per the demands of the psycho-physical approach we had been exploring, we were to continue to give primacy to the physicality that resulted from working with images, proceed from image to movement, and then, arrive at working with sound.

The text begins, "One night, before heading to Ultra Supper Club, I pop an Ativan."[10] Her physicality as she spoke the text embodied the spider, hands teasing her hair, and then shifted to the gliding walk of the model as she made her entrance into the club: "As I glide into Ultra Supper Club, the restaurant manager, Neil, leads me by the hand, passing a lineup of over-the-top, skeleton-thin, silicone-enhanced women. Lots of extensions. Lots of rocker chicks. Neil says, 'Ugh! All wannabe star-fuckers. Here for the biggest-dicked rocker in the world.'"[11] As I watch Nina, I can see that the integration is going well. I side coach with directions such as "glide, just glide, forget about the text. Exaggerate the spider. No meaning, just consonants and vowels!"

As the final exploration we would undertake together, Nina introduces the idea of another animal: a great white shark. We spend time developing the image of the shark and connecting it to her movement. I like the effect that the shark has on Nina's gaze; there is darkness in her eyes brought on by embodying the shark. I comment that her gaze is in an unemotional, nonperformative state and Nina agrees, "that to me is not performing. The shark has an internal movement. The image of a shark lets me ride to the moment with no responsibility to be warm. There is a single purpose to it. There is no thinking. There is the water and the movement. There is also a hunger. It feels sinister."

We work on the image at slow, fast, and medium speeds and Nina comments that she feels self-possessed. "Nothing can hurt me. Nothing penetrates." Her outside expression matches this, as I observe that she really does seem to be unstoppable, but that she also appears to be a cold person. Nina is frightened by this possibility, as it has a connotation of inhumanity or cruelty. Still, we continue with the great white shark: "It feels like nothing matters. I feel nothing." Just as Nina is commenting how she isn't feeling anything, I, in observer mode, am beginning to feel a lot. Once again we have encountered the paradox of our art form through the eternal opposition of process and result: one must not look for the result, yet the deciding factor in the successful outcome of art is the result. As she is embodying the shark and not seeking a result, I am getting goosebumps from her performance.

When we stop, Nina observes that her actor training has never allowed her "not to be concerned about the storytelling." Even to abandon it for a short while is outside her performance paradigm to such a degree that the moment calls for a theoretical explanation, which I have avoided in our previous sessions so as not to complicate the process. I explain, "we are adding something to the performance and it is called the Imaginary Body. It is a tool. We work with an image and integrate that image." Curiously, this makes Nina break into a wonderful laugh. "Why are you laughing?" I ask. "Because," she answers, "when I was working with different acting teachers they would say 'stop worrying about yourself, just be with the other person.' The whole idea of 'don't think about your body' has been just impossible." I was delighted that Nina brought up a topic of which I have always been very aware while teaching the psycho-physical acting approach. Unlike the American Method,[12] which is most often used by North American teachers, and, for the most part, seeks to find a life-like expression on the level of the performer's own personality and behaviour,[13] the psycho-physical approach trains an actor to develop a distinctive manner of expression that is also truthful.[14] This means that a performer does not solely strive for verisimilitude and psychological realism in expression. Rather s/he creates a new reality through a specific quality of action, which draws upon such concepts as inner movement and working with an image. Clearly, Nina is the kind of actor for whom this approach is well suited. Not only does it offer a good way out of self-consciousness, but it also offers a way into Nina's creative process (again, these are inextricably connected).

In working with Nina, my own exploration was focused in large part on what happens when the actor's Imaginary Body becomes her permanent body. Nina responded thus:

> I built [my body] over time. There is a difference between being thirty and thirty-six and how comfortable I can be in my constructed body. Now, I need to work with the image/ Imaginary Body in order not to feel like I don't really fit in this body any longer, as I am changing and becoming older. There are new ways that I can be in this body.

Indeed, at this point, the challenges to relate to the body seem to be internal rather than external in Nina's case. This is somewhat of a paradox in that this is a person who has gone through sixty operations in order to match her inner thoughts and feelings to her outward appearance. Or, instead of being a paradox, it is a confirmation of a very simple principle: when working with an image in a psycho-physical way, the inner and outer are interconnected and part of a greater sense of the whole that is constantly shifting. For example, inhabiting an image of a king cobra or a spider will give a performer an external but also an internal consistency, which, if done well, will also be surprising and inconsistent. The operative word in this statement is "inhabiting." The permanent Imaginary Body poses the very same challenge. It needs to be inhabited.

Conclusion

After our sessions, I return to my original questions to Nina and I ponder our discoveries. What does it mean "to act" once a performer has physically transformed into a role permanently? *It means to inhabit the role.* Is this still acting? *Yes. Working with an outer image requires an adequate inner life, and, conversely, all inner impulses must be expressed adequately.* When she acts, does she still play a part or is the part playing her? *Both. Chekhov talks about a dual consciousness that can develop in an involved performance. A person can* simultaneously *play but also observe the performance. This is a desired state and a completely different one than "being in one's head."*[15] When doesn't she play a part? *The moment an actor is inspired, she stops playing a part and abides in that cherished place of emptiness where impulses flow freely. This occurred when Nina was working with an image in a psycho-physical way.* How could she (and would she) want to step outside the role/s she has created for herself? *No, Nina didn't want to step outside the realm of playing "beautiful." However, she also said "If I were to be cast against the type, I would be cast as a natural beauty." All her choices are determined by her idea of female beauty.* Is one type of role enough to keep her interested? *Yes. Nina is constantly searching for moments of presence, as she is performing her life. This is a continuous process of looking deeply into her own truth and expressing it.* Does she desire to play outside the type she has created? *Yes, as long as it is not the role of "the girl next door."*

Beyond all of our questions and answers, it is Nina's Imaginary Body that continually fascinates and engages the viewer. Yet the Imaginary Body also provides an identity, providing a mechanism and a container for both internal and external transformation: the internal transformation of the actor's consciousness, and the external, physical transformation.

Nina's Imaginary Body frees her from having to create a self-portrait and allows her to simultaneously be objective and subjective. Her dual consciousness is equally her blessing and her curse. In something akin to a permanent trance-like state in the Imaginary Body, a part of her is doing the action as another part of her is watching the action. Nina calls this her willing self-objectification, and indeed this has resulted in the object being watched by the self.

My experiences working with Nina have drawn me back to Hans Christian Anderson's telling of *The Little Mermaid*, which I loved when I was a young girl. In this telling, the Little Mermaid longs for a soul and an eternity in heaven, a destiny which only belongs to humans, not Merfolk. She falls in love with a prince, whose life she saves, but to earn his love she must become human and bargains her intoxicating voice and mermaid tail for human legs. Every step the Little Mermaid takes on those new legs is as painful as if a hundred daggers are being driven into the soles of her feet. Naturally, the prince loves to watch her dance and she dances for him despite the excruciating pain. The narrative worsens when he chooses another maiden as his mate, one who he mistakenly thinks has saved his life. Heart-broken, the Little Mermaid returns to the sea, and the agony she feels transforms her body into sea foam. But instead of ceasing to exist, she becomes a spirit, a Daughter of the Air. Because she loves truly, she gains an eternal soul. The tale is about passion, sacrifice, risk, and the desire for transformation.

In Anderson's version, the Little Mermaid willingly became an object for the prince. However, in an alternate ending that he also wrote, as she is dying of a broken heart, but before she turns into the foam, the Little Mermaid is given a choice. If she slays the prince and lets his blood drip on her feet, she will become a mermaid again, all her suffering will end, and she will live out her full life. The Little Mermaid cannot bring herself to kill the sleeping prince, lying with his bride, and, as dawn breaks, she throws herself into the sea. Her body dissolves into foam, but instead of ceasing to exist, she feels the warmth of the sun; she has evolved into a spirit, a Daughter of the Air. Anderson originally ended the tale with the mermaid dissolving, but then later added the "Daughter of the Air" coda, stating that it was his original intention and, in fact, the working title of the story. He saw her sacrifice as a means of transformation and a conscious choice to relinquish her body in service of a more beautiful wholeness. And to me Nina has done just that, and in so doing she has and continues to become a Daughter of the Air.

Dr. Cynthia Ashperger was born in Zagreb, Croatia (formerly Yugoslavia), where she had extensive experience in theatre, film, and television industry as an actor. She holds a PhD from University of Toronto's Graduate Centre for Study of Drama. She has taught acting at Ryerson Theatre School since 1994, where she is also the director of the Acting program. In 2008 she published a book on Chekhov's acting technique titled *The Rhythm of Space and the Sound of Time: Michael Chekhov's Acting Technique in the 21st Century* (2008). Her contribution to *Stanislavski and Directing: Theory, Practice and Influence* was published in 2009.

Ashperger has taught workshops and lectured on Chekhov's technique nationally and internationally. Her recent work has been two-fold: she is researching how process-oriented psychology and Chekhov technique can come together to aid actors in overcoming creative blocks, and she is developing new methods within the rehearsal process. Recently she contributed a paper at the International Federation for Theatre Research Congress (IFTR) in Munich, Germany. Other recent credits include facilitating a workshop at the Staging Sustainability Symposium (York University, Toronto), contributing a paper at IFTR (Osaka, Japan), and playing the role of Birgit in *Berlin Blues* by acclaimed First Nations Canadian playwright Drew Hayden-Taylor at 4th Line Theatre (Ontario).

Bibliography

Arsenault, Nina. *The Silicone Diaries*. In *TRANS(per)FORMING Nina Arsenault*, edited by Judith Rudakoff, 191–227. Bristol: Intellect Press, 2012.

Ashperger, Cynthia. "The First Session." Toronto, ON, October 21, 2010.

———. "The Second Session." Toronto, ON, October 22, 2010.

———. "The Third Session." Toronto, ON, November 5, 2010.

Chekhov, Michael. *The Actor Is the Theatre. A Collection of Michael Chekhov's Unpublished Notes and Manuscripts on the Art of Acting and the Theatre*, "Skid." Compiled by Deirdre Hurst du Prey, 1977.

Mindell, Amy. *The Dreaming Source of Creativity*. Portland, Oregon: Lao Tse Press, 2005.

Notes

1. Nina Arsenault, e-mail message to author, September 30, 2010.
2. Unless otherwise indicated, all of the quotations in the three sessions refer to their respective number in the bibliography. These sessions were audio-taped and transcribed by the author.

3. Amy Mindell, *The Dreaming Source of Creativity* (Portland, Oregon: Lao Tse Press, 2005), 202.
4. Ibid., 204.
5. Ibid.
6. Ibid., 206.
7. Ibid., 202.
8. In the final stage of the exercise when the actor *transforms* the negative aspect of the figure into a positive essence of its pent-up energy by imagining its core and its essence in terms of a piece of nature, the actor needs to learn how to express this essence in a large gesture. This is where I usually introduce Chekhov's Psychological-Gesture (PG). PG is a large, archetypal, continuous gesture, which has a beginning, middle, and an end, and which can serve many functions, such as capturing the essence of the character or several aspects of it, specifying a relationship, or creating an important moment in the play etc. A PG needs to be internalized and one is ready to internalize the movement of the PG only once it has sufficiently changed his/her psychology while done externally.
9. Church Street is the central street of Toronto's gay community.
10. Nina Arsenault, *The Silicone Diaries*, in *TRANS(per)FORMING Nina Arsenault*, ed. Judith Rudakoff (Bristol: Intellect Press, 2012), 217.
11. Ibid.
12. American Method is a general term for an extremely valuable acting approach used by teachers such as Stella Adler, Uta Hagen, Sanford Meisner, and Lee Strasberg (to name a few). Although their approaches differ, they have all grown from the common root of early findings within Konstantin Stanislavsky's system.
13. As Stanislavsky's productions entered America in the 1920s, North America was in need of a basic, cohesive acting training. It was the "lifelike" feelings of the actors of the Moscow Art Theatre (MAT) that attracted those who then became the system's proponents in the United States.
14. A suitable definition of style in the context of Chekhov's technique is the quality that results from a distinctive manner of expression. Creating a style has been and continues to be a contentious issue between the proponents of this technique and those of the American Method, where naturalism is a default style in all its branches.
15. Michael Chekhov, *The Actor Is the Theatre. A Collection of Michael Chekhov's Unpublished Notes and Manuscripts on the Art of Acting and the Theatre, "Skid,"* compiled by Deirdre Hurst du Prey (1977).

Chapter 4

Nina, Amber, and the Evolution of a Commodified Sexual Being

Todd Klinck

I met Rodney Arsenault in September 1993, on my first day of university. Rodney was my frosh boss during Orientation Week. I didn't get to know him that well; we were just (I thought) fellow gay guys in the same theatre program and we lived in the same residence. I remember him as a highly talented, creative theatre director, and a somewhat quiet individual.

Approximately five years later, I met Nina Arsenault. She had moved to South Africa to get a Master of Fine Arts degree, and I'd heard through the grapevine that she had transitioned from male to female while living there. In the time since we had last seen each other, I had written a book about the after-hours club scene titled *Taccones*[1] and I had become a photographer of shemale pornography. I had also worked as a male escort. During the same period, Nina had been working as a cybersex model and had been undergoing a lot of plastic surgery. She phoned me out of the blue one day and asked if we could meet to discuss tranny sex work stuff. That's when our friendship really began.

When Nina came to my place, I almost cried as I saw her. I had a deep, visceral reaction to the extensive plastic surgery she had undertaken. This was during the initial years of the Internet and knowledge revolution, and although I was involved in the T-girl[2] porn scene, very few girls were getting facial feminization surgery.[3] Rodney was a handsome guy, but with very male squarish features, and Nina told me in that meeting that she was determined to get as much surgery as necessary to be content with her look. While it turned out that she was only part way towards her goal when it came to surgery, the dramatic changes I saw both shocked and inspired me.

Nina's approach to surgery, beauty, and femininity is unconventional, controversial, and fascinating. Nina has explored this in her writing and video work, and academics and journalists continue to weigh in. I have always supported and celebrated Nina's approach, but my contribution to this book will not directly address this topic. Perhaps because of our long friendship, perhaps because we both spent many years as sex workers, Nina has granted me access to an area of her life that has not yet been explored or even delineated. That area is yet another unconventional aspect of Nina: her sexuality and its commodification. In this chapter, I will catalogue Nina's evolution as a commodified sexual being, focusing on her own frank analysis and commentary throughout.

I was present and involved during much of Nina's sexual evolution, as a friend and colleague in the industry,[4] so my primary research for this chapter took the form of an afternoon spent together collectively remembering and documenting the evolution of her sexual being. I have chosen to include much of what Nina said during our lengthy conversation,[5] rather than intruding with a great deal of commentary, because the conversation was so real, exploratory, and because, as usual, Nina is an excellent source of self-analysis. What the conversation made most clear to me is that Nina is an experimental person, navigating her way through life, moment to moment, and that she is not scared to reveal and share the insights she gains along the way. These insights are not always pretty, nor do they fit into society's conventional boxes, but they are authentic, human, and honest.

The Chronology of Nina's Sexual Commodification

Nina summarizes her sexual chronology as follows:

- Webcam Model Period[6]
- The Comfort Zone Era[7]
- The Escort Period
- Shemale Stripper Period[8]
- Militaristic Hooker Period
- Girlfriend Period[9]
- Mistress Period[10]

The Comfort Zone Era and the Appearance of Amber

When Nina stripped at The Lounge, her stage name was Amber. Amber was a persona she created, and during our interview she explained that Amber started to evolve during the Comfort Zone Era.

I was going to the Comfort Zone, getting high and having sex with a bunch of guys and not getting paid, just for the fun of having sex, being drunk and high. I started developing Amber at CZ, before the sex work started. I wanted a boyfriend and the way I was going to get a boyfriend was that I would be super sexual and do anything, like a nymphomaniac. My sexuality was super robust. I wasn't on hormones at the time, so I just wanted to have a lot of anonymous sex and it was anything goes, and the wilder the better: orgies, threesomes, or five guys at one time. I wasn't sure if I was playing a role as Amber, or if I was being real, or if I was playing an image of a woman.

I desperately wanted to be loved, and I thought the way to get love was to be everything a man could desire sexually, to be a man's personal pornstar, that then he'd come over and fuck me all the time and then eventually we would bond and he would fall in love with me. But that never worked. Then when I started escorting, I integrated that mentality—the way I was picking up guys and having sex—into my sex work, because when I was picking up those guys at the Comfort Zone and having all that sex with them, a lot of times after the sex or after they would cum they'd be like "I can't believe I did this, I'm fucking straight" or "I have a fucking girlfriend" or "Fuck, like, you tricked me" and I'd always be like "Fuck, as soon as they cum they become completely transphobic" and so I thought I might as well be fucking getting paid for this.

From the creation of Amber at the Comfort Zone, which led to her decision to begin charging for sex, Nina began to explore and express her frustration with the paradox of men's desire/repulsion for shemale sex. Her own growing understanding of issues of real versus fake versus authentic and how she was negotiating those territories followed her into the next stage of her development, the Escort Period. And so did Amber.

The Escort Period and the Evolution of Amber

So that took me into escorting. Those men made me so angry. They lied to me over and over: "Oh, you're really special, I want to get to know you." All those stupid-ass lies that straight guys have to tell to get laid. And I would believe them, time after time. Maybe that was because I was new to being a woman and new to having breasts and new to being sexually desirable.

I was angry at men when I started, but as soon as I was getting paid for sexual experiences, I was like, "This is great" and so I started sort of developing Amber. She was a piece of my personality. I splintered Amber off and commodified that persona. I found ways to seduce men. Drugs enabled me to be in touch with a greater piece of my sexuality and I could bring that to the forefront, and that made me more seductive to straight men. Then I would try to seduce straight men all the time because I wanted one of them to love me. Then I learned how I could seduce them. Sometimes it felt like I would open a psychological door in my head to find that I was really needy, and this really needy part of me wanted to be loved. I would drop into that damaged part of me that wanted to be overstimulated and hypersexual and I would do anything for the slightest bit of attention. That persona became Amber.

In time, I got her a tan, I got her a weave, and I started to sculpt that damaged part of me. In certain ways, I empowered and then fortified her and Amber was a piece of me. It was like going back to that damaged inner child and building her up. And styling her.

I made a lot of money as Amber, and I also want to say that I'm not judging or saying "that's a really damaged part of me, so as a result I was a damaged hooker." In going into that piece of my psyche, I found incredible pleasure, because I wanted love, I wanted attention and I was getting fulfilled.

The Shemale Stripper Period and the Paradox of Authenticity

I witnessed the continued evolution of the Amber persona in my role as Nina's DJ, waiter, and manager at The Lounge. She tipped me at the end of each shift, so technically I was also her pimp. She often talked to me during slow periods about authenticity, and how it related to her approach to stripping, sex work, and theatre. This period was clearly experimental for her in terms of how she positioned herself and how she presented and engaged with her constructed public image and performed sexual persona; in the early days, she summoned and inhabited the character of Nomi Malone from the movie *Showgirls*. At one point, she asked me to introduce her as The Shemale Nympho, and a few times, to explore further aspects of her evolving sexual persona, she experimented with the drug GHB (which amongst other things, can cause an increase in libido and reduce inhibitions). We revisited these topics during our interview.

The songs were three minutes each, $20 a song for a private dance. For me, the number one way to keep it going was to keep it authentic. Because the clients could sniff out fake sexiness if you were faking it. What the guys wanted, I found, was not any kind of mechanical sex act. It wasn't that they wanted a blowjob or to suck your dick. They wanted an authentic experience of either intimacy or passion. So for me the best way to work it, to make the money, to have the most positive experience, was to do everything I could do to encounter each man as authentically as I could. I would take the guy back to the private booth and think of that booth as a confessional: they were going to show me things that they couldn't show their girlfriends or wives, or do things with me that their buddies couldn't know about, probably just because I was a transsexual and had a dick. This was a private experience of maybe something they had thought about for a really long time, or a really important piece of them that no one could know about, or a primal piece of them that they felt society was oppressing. If I remembered that, it was easy to be authentically interested in them. How could I turn myself on, take the clues from what each guy was giving me and find a way to make that real, and what I mean by real is emotionally intense or intimate.

That would keep the money coming, but it also meant that I was having fun. Sometimes it meant having secrets. (For me being authentic doesn't mean that you get to know everything about me; part of being authentic in the case I'm describing was that there was always this secret part of my mind that was working.)

Sometimes I would make the seduction authentic by activating Amber. I would unlock the psychological doors in my mind and go inside: I would even go into trauma, or whatever it took. Sometimes being authentic meant pretending I was someone else, so for that I had my Amber persona. I thought of her as a compartmentalized personality that I had created. Moving into Amber was a shift I could make to a place where I could be her, and she came from inside me, was me, so I guess that's part of the paradox of authenticity.

The Militaristic Hooker Period and Being Amber

There was a period when working at The Lounge became difficult for Nina due to a group of other strippers ganging up on her. Thus began Nina's period of "militaristic" hooking. She wanted to make as much money as quickly as possible to get as much surgery as she felt she needed, as fast as possible. Her hooking was extreme: she would see up to twelve guys in one day, back to back. In my own escorting days, I found it emotionally challenging to see even four guys in one day, but Nina dug deep, summoned Amber, and survived this athletic sexual period.

It got so tough I couldn't work there. I started crying at work because they were so rude to me, so I thought "fuck this, I'm just going back into hooking." So I left stripping and started hooking hardcore. Like twelve guys a day.

There was a time when my hooking was militaristic. I would even sleep with my makeup on, so if I would get a call in the middle of the night, I would take a caffeine pill and do the trick. In the morning I would wake up, clean my apartment, and I'd be picking up the phone as I was doing my makeup: I would do back to back to back guys all day.

I was obsessed with earning money and getting the next surgery. I made a lot of money and I spent a lot of money on my surgery, and while I didn't go out, and I didn't buy dresses, I wasn't frugal either: it was an expensive lifestyle. I took cabs everywhere. I ordered in every meal: my food bill was crazy, like $60 a day. When I was hooking one summer, I was high on marijuana from the moment I woke up until the moment I went to bed, and that helped me. Eventually I needed the marijuana just to get through the tricks, to get through the day. Then gradually, I felt like I had to get into guys hitting me because that was real.

Sex had become such a performance of authenticity for me that it was fucking me up. Because I was always having to find a way in, to make it real, a little bit of marijuana helped to open up that trauma file in my brain, to become, to be Amber.

Eventually it got to the point that I was living inside the Amber persona all day, every day: I was Amber. I was building up this compartmentalized personality who was really quite fabulous and agreeable and treated men with respect and was interested in whatever sexually made them tick and who wanted to be loved. And the thing that I really came to peace with about her was that she was insatiable. She wanted to be loved so badly that nothing could fill that void.

In a way, Amber was like a cup that couldn't be filled. Even if there was a guy that came over and was really into me, it could never be enough. I felt that I was working it so much and working it so well that I could even fool myself. And then I didn't know how to get out of that role. Once I started having sex for money that was pretty much it: sex was for money. I didn't have sex for fun anymore.

And then I met this guy Anthony,[11] who was one of my last tricks when I was going to quit escorting because it was fucking with my head too much. When I saw him, I immediately knew that I would be in love with him, and I knew that he would be my next relationship. I started to let him come over for free, and one thing that was really good about him was that he hit me and that kind of deconstructed my whoreness.

All of the fake stuff that I was doing, the performative stuff—you know, the stomach in, tits out, ass up routine—he would fuck me so brutally and beat me and take me to the limits of my endurance so that I couldn't control myself in that or any other way anymore. I couldn't work it any more. I was barely able to keep up with what was happening, the way he was hitting me or the overstimulation of the sex: I couldn't do anything but hang on, it was that intense. That was a real thrill. And then I fell in love with him.

Nina stopped escorting and dated Anthony exclusively. To support herself, she went back to stripping (the other girls were nicer to her this time), and she was diligent about never doing anything sexual with men during private dances; it was just dancing. She also still did webcamming from home. Nina's relationship with Anthony lasted for sixteen months, and then he dumped her. I know she was conflicted about her relationship with Anthony because it was located on that line between real abuse and consensual sadomasochism. She had detached from her body so much during the militant escorting period that she needed the physical beating to help her to get back into her body. She had, in my opinion, been using her body while protecting her inner self by retreating to a place inside her mind. Conflicted or not, the break up with Anthony put her into an extreme depression. Despite her emotional turmoil she continued working as a webcam model from home and as a stripper at The Lounge, which is where she met Maurizio.

The Full-Time Mistress Period and Releasing Amber

Nina's relationship with Maurizio is the most positive relationship I have seen her engage in during the lengthy duration of our friendship. As she says frequently, "it works." There is still clearly a business component to this relationship, but she is no longer "working it" in such an intense way.[12] I think she has found a healthy balance. Though Nina maintains that she loves both Maurizio and Anthony, it is clear that there are differences in the relationships and that "love" is not the differentiating component in these complex and complicated interactions.

My next relationship was with Maurizio. He would come to The Lounge every day I stripped, spending an enormous amount of money on me, you know, $20 a song for two hours a day, for over a year until I said to him "why don't you just get me out of here? You're spending this much money on me every week, why not just pay this much more and you can have me exclusively to yourself?" So Maurizio and I came to an agreement about what that amount would be and so then in a way, well, I wouldn't call him my sugar daddy: he is my boyfriend. He also has a wife and children.

I see him for a few hours a week, it's always during the same time slot and during that time slot, I have to be "on." I have to be sexually hot and yet it isn't really that hard because it works between us. I'm attracted to him.

It's exclusive. On my part. He owns the rights to my body, to my sexuality. That's part of the deal and I've never broken that deal. I'd have to look him in the eyes and I think he'd know. Part of the hotness for me is his ownership.

I'm not sure how long it's going to last, but I do know that when I told him how much I wanted per week, in my mind I thought "he could dump me tomorrow and I would think I got what I was worth the whole time." I am very content with this arrangement. Of course now that we've been together for four years, he would have to give me six weeks severance pay.

If I saw him at a store with his family, he wouldn't even say hi to me. We do things publicly together, but in places that he knows his family is not going to see him. A couple of his guy friends who also have mistresses know that he and I are together; I feel like I should be compensated because he's a married man and won't fully acknowledge his mistress in public. His wife knows he has a mistress. They are Italian, he's wealthy, he's older, from the old country and the wife is taken care of in her own way. She's comfortable knowing that he has a mistress. She's relieved of some of her wifely duties.

At this point in my conversation with Nina, I noted that even with Maurizio, her sexuality is still being commodified in their relationship. She clarified that in her relationship with Maurizio there are differences from earlier interactions. With him, she is actually emotionally engaged.

In a certain way, yeah, but it's blurry now, because what happens between me and him works. It's authentic. It's also real. I don't have to find a way into it to be attracted to him. I don't need to become Amber. The very first time I danced for him, he put his hands on me and I thought "oh yes, this is going to work," just the way he touched me, I knew he'd be the next one. I knew it right away. Love at first touch.

I asked Nina to clarify the term "boyfriend" and how that might differ from the term "trick" given that she and Maurizio are still technically in a business relationship. She made it clear that one aspect of a boyfriend relationship was the important validation of public acknowledgement. And that she was relating to Maurizio as herself, not as Amber.

I knew I couldn't have Anthony as my boyfriend, because above all else he wouldn't go out in public with me. I realized then that it was going to be very hard to meet a straight guy who was OK with being seen with someone who is visibly transgendered in public.

Nina also made it clear that the boundaries of her relationship with Maurizio do not make it any less authentic or pleasurable. She also claimed that in all her dealings with her boyfriend, even when she is enacting her sexual persona for him, it is not as Amber, but as Nina.

Maurizio has seen enough of my plays and he is mature enough to know that my sexuality is a performance, but with him it is a performance of revealing, like a dance of the seven veils. I'm not "working it" so much as he comes over and we fool around and I see just how much carnality I can drop into, how much I can reveal. In a way that's one of the reasons why I don't feel I need a pussy. Because my sexuality now is about how much I can open myself up, how receptive can I be to sensation, emotion, and obviously Maurizio's physicality.

We never get bored of each other because we only see each other once a week. The other six days a week I have for my life and my work. I'm devoting myself to my artwork and theatre really is of the utmost importance to me. I don't want a man around all the time, I don't want a man sleeping over, seeing me in the morning without my makeup on, I don't want any of that. I don't want a boring conventional relationship that gets stale.

I have a boyfriend, I get to be loved and I get to be financially supported. I get to do my work as an artist and I don't have to fill out arts grants ... it's amazing.

Conclusion

Through an abbreviated journey through a selected chronology of Nina's sexual commodification, I have demonstrated how Nina created inner and outer safeguards to protect her emerging authentic sexual self. From the protective barrier of the electronic stage to inhabiting a series of increasingly real characters that interacted with the public, and eventually culminating in a fully fledged persona named Amber, Nina has been able to discover and embrace both her evolving personal identity and the ongoing commodification of her sexuality.

As stated above, Nina is more content today in her relationship with Maurizio than I've ever known her to be during the nearly two decades we've shared as friends and associates. As well, while she may have, in large part, relinquished the sheltering presence of Amber, and she may have done so without judging or devaluing this and other important parts of her evolutionary journey, she remains, undeniably and willingly, a sexual commodity. And that, in and of itself, presents another unique facet of the unconventional being that is Nina Arsenault.

Todd Klinck is an award-winning author and screenwriter. He is an advocate for the decriminalization of sex work, and was a sex worker for many years. He has produced approximately 150 pornographic films (mainly gay and transsexual themed) and manages a nightclub in Toronto called Goodhandy's.

Notes

1. One of Nina's earlier club-kid alter egos, a girl named Breezy, made a brief appearance in one of the stories.
2. "T-girl" refers to a transsexual woman.

3. A highly specialized plastic surgery technique for Male-to-Female transsexuals.
4. I started working as a webcam model when I was twenty-one, and also escorted. I did photography for adult shemale websites, I consulted with escorts who needed their own website or Internet advice, and I eventually formed a porn video business with my business partner Mandy Goodhandy. There has always been an "adult" facet to my very diverse resume of experiences.
5. All quotations in this article are from a four-hour conversation Nina and I had in Toronto on January 9, 2011.
6. Webcam modeling was one of Nina's ongoing skills and jobs. She started out at Toronto's VideoSecrets, where she worked in a studio environment, but then, as technology evolved, it became possible for her to continue her webcam modeling from her home. Webcam modeling was more often than not part of the chronology, so its placement is, in some ways, fluid. It took place, in any case, at the start of what I'm categorizing as a chronology.
7. The Comfort Zone is a legendary Toronto after-hours club known as a place to go to do drugs and dance to electronic music. Even though the clients are often totally straight suburban kids, there has always been a queer element to the place. Late at night when everyone's fucked up on drugs, labels like straight, gay, trans, all start blurring together and there is a general tendency for people to get along.
8. In April 2003, my current business partner Mandy Goodhandy opened up a revolutionary club event in the basement of a divey, filthy Mississauga strip club featuring shemale strippers. She rented the party room of the club, called it "The Lounge," charged customers $40 cover, and the girls made $20 a song doing private dances for guys who had primarily learned about their interest in transsexuals through Internet porn and backpage ads of weekly magazines. I worked for Mandy as the DJ and waiter, and Nina was one of the very first girls to take a leap of faith and travel to the dingy airport strip hoping to make at least a couple hundred bucks. It became a lucrative source of income for Nina and other girls: some days she made more than $2000.
9. Nina entered into a sixteen-month-long, non-commercial, sadomasochistic relationship during this period.
10. Nina entered into a long-term commercial relationship with a wealthy Italian man who does not hit her.
11. Names have been changed to maintain anonymity. Anthony and Maurizio are pseudonyms.
12. There is, it should be clarified, a major distinction between letting the relationship work and working the relationship. The former speaks to a type of trust while the latter implies a need to maintain a level of control.

Chapter 5

Sexed Life is a Cabaret: The Body Politics of Nina Arsenault's
The Silicone Diaries

Frances J. Latchford

What does it cost to parody sex and should it be tried? At a time when queer and transgender theories often follow different trajectories concerning the social and political value of parody, camp, and drag, Nina Arsenault's work on the stage is unique as sex parody. She reimagines sex, not merely gender, as burlesque spectacle. She exposes what is phantasmagoric in sexed embodiment to demonstrate the body's possibility as temporal-corporeal-plasticity in sense, meaning, and form. She does so through critical camp performances that (re) present desire as a basis for better understanding the ontological (in)authenticity of the genitals, sexed embodiment, and "female" and "male" subjectivities, as well as gender. By doing so, Arsenault's work provokes a dialogue in and between theories that concern queer and transsexual subjects, theories that increasingly articulate a difference between gendered and sexed subjectivities as respectively *on* the skin (i.e. performative) and *in* the skin (i.e. embodied). Her burlesques of sex frustrate the (perhaps inadvertent) knowledge effects of a *will to difference* in queer and transgender theory, a will that generates a powerful discursive undercurrent of division between queer and transsexual folk that can have further effects socially and politically.

Where it is likened to, or coupled with, drag and camp, the idea that queerness is different in kind from what is enlivened by and through transsexuality is an important theme that emerges in and between queer theory and theories of transsexual embodiment. The difference, in Jay Prosser's words, is the fact that "there is much about transsexuality that must remain irreconcilable to queer: the specificity of transsexual experience; the importance of the flesh to self; the difference between sex and gender identity; the desire to pass as 'real-ly gendered' in the world without trouble."[1]

Indeed, the work of many important queer and transsexual theorists reiterates this difference as both psychic and essential, and as such it separates queer and transsexual experiences one from another.[2] For instance, this difference is implicit in Pat Califia's rejection of Kate Bornstein's political praxis, wherein Bornstein argues that "camp is the safety valve that can keep any gender activism from becoming fanaticism," whether or not it pertains to "transgendered people who would subscribe fully to culture's definitions of gender, and seek to embody those definitions within themselves"[3]; there are, according to Califia, "more concrete items that should appear on a political agenda for transsexual activists" than camp or humour.[4] One of the earliest queer theorists Judith Butler also marks "the difference between dressing up, drag, transgender, and transsexual, and what this says about performance and its relationship to audience."[5] Drag, she explains, "demands its stage and its club," where transgender "ask[s] us to think performance off the proscenium stage …

more on the street and in relation to family, workplace … airports, immigration, authorities and the rest."[6] And "*transsexuality* has another set of institutional implications, ones that involve questions of legal and medical status as well as how the meaning of *performance* changes when it becomes less based on a theatrical space and more about the vicissitudes of daily life and even psychic survival."[7] In one sense, the psychic distinction that is made in theory between queer-gender-drag and transsexual-sex-embodiment has social and political implications; the former is said to take gender subversion as its goal, while the latter's aim is said to be meaningful access to the achievement of a desired sex. The life of the transsexual subject is not meant to be a cabaret, my friend, or so it seems in light of how this difference is repeatedly articulated in theory. In another sense, this difference, as it is said and re-said is becoming categorical and, as a result, it has ontological effects that can undermine queer and transsexual lives. In a world where gender and sexuality is staged as a comedy and sex is staged as a tragic drama, queers can't die and transsexuals can't laugh.

With an eye to Nina Arsenault's sex parodies, this chapter suggests that either existence, on its own, is perilous. It initially examines how queer and transsexual subjects are differentiated in theory, particularly in relation to comedy and tragedy. It sets out to challenge this binary of queer comedy and transsexual tragedy. It does so by showing how burlesque elements in Arsenault's performance elicit a parody of sex. It examines *The Silicone Diaries* as a play that refuses conflations of transsexuality with interiority and corporeality and queerness with exteriority and fluidity, both of which are effects of this troublesome and divisive binary. It finally suggests that *The Silicone Diaries* inspires what I call transsubjective identifications; it argues that the play's ability to engender these identifications, amongst diverse members of an audience, founds a basis for critically rethinking the ontological effects of the binary of levity and gravity at work in queer and transgender theories, a binary that is (re)produced through a will to difference that categorically sets out to separate our desires for sex, gender, and sexuality.

Queer and Transsexual Difference in Theory

Today, the idea that the transsexual subject has a physical body that, barring access to hormone therapies and/or surgery, is not in harmony with an authentic or essential sex is cited often as that which fundamentally differentiates transsexual and queer subjects. Transsexuality, therefore, is distinct from queer subjectivity in that it is not centred on the question of "sexual object choice."[8] It is concerned with embodiment as the desire or need to bring the body in line with a "deep, essential truth" about one's sex.[9] This is not to say that transsexual subjects never experience same-sex or queer desire and gender, but only that when they do, this is a question of sexuality, *not* transsexuality.

In theories of transsexual embodiment, the matter of sex is neither biophysical, nor socially constructed. It is characterized, more precisely, as a matter that is existential and phenomenological, wherein the self's experience of a true sex is at odds with *both* the biological body and any social meanings this given body elicits or is constructed, *as* materiality, to sustain as social, in the sense that Judith Butler has described so well.[10] Sex, therefore, is lodged elsewhere in a "*deeply felt conflict between body and image of self*," in a "core self" or a "gendered soul" that structures the psyche.[11] Paradoxically, the truth of sex is characterized by these theories as one that resides *in* the skin; and this is because these theories understand transsexuality as a psychic demand or interior need wherein the physical body must be made to comply with the self's authentic experience of its sex. The transsexual subject's existential and phenomenological aim is to master a "psychic/corporeal harmony" in which the body, not the psyche, is re-sexed to enable the self *to become* "at home in one's skin."[12] Theories of transsexual embodiment, while they do not agree on all fronts, do typically agree that where the given physical body does not operate as a material foundation or referent that is allied with the self's experience of its authentic sex—or is not a body with which the self can identify—*that* body is not encompassed by the transsexual's skin at all.[13] It is for this reason that theories of transsexual embodiment treat the self that solely enacts an atypical gender and/or sexual desire (e.g. the butch lesbian) as something *other* than transsexual, because these kinds of desires are really only manifested *on* or *between* skins, rather than *in* the skin.

There are then two categorical differences that fundamentally separate transsness from queerness, even as transsexual and queer subjectivities are often understood to be encompassed by the broader category of "transgender" experience, a category "which includes anyone who crosses boundaries of either sex or gender" or both.[14] In essence, transsness is unlike queerness because the conflict that surrounds sex is interior and corporeal; so, even as transsexuals' sexual object choices and genders can be queer, that they *are* is irrelevant to the experience of transsexuality. And conversely, queerness is unlike transsness because the conflict between sex and sexual object choice (and gender, since sexual object choice has inherent implications for non/normative gender) is an experience that is exterior and social; queer identities occur out of desires directed towards (non-normative) external objects— other selves—with whom the self wants to commune.

Where the defining experience of transsexual subjectivity is constituted as an interior affair, and queer subjectivity is relegated to the province of exteriority, the logic of this distinction, as it occurs in theories of transsexual embodiment, is bound to produce ontological effects that elide the possibility of transsexuals being social and communal, and queers being private and individual. In theatrical terms, it is a logic that fashions transsexual lives as tragedies and queer lives as comedies, a polarization that threatens the existence of either subject psychically, socially, and politically. Indeed, traces of this logic are evident in theories of transsexual embodiment, which emerge variously in contemporary transsexual, queer, transgender, and/or feminist theories that are psychoanalytic and/or postmodern; theories of transsexual embodiment can also be proposed in conjunction or contrast with theories of performativity, the latter of which is allied with the former within transgender rubric, but nonetheless serves increasingly as a foil against which transsexual subjects are differentiated from queer subjects.[15] In addition, the tragedy of this logic commonly manifests as a discourse of psychic "suffering" that haunts the interiority of the transsexual subject, while its comedic effect is a discourse of "play" that queer gender and sexuality invites at the expense of meaningful self-reflection or concern with the real.[16]

Theories of transsexual embodiment, in all their diversity, invoke tragedy, for instance, when they furtively or boldly depict "transsexuals not as 'exotic' but as persons who suffer (for both personal and political reasons)."[17] They do so as they locate the origins of transsexual suffering in: identities that are "potentially dangerous," the "long[ing] to restore the link between their bodies and their core identities," or the experience of "an internalized subjectivity that is sealed off from other subjects."[18] They emit it in sentences careful to qualify that for "some" transsexuals the "dissonance of identity and physical body is unbearable."[19] And they demonstrate its ontological magnitude as a characteristic of transsexual experience in affirmations that "*I am alienated from Being*" and that "we transsexuals often suffer for the pain of others."[20] That transsexual people can and do suffer is not in question, that psychic suffering and tragedy operates uncritically in embodiment theories as a defining feature of transsexual subjectivity is a profound existential concern. It is a concern because interior subjects "sealed off" in "unbearable" states of "alienated being" are ones that cannot act in their own defense, or the defense of others, either socially or politically; they are effectively incapable of community and laughter because both entail an interest and ability to enter the exterior world, even as the world puts the self at risk. It is also a concern because producing transsexuals as tragic subjects marginalizes them further. While theories of transsexual embodiment do bring an understanding of transsexual subjectivity to the world, the subject they construct, arguably, is not one that easily enters the world.

Conversely, the queer subject is the comedic binary to the transsexual subject's tragedy. In part, this is the vestigial heritage of strategic AIDS and queer activism that politicized many queers as such, for example, in and through camp, drag, and guerilla theatre. Increasingly, however, the queer's pairing with comedy is the effect of theories of performativity (which sometimes are misread) and the queer's use as a foil against which embodiment theories choose to differentiate transsexual subjects within transgender discourse more broadly. The queer subject is cast apart from trauma and at play with others in the world, orientated always outward toward sexual objects, in a constant social state of uncompromising sexual celebration and gender-fucking pride. This subject subverts and parodies heteronormativity with a camp sensibility, a fluid gender and/or desire that, in theory at least, can potentially *drag* all manner of *other* toward it through the mimetic arts.

The queer subject is thrust onto a stage, for instance, by Judith Butler because she likens gender performativity to the queer practice of drag, an idea that is (mis)read as often as not to suggest that gender is "voluntarist" or entails "theatrical" agency.[21] While Butler did intend performativity to elicit an idea "of pastiche" or "a postmodern form of parody without laughter, a parody that has lost its satirical impulse," her coupling of this idea with her now infamous illustrative example of drag, nonetheless, reinstates this impulse in the queer subject.[22] The impact of Butler's thought on the queer subject, inadvertent though it may be, is that it inculcates an epistemic continuum between queer gender performance and drag, particularly within queer and transgender theory that addresses queer and transsexual subjects; queerness is tethered to comedy because Butler plays an undeniably formative role in thinking the queer subject, a role as powerful as Michel Foucault's works are relative to the homosexual subject. This effect is sustained also because queer and transgender theorists continue to reiterate Butler's drag example (as I do now), for any number of reasons. So regardless of whether she is accepted or understood, the ongoing reiteration of Butler not only represents queer subjectivity as parodic, it renders queerness ever more impervious to her less audible warning that "not … all performativity is to be understood as drag."[23] This notion of queer subjectivity is also reiterated often in theories of transsexual embodiment, and sometimes to acknowledge (mis)readings of Butler and/or the effects of her theories: "*gender* performativity has become so coextensive with *queer* performativity as to render them interchangeable."[24] At the same time, these embodiment theories often treat Butler's notion of performativity, or its effects, as an opportunity to reiterate a difference between queer and transsexual subjects, and in doing so, the possibility of transsexual subjectivity is cleaved away from comedy toward tragedy. For instance, Prosser rejects performativity (read any way) because it is unable to address transsexuals for whom gender is "an *end* of narrative *becoming*," and not a series of "performative moments all along a process" that are "above all, unpredictable and necessarily incomplete"[25]; and by doing so, he effectively rejects the relevance of queerness—performativity's sidekick—to the essence of transsness.[26]

Notably, Prosser also illustrates the fact that the queer's history as comedy is long and well known. He does so because he argues, "Butler's centrality in queer theory is in part an effect of queer's recuperation of camp and queer's recuperation *through* camp."[27] He therefore demonstrates not only the conflation of queer with comedy that is a corollary of performative discourse, but that prior to Butler this conflation is well established as an effect of the "community pride" that is founded upon a history of queer activism.[28]

But to recuperate from what precisely can queers be said to use camp? The answer to this question sets the stage for my discussion of *The Silicone Diaries* as a play that undercuts the will to difference that, increasingly, is at work in knowledge production that surrounds queer and transsexual subjects: queers use camp to recuperate from the shame and trauma that dominates queer life prior to Stonewall and the liberation movement it initiates. In other words, camp has fuelled queer politics and activism on the stage and in the streets in manifold ways, ranging from drag, kiss-ins, die-ins, and threats, such as, "we're here, we're queer, and we're not going shopping!" The problem of camp praxis, however, is that as it becomes an object of study in queer and transgender theory, it begins to operate as a stand-in for the queer subject. For instance, Heather K. Love demonstrates this effect in her critique of "queer existence," one which contends that—because "[c]elebration only gets us so far, for pride can be toxic when it is sealed off from the shame that has nurtured it"—a genealogical return to a pre-pride consciousness of shame is in order for queers.[29] In other words, the idea that queer subjects, through camp politics, have somehow exempted themselves, in life, from tragedy is implicit in Love's theoretical idea that a return to shame is necessary; Love's work effectively theorizes contemporary queer subjectivity as an outright refusal of tragedy.[30] Moreover, this effect sustains its converse effect in queer and transgender knowledge production: it seals the transsexual subject off from the laughter and comedy that also nurtures it in life. For example, a sign of this effect, which would deny the transsexual subject its share in laughter, is arguably reflected in the inability of theories of transsexual embodiment to account for the subjectivity of transsexuals like Kate Bornstein, who argues "camp is a safety valve," as I mentioned, and further that "real gender freedom begins with fun."[31]

The Silicone Diaries and the Subversion of Binary Difference

To the degree that I have established the reiteration of queer comedy and transsexual tragedy is both real in theory and dangerous in reality for subjects who are constituted thus, Nina Arsenault's tragicomic depiction of transsexual subjectivity on the stage in *The Silicone Diaries* is potent in its ability to subvert this binary. Arsenault's performance of sexed embodiment disrupts this binary because it burlesques sex, deposes the (sometimes inadvertent) conflation of transsexuality with interiority and corporeality and the reduction of queerness to exteriority and fluidity, and elicits transsubjective identifications that invite a critical rethinking of a will to difference that categorically and discursively isolates queer and transsexual subjects one from another.

Even though it can be likened to drag, because "burlesque performance must be aligned with camp," burlesque is distinct from drag in that it does not typically entail cross-dressing.[32] Historically, it is a nineteenth-century *female* genre of performance, wherein what are regarded as lower-class modes of femininity and female sexuality are parodied by women through comedic and "grotesque" exhibitions of the female body; indeed, some of the earliest audience responses to burlesque are said to have "alternated between desire, humor, and disgust."[33] Early burlesque, however, "loot[ed] and adapt[ed] the stage business of other theatrical forms" of comedy that were male.[34] As Robert C. Allen observes, it "drew particularly upon the conventions of the minstrel show" in which white men performed what is known as "black face".[35] It borrowed from minstrelsy a comedic mode of contempt that it redirected toward white, lower-class women's sexualities. These two theatrical forms were alike then, in that "[b]oth were constructed around ironic, low-other characters, whose speech, costume, behavior and demeanor helped to structure different but homologous ideological problematics: gender and race."[36] The "English idea that a burlesque had to be a parody," it is worth noting, was not ultimately sustained in nineteenth-century American burlesque, because it "disappeared behind the voluminous thighs of bare blonds dressed in tights," but in neo-burlesque, parody again becomes central to the performance as it is revived in various European and North American contexts.[37] Neo-burlesque, which emerges at the end of the 1980s, is distinct from traditional burlesque, especially as it concerns objectification, because here the "performer … by 'speaking back' to her audience, challenges received notions of sexual objectification."[38] In other words, "new burlesque parodies femininity not through self-hating mockery, but through the production of an excessive feminine self that is experienced as a source of pleasure," a pleasure that is shared by the audience and the performing subject.[39]

In *The Silicone Diaries*, important aspects of Arsenault's performance are comedic precisely because they are odes to old and new elements of burlesque, a theatrical term that literally "means 'to parody or ridicule.'"[40] These odes are evident in "studied" feminine poses that Arsenault strikes at the start of each scene and her "dramatic and deliberate display of the female body," which is relentless in the play, and a crucial tactic in burlesque and neo-burlesque performance.[41] The intentional overplay and success of her poses, particularly, as "a ballsy, glamour-puss-type of chick," magnifies stereotypes of hyperfeminine glamour and female sexuality that, when combined precisely with the audience's knowledge of her transsexuality, demonstrates the degree to which sex and gender are uncanny achievements on the part of any woman.[42] Thus, Arsenault's performance is burlesque because it "works to destabilize the ways in which dominant feminine identities become normalized," and I would add to this, the ways in which dominant female identities become normalized.[43] Her cosmetic narrative surfaces and contours the female body as it "draw[s] a dark line where my red lip meets white skin," giving "people" pause to "say, 'Don't do that. Don't do that. You won't look like a real woman if you do that. You'll look like a drag queen,'" all of which indicates that female sex and feminine gender are not her only accomplishments.[44] In what is a modern-techno-neo-burlesque style of "'high maintenance' femininity," she subverts sex and gender as "artifice" because she uncovers the spectacular nature of each as life-long quests at which human beings must always fail, precisely, because "it's not enough."[45] Thus, Arsenault's parody of sex manifests as she exposes not only herself, but all "women" as "caricatures" or "imitation[s] of an imitation of an idea of a woman. An image which has never existed in nature."[46]

In one of the most dramatic moments of the play, Arsenault performs a "grotesque" striptease and further achieves a dual parody of sex that simultaneously invokes burlesque and subverts it as the *nonpareil* genre of female performance. Very much like striptease in the context of classic and neo-burlesque style, Arsenault's striptease is a climactic centrepiece in the final movement of the play, "Venus/machine (2007–2009)."[47] As is the case in burlesque, her striptease is also critical to her play's function as parody: the social and political fecundity of burlesque, as a "site of anxiety about traditional female roles," occurs through its "public display of sexuality," a display that "depend[s] first and foremost on excessive femininity of appearance and gesture."[48] Arsenault creates even greater anxiety, however, because her striptease is coupled with the "grotesque"; a cornerstone of burlesque that dates back to the nineteenth century, the grotesque is an acute instrument of parody that, like the striptease, provokes a critique of normative bodies and roles through a theatrical display of excess, because much "like comic bodies, grotesque bodies are out of bounds in terms of behavior."[49] In the play, Arsenault's use of the grotesque is also reminiscent of its historical use in burlesque, wherein the grotesque was considered a "subspecies of the comic, designating the more fantastic side of humour."[50] Arsenault's striptease is comically grotesque: she never removes her clothes. She removes her wig—audaciously—to expose her scalp and its surgical map of scars that detail, in relief, her journey to a woman. In effect, she melodramatically grotesques the striptease and, in doing so, exposes the extent to which the female, and not merely the feminine, subject is mutable. What is more, because Arsenault grotesques the striptease as a transsexual woman—and not as a Male-to-Female impersonator or drag artist—she accomplishes a further parody of the sexed meaning of burlesque itself, in that she literally subverts a pinnacle of female, and not merely feminine, performance. The social and political import of Arsenault's burlesquing by grotesquing the striptease is that she effectively *re*presents herself as a metaphor for all women who love their sex, and for all women who are scarred by it, and gender, in that, all women, once stripped, "look[s] like no woman I have ever seen before."[51]

While Arsenault does enlist many comedic aspects of burlesque theatricality, *The Silicone Diaries* also enlists tragedy because it is an autobiographical play. It recounts various crossroads in Arsenault's voyage toward the embodiment of female sex, a voyage that, while often joyous and pleasurable, is also at times painful, humiliating, and textured by existential loss and trauma. It is painful physically because of surgery and silicone injections, and psychically because of the potential failure, breakdown, and long-term effects of each. It is alienating and humiliating when her image "unaltered by digitization" prompts an exodus of horrified male viewers in her porn-chat-room, an exodus that threatens the longevity of the online she-persona she enlivens to pay for her surgeries.[52] It is disenfranchising, much like race and disability, particularly, in terms of class, because her visibly embodied difference, as a pre-operative *and* post-operative transsexual, delimits her employment access to sex work—she cannot "pass" over the transphobic sexism that is her obstacle to normative social intercourse and labour. It is also textured by existential loss and trauma when she tells the story of her transsexual sister Nancy Bianca Valentino, who "die[s] due to complications of surgery that she had been warned about, but which she felt she could not live without."[53] Indeed, this loss emphasizes the life-and-death reality of Arsenault's and many *othered* women's desires to bring their bodies in line with an ideal of female sexed life, a desire Arsenault tells us she, like so many women, must realize "so I could live with myself. So I could look at myself."[54] Even Arsenault's near to last confession in the play is as heartbreaking as it is honest: "the next phase of my work with my body" is "to breathe through the trauma I have put inside my body."[55] And yet, Arsenault's autobiographical play never fails to couple sexed life's tragedies with its comedies. She repeatedly accomplishes this through her burlesque brand of melodrama and existential camp, for instance, when she utters her final words "that my pleasure and my sublime privilege is to suffer. And to live. With. Beauty."[56] It is, in part, Arsenault's insistence on this coupling throughout *The Silicone Diaries* that suggests the binary opposition of transsexual and queer subjects is suspect in queer and transgender knowledge production.

Arsenault's use of burlesque with autobiography in *The Silicone Diaries* enables her to parody sexed embodiment and gender without negating the significance of tragedy's equality with comedy in both the performance and reality of her transsexual subjectivity.

In other words, Arsenault's performance embodies a critique of queer and transgender knowledge that fails transsexual and queer subjects when that knowledge does not unite them along a tragicomic continuum, but rather opposes them with the binary of tragedy and comedy. She does so through a powerful rendering of transsexual existence that is undivided on the inherent gravity and levity of sexed being.

The Silicone Diaries explicitly troubles the conflation of transsexuality with interiority and corporeality and implicitly challenges the reduction of queer existence to exteriority and fluid play as these divisions occur in and through queer and transgender knowledge production. In an obvious sense, it reclaims the exteriority and play denied the transsexual subject in theory because it is both a play that takes place on "the proscenium stage," and an autobiographical narrative that concerns transsexuality and "the vicissitudes of daily life and even psychic survival."[57] On top of this, the play's narrative, scenography, and moments of direct address intend to draw the audience in as Arsenault's company—and community, as I later discuss, through transsubjective identification—while she performs the nuances of her interior life. That psychic exteriority is an aim of the play is evident in its narrative because Arsenault repeatedly directs the audience's attention to the psychic life of her sex, for instance, by repeating the phrase, "I'm visualizing on my interior screen, in my mind's eye."[58] The goal of exteriority is also visceral and tangible in the flow of images that are projected on a screen that is the play's stage backdrop; these images document Arsenault's transitions and interrupt or accompany her narratives of bodily history, fantasy, and metamorphoses. Simply put, the stage's backdrop operates as a literal externalization of Arsenault's interior screen. Furthermore, the interplay between these interior and exterior screens makes her desire for sexed subjectivity uncanny—it is eerily un/familiar in the psychoanalytic sense— because no subject escapes the knowledge and experience of what is a social-historical-political imperative of sexed life.[59] Ultimately, the uncanny effect of *The Silicone Diaries* is that it opens a window, partway, onto each self's familiarity or identification with the demand that life be sexed; and this makes Arsenault's desire that much more intelligible and, thereby, communal for an audience born to either sex.

The play's use of direct address, a technique frequently used in comedy and neo-burlesque, further heightens the sense of community and play that Arsenault clearly wants to build between her audience and herself, as both a performer and transsexual subject. This is evident, for instance, when Arsenault speaks to the audience to let it in on transsexual codes, cultures, and (camp) language wherein she defines terms such as "Fishy"—"That's what American trannies say when they mean you look like a biological female. That's something we say amongst ourselves. We mean it as a compliment. It means she looks real. It's like this: 'She's … she's … she's fishy.' Work"—or "boy-holes—that's what we call the little indentations men have between their hips and ass."[60] Where Arsenault edifies the audience directly with respect to transsexual mores, she turns outward and playfully away from interiority. Her willingness to confide in the audience tangibly demonstrates the reality of her exteriority as a transsexual subject and, in this way, *The Silicone Diaries* further disrupts the binary that divides transsexuals and queers in theory.

With respect to the binary distinction between corporeal sexed embodiment and the fluidity of gender, the play's narrative and scenography not only disrupt the artificial divide as it occurs between transsexual sex and queer gender in theory, they also replace this sex/gender binary with a continuum of corporeal, sex–gender fluidity. For instance, Arsenault's embody-works in the interests of her sex do not simply undergird her feminine gender solely as a referent, they also (re)produce it once the referent, in the main, is established. Indeed, her narrative of beauty coupled with the images that document the visual history of her transitions suggests this referent is not the sole aim of her sixty-plus surgical interventions: gender is also at issue and even more so with the success of each new surgery. Thus, at least some of Arsenault's embody-works are akin to the "cosmetic" surgical interventions cisgendered women pursue to embody their gender, not sex, because sex is not primarily in question for them. Therefore, where queer genders are concerned, the play implies that the body can corporeally confound gender and not sex, even as it also confounds sex and gender for transsexuals; for example, *there are* big-busted butches who opt for gender-change via embody-works such as breast reduction. To put it simply, *The Silicone Diaries* is uncanny also in its ability to show the degree to which gender, queer or otherwise, is often a corporeal issue of embodiment too. The play's narrative of embody-works, parceled with Arsenault's sex parodies, effectively brings fluidity to sex and corporeality to gender, without negating the inverse's reality.

Through the provocation of transsubjective identifications, *The Silicone Diaries* undoes the will to difference at work in queer and transgender discourse. The play, combined with Arsenault's performance, urges a critical rethinking of transsexual and queer being in theory; it redresses theory's division and effacement of common ground that can otherwise fortify collective social and political movement on the part of queer and transsexual subjects and, really, any subject that is marginalized by virtue of sex, gender, and/or sexuality. While the play centres on Arsenault's transsexual journey and identity, many scenes also create the possibility for transsubjective identification in an audience made up of diverse subjects; this is because transsubjective identification, as I propose it, does not turn on a common identity or subject position—it occurs between differentiated subjects on the basis of common experience and/or desire, whether that desire is a desire *to be* or *to be with*.

Two scenes in the play are particularly obvious as platforms for the possibility of transsubjective identification: the one in which the mannequin that is "more beautiful than Barbie" is encountered and another in which the "girlie magazine" that is "magic" is excitedly studied.[61] The potency of these scenes is that they recount childhood experiences on the part of Arsenault that are oh-so-like the charged experiences so many adults have also had as children, and in relation to similar objects, whether it be a mannequin, Barbie, Ken, G. I. Joe, a television or athletic persona, a *Playboy* or *Hustler* centrefold, or even a chance happening upon a naked body or a sexual scene.

In the encounter with the mannequin, for instance, Rodney (Arsenault's former first name) recognizes herself, like so many girls do, in an idealized objectification of "female" being in the world. And as she "stare[s] at her. Into her eyes" and asks "Is she real?" and later "imitat[es] the mannequin poses. Breathing life into them. The way a child would believe," Rodney reveals another kind of experience, one with which all former children, and not just girls, can identify—the imaginary experience of a future, perfect in childhood desire as the infinite possibility of existence, a possibility that too soon is painfully rejected as fantasy, or pathology, in the real by adult knowledge.[62] The breathtaking experience of the possibility of existence, now distantly familiar in what, for most of us, was once an electric childhood imagination, is echoed again by Arsenault in the story of naked centrefolds that she and the boys look at together in the woods: "I have never had this much breath inside my body before. There is so much air inside me. I don't know how I know it. Or why I know it. But I know that this is exactly what I will be when I grow up."[63]

What the play recovers from childhood for most audience members, I suspect, is the shockingly intense and "magic" pull of desire itself, and, again, this is regardless of whether it is a desire to be or to be with. It calls to mind a desire of old that was less constrained by a meaning of sex and/or object-choice than it was the simple and unself-conscious experience of being drawn to beauty and pleasure. In recovering the intensity of childhood desire *per se*, whether it manifests as a desire to be sexed, to be with a sex, or to fashion the appurtenances of sex, *The Silicone Diaries* creates a visceral emotional surface upon which the audience is invited to understand Arsenault's desire. It does so through neither an identification with embodiment, nor object-choice, but through the primary intensity and drive of one's own history of desire. Thus, insofar as it elicits transsubjective identifications that enable audience members to be with Arsenault in desire, the play gives rise to community. It also facilitates play both with the meaning and, maybe even, the end of the audience's own desires of sex, gender, and sexuality, all of which have implications for (re)thinking the subject in life and theory. In this light, *The Silicone Diaries* provokes an epistemological shift that serves up a phenomenology of desire to queer and transgender theory, one that builds bridges rather than categorical and ontological binaries between queer and transsexual subjects.

Nina Arsenault's burlesque sex parodies render the binary differentiation of queer and transsexual subjects, in relation to comedy and tragedy, highly suspect in queer and transsexual knowledge production. Her autobiographical narrative and sexed performance in *The Silicone Diaries* disjoins this binary, as well as its conflations of transsexuality with interiority and corporeality and queerness with exteriority and fluidity. Through the possibility of transsubjective identification—a possibility the play creates no matter the heterogeneity of the audience—*The Silicone Diaries* opens onto an opportunity for critically rethinking the ontological effects of this binary, and really the will to difference that effectively divides *us* through its division of our desires for sex, gender, and sexuality.

Frances J. Latchford is an associate professor in the School of Women's Studies at York University in Toronto; she teaches courses in Women's Studies and Sexuality Studies. Her research and teaching is informed by feminist social and political philosophy that utilizes continental, post-structuralist, postcolonial, psychoanalytic, and queer theories of subjectivity. She has published articles that examine drag, queer identities, sexualities, and subjectivities, as well as rights and ethical knowledge. She has performed drag on the stage and utilized it in the classroom as a pedagogical device. She is completing a monograph, *Steeped in Blood: Crimes against the Family under the Tyranny of a Bio-Genealogical Imperative*, which considers the production of "family" identities and experiences; it examines the devaluation of adoptive families through discourses of family, adoption, sexuality, and incest in the modern Western context. She is currently editing *Adoption and Mothering*, an international and interdisciplinary collection of essays that examines discourses, debates, and the politics that surround the "mother" in the context of adoption. Her latest research project, *Distant Family: A Genealogy of Transracial, Adoptive Family Discourse and Subjectivity*, looks at the ontological status of transracial adoptive ties and interrogates the effects of "scientific racism" in historical and contemporary discourse about transracial adoption.

Bibliography

Allen, Robert C. "'The Legs Business': Transgression and Containment in American Burlesque." *Camera Obscura*, 23 (1990): 43–68.

Arsenault, Nina. *The Silicone Diaries*. In *TRANS(per)FORMING Nina Arsenault*, edited by Judith Rudakoff, 191–227. Bristol: Intellect Press, 2012.

Bornstein, Kate. *Gender Outlaw: On Men, Women, and the Rest of Us*. New York: Vintage Books, 1995.

Butler, Judith. *Bodies That Matter: On the Discursive Limits of Sex*. New York: Routledge, 1993.

———. *Gender Trouble: Feminism and the Subversion of Identity*. New York Routledge, 1990.

———. *Judith Butler in Conversation: Analyzing the Texts and Talk of Everyday Life*. Edited by Bronwyn Davies. New York: Routledge, 2008.

Califia, Pat. *Sex Changes: The Politics of Transgenderism*. San Francisco: Cleis Press, 1997.

Elliot, Patricia. "A Psychoanalytic Reading of Transsexual Embodiment." *Studies in Gender and Sexuality* 2, no. 4 (2001): 295–325.

Evans, Chad. *Frontier Theatre: A History of Nineteenth-Century Theatrical Entertainment in the Canadian Far West and Alaska*. Victoria: Sono Nis Press, 1983.

Ferreday, Debra. Review of *The Happy Stripper: Pleasures and Politics of the New Burlesque*, by Jackie Wilson. *Feminist Theory* 11, no. 1 (2010): 106–108.

———. "'Showing the Girl': The New Burlesque." *Feminist Theory* 9, no.1 (2008): 47–65.

Freud, Sigmund. "The 'Uncanny.'" In *An Infantile Neurosis and Other Works, Volume XVII of The Standard Edition of the Complete Psychological Works of Sigmund Freud*. Translated by James Strachey. London: Hogarth Press, 1986.

Gherovici, Patricia. *Please Select Your Gender: From the Invention of Hysteria to the Democratizing of Transgenderism*. New York: Routledge, 2010.

Halperin, David, and Valerie Traub, eds. *Gay Shame*. London: University of Chicago Press, 2009.

Love, Heather K. "Selections from 'Spoiled Identity': Stephen Gordon's Loneliness and the Difficulties of Queer Theory." In *The Transgender Studies Reader*, edited by Susan Stryker and Stephen Whittle, 534. New York: Routledge, 2006.

Nally, Claire. "Grrrly Hurly Burly: Neo Burlesque and the Performance of Gender." *Textual Practice* 23, no. 4 (2009): 621–643.

Nataf, Zachary I. "Selection from *Lesbians Talk Transgender*." In *The Transgender Studies Reader*, edited by Susan Stryker and Stephen Whittle, 439–448. New York: Routledge, 2006.

Prosser, Jay. "Judith Butler: Queer Feminism, Transgender, and the Transubstitution of Sex." In *The Transgender Studies Reader*, edited by Susan Stryker and Stephen Whittle, 257–280. New York: Routledge, 2006.

———. *Second Skins: The Body Narratives of Transsexuality*. New York: Columbia University Press, 1998.

Rubin, Henry. *Self-Made Men: Identity and Embodiment among Transsexual Men*. Nashville: Vanderbilt University Press, 2003.

Spies, Kathleen. "'Girls and Gags': Sexual Display and Humour in Reginald Walsh's Burlesque Images." *American Art* 18, no. 2 (2004): 32–57.

Stryker, Susan. "(De)Subjugated Knowledges: An Introduction to Transgender Studies." In *The Transgender Studies Reader*, edited by Susan Stryker and Stephen Whittle, 1–17. New York: Routledge, 2006.

———. "My Words to Victor Frankenstein Above the Village of Chamounix: Performing Transgender Rage." In *The Transgender Studies Reader*, edited by Susan Stryker and Stephen Whittle, 244–256. New York: Routledge, 2006.

Notes

1. Jay Prosser, "Judith Butler: Queer Feminism, Transgender, and the Transubstitution of Sex," in *The Transgender Studies Reader*, eds. Susan Stryker and Stephen Whittle (New York: Routledge, 2006), 279.
2. Since queer and transsexual people and theory can be referred to collectively as transgender people and theory, I rarely use the term transgender in this chapter and only in this collective sense to avoid confusion.
3. Kate Bornstein is quoted in Pat Califia, *Sex Changes: The Politics of Transgenderism* (San Francisco: Cleis Press, 1997), 273.
4. Ibid.
5. Judith Butler, *Judith Butler in Conversation: Analyzing the Texts and Talk of Everyday Life*, ed. Bronwyn Davies (New York: Routledge, 2008), 239.
6. Ibid., 239–40.
7. Ibid.
8. Susan Stryker, "(De)Subjugated Knowledges: An Introduction to Transgender Studies," in Stryker and Whittle, *The Transgender Studies Reader*, 7.
9. Ibid., 9.
10. Judith Butler, *Bodies That Matter: On the Discursive Limits of Sex* (New York: Routledge, 1993).
11. Patricia Elliot, "A Psychoanalytic Reading of Transsexual Embodiment," *Studies in Gender and Sexuality* 2, no. 4 (2001): 299; Henry Rubin, *Self-Made Men: Identity and Embodiment among Transsexual Men* (Nashville: Vanderbilt University Press, 2003), 145.

12. Jay Prosser, *Second Skins: The Body Narratives of Transsexuality* (New York: Columbia University Press, 1998), 73.

13. Ibid., 73.

14. Elliot, "Transsexual Embodiment," 300. I specifically use the word "transsness," as opposed to "transness," to signify transsexual subjects, and not the broader categories of trans or transgender subjects, because while these latter categories both include transsexual subjects, they do not refer to them alone. This exclusion, therefore, is intentional for the purposes of this discussion.

15. Jay Prosser, Susan Stryker, Judith Butler, Pat Elliott, and Henry Rubin theorize transsexual embodiment in what are, arguably, fundamentally similar ways in terms of some of the main differences they identify between queer and transsexual subjects, even as it can be said their approaches to this question utilize different frameworks and/or blends of transgender, queer, postmodern, and/or psychoanalytic theories.

16. Historically, of course, transsexual and queer lives converge in tragedy in the context of late nineteenth- and early twentieth-century sexology discourse, which pathologized and punished both as inverts.

17. Elliott, "Transsexual Embodiment," 297.

18. Rubin, *Self-Made Men*, 3–13.

19. Zachary I. Nataf, "Selection from *Lesbians Talk Transgender*," in Stryker and Whittle, *The Transgender Studies Reader*, 445.

20. Susan Stryker, "My Words to Victor Frankenstein Above the Village of Chamounix: Performing Transgender Rage," in Stryker and Whittle, *The Transgender Studies Reader*, 251.

21. Judith Butler, *Gender Trouble: Feminism and the Subversion of Identity* (New York Routledge, 1990), 137–9; Butler, *Bodies that Matter*, 7–12.

22. Patricia Gherovici, *Please Select Your Gender: From the Invention of Hysteria to the Democratizing of Transgenderism* (New York: Routledge, 2010): 114; Butler, *Gender Trouble*, 136–9.

23. Butler, *Bodies that Matter*, 230–1.

24. Prosser, *Second Skins*, 27.

25. Ibid., 29–30.

26. Ibid.

27. Ibid., 25.

28. Ibid.

29. Heather K. Love, "Selections from 'Spoiled Identity': Stephen Gordon's Loneliness and the Difficulties of Queer Theory," in Stryker and Whittle, *The Transgender Studies Reader*, 534.

30. While Love's call for a return to shame comes as early as 2001, David Halperin and Valerie Traub's recent anthology, *Gay Shame* (to which Love also contributes as an author), is really the first in-depth examination of the social and political import of a post-pride return to shame in queer theory, literature, art, and performance. See David Halperin and Valerie Traub, eds., *Gay Shame* (London: University of Chicago Press, 2009).

31. Kate Bornstein, *Gender Outlaw: On Men, Women, and the Rest of Us* (New York: Vintage Books, 1995), 87–138.

32. Claire Nally, "Grrrly Hurly Burly: Neo Burlesque and the Performance of Gender," *Textual Practice* 23, no. 4 (2009): 625.

33. Ibid., 622; Kathleen Spies, "'Girls and Gags': Sexual Display and Humour in Reginald Walsh's Burlesque Images," *American Art* 18, no. 2 (2004): 53. Notably, this does not mean that male-to-female drag performers never enact burlesque styles or tropes. Instead, there is a long tradition and established understanding that burlesque is performed by females, and especially because of its emphasis on striptease and the revelation of a female form.

34. Robert C. Allen, "'The Legs Business': Transgression and Containment in American Burlesque," *Camera Obscura*, 23(1990): 54.

35. Ibid., 54.

36. Ibid., 58.

37. Chad Evans, *Frontier Theatre: A History of Nineteenth-Century Theatrical Entertainment in the Canadian Far West and Alaska* (Victoria: Sono Nis Press, 1983), 174.

38. Nally, "Grrrly Hurly Burly," 631; Debra Ferreday, review of *The Happy Stripper: Pleasures and Politics of the New Burlesque*, by Jackie Wilson, *Feminist Theory* 11, no. 1 (2010): 107.

39. Debra Ferreday, "'Showing the Girl': The New Burlesque," *Feminist Theory* 9, no.1 (2008): 60.

40. Ibid., 49.

41. Nally, "Grrrly Hurly Burly," 622.

42. Nina Arsenault, *The Silicone Diaries*, in *TRANS(per)FORMING Nina Arsenault*, ed. Judith Rudakoff (Bristol: Intellect Press, 2012), 220.

43. Ferreday, "Showing the Girl," 49.

44. Arsenault, *The Silicone Diaries*, 215.

45. Ferreday, "Showing the Girl," 53–4; Arsenault, *The Silicone Diaries*, 215.

46. Arsenault, *The Silicone Diaries*, 219.

47. Ibid., 224.

48. Ferreday, "Showing the Girl," 50.

49. Spies, "Girls and Gags," 35.

50. Ibid.

51. Arsenault, *The Silicone Diaries*, 226.

52. Ibid., 209.

53. Ibid., 224.

54. Ibid., 213.

55. Ibid., 225.

56. Ibid., 227.

57. Butler, *Judith Butler in Conversation*, 239–40.

58. Arsenault, *The Silicone Diaries*, 216–18.

59. Freud discussed the uncanny in his 1919 paper: Sigmund Freud, "The 'Uncanny,'" in *An Infantile Neurosis and Other Works, Volume XVII of The Standard Edition of the Complete Psychological Works of Sigmund Freud*, trans. James Strachey (London: Hogarth Press, 1986), 219–56.

60. Arsenault, *The Silicone Diaries*, 212–14.

61. Ibid., 206–7.

62. Ibid., 206.

63. Ibid., 207.

Chapter 6

Chopping at the Sexy Bits: [Trans]cending the Body with Surgical Conundrums

J Mase III

If we take our cue from Eve Ensler's *The Vagina Monologues*, I'm sure there was a time when Nina Arsenault was worried. We've all been worried. We've been worried about what to do with our sexy bits. Nina Arsenault, like many transgender and transsexual people all over the world, has taken a hard road by embodying a gender not typically assigned to what has been traditionally interpreted as a very male body. Sixty surgeries into creating her body and fierce femme identity, one question that might strike people with a rigid understanding of gender: Why would anyone who identifies as a woman choose to keep her dick?

As a transmasculine individual, the question of whether to cut, or not to cut, has come up in my life as well; indeed, it is a common question in the lives of many other transpersons I have met. If being trans is, in part, accepting that the body does not define our internal sense of gender, what roles do surgery and hormonal intervention play in the lives of most trans folk? Is the act of surgery a defiant gesture against biological essentialism? Or, is it a survival tactic that trans folk, such as Nina, must endure to be seen? These and other possibilities regarding the realities of transidentity and its relationship to surgical and medical procedures are issues I explore as I take a look at Ms. Arsenault's relationship to her genitals.

External and Internal Beauty

According to a CBC TV news item aired on December 19, 2010, Nina Arsenault is still a man.[1] What I imagine the reporter to mean is that Ms. Arsenault still has her penis. This starts what can be a very hard conversation with a mainstream culture that cannot always recognize the complexities of identities on the fringe. Much like the 2008 hailstorm of sensationalized media reports that surrounded the well-documented existence of Thomas Beatie, an Oregon-based pregnant man, the biology and psychology of transgender identities is still a thing of wonder for many.[2]

In her autobiographical one-person plays, *The Silicone Diaries* and "I W@s B*arbie," Nina takes us on fabulous trips that address what it takes to create her own vision of gender and beauty. As Milton Diamond suggests, the idea of beauty often leads to a quest for the feminine;[3] in Arsenault's play *The Silicone Diaries*, we discover that for Nina a primary source of physical beauty and femininity is silicone! And because beauty is a commodity that can be shaped, bought, and cosmetically enhanced, Nina's relationship to her own femininity appears to be rooted (at least for a time) in her ability to acquire surgical modifications.[4]

If Nina is able to change body parts that are incongruent with her view of her own gender, it is possible that the paradox of maintaining her penis means that it is purposely part of the transgressive way she expresses her transfeminine gender. As she has explained:

> It's not something I think about getting rid of. I have transsexual girlfriends and some of them think of that part of themselves like it's a tumor. I believe I am a woman inside, there's no doubt about that. But I don't have that relationship with that part of me that it grosses me out. It's more important to be socially accepted as a woman and look like a woman. At this point, my body is so different anyways. I just think I'm a woman with a very unique body.[5]

In a world of pussies, the chick with a dick is queen: or is she? In many communities (including the ones that Nina inhabits in *The Silicone Diaries*), being able to pass as a bio-woman is central to one's identification with being feminine.[6] Being able to have the look of natural hips, tits, and hair, amongst other things, can dictate a hierarchy of power in transfeminine communities. On first glance, Nina's hyperfeminine beauty appears to be aligned with this idea: that being a "real" transsexual woman means affecting a look that passes as female. This is to say that early on in *The Silicone Diaries* Nina seems to follow a sort of biological essentialism, chiseling away at every feature she views as "masculine" in appearance, and affecting femininity on and from the outside. But just when you think Nina is rehearsing a typical transnarrative, she gets subversive.

In the fourth monologue in *The Silicone Diaries*, titled, "I am my own self-portrait," Nina begins to chart a new course. She surprises her audience by revealing that her surgical procedures are first predicated upon her own conception of feminine beauty, rather than an authentic notion of embodied "sex." In this monologue, Nina recounts how her testicles were removed, because of the toxic testosterone they produced—a substance that will have negative effects on the beauty of her skin—and positions her penis/genitals as a source of power. Whether it is the place from which she is drawing her breath, or the means by which she attracts her clients, there is something powerful and mysterious about Nina's penis, as it becomes a semi-acknowledged entity. Along with an intense sexual power and seductiveness, Nina also telegraphs what I perceive as a sense of shame about her genitals, which presents an interesting paradox. Whether her penis is cradled in the lap of Tommy Lee, trying not to get too excited, or whether it is preventing her perfect presentation of a full Barbie persona, this dick is having a bit of an identity crisis.

Real versus Authentic Beauty

From the very first time she witnessed the lifeless beauty of a mannequin, Nina makes no apology for creating herself in the image of a doll, when so many transpeople are fighting to become "real" boys and girls. In the opening sequence of *The Silicone Diaries*, she recalls being completely overcome by feminine beauty when, as a young boy, she witnessed a creature unlike any other: the still, poised, polished, and plastic mannequin. In noticing its delicately nuanced and doe-eyed features, Arsenault began to shape her relationship with beauty. But like most dolls, tiny or tall, mannequins are usually missing one essentially human characteristic: genitals. It appears that through surgery and body modifications, Nina opened the window to feminine perfection and identified it as the goal towards which she wished to transition. Even as an online sex worker, before she achieved the fiercely fake physicality she wanted, she manipulated the camera's settings so that she broadcast a Warhol-like image, keeping her own face hidden behind these filters, creating a simulated vision of perfect beauty.[7] Nina clarifies this point further: "My story has now become about a transition from being ugly to becoming beautiful, even if beautiful means looking plastic. At some point looking beautiful became more important than looking like a woman."[8]

In "I W@s B*rbie," Nina explains how she tucks away the parts that don't align with her Barbie costume and persona, and yet draws confidence and Buddha-like breath from this hidden element. For Arsenault, breath and breathing into and from her genitals is an important source of authenticity and power. Her feeling of the sensuality, sexuality, and even the persona that emanates from a part that cannot be shared with the public is striking to me, as a tranny trying to make peace with my own parts. It seems that Nina is pushing beyond the idea of biological essentialism into a realm of public manufacturing; she creates how she wants to be seen by the public by altering the parts that they can see, but still using her genitals as a source of power and change. Describing how she transformed a servile role as Barbie at the launch of Toronto Fashion week, where she was asked to distribute cupcakes to the partygoers, Nina explains that she breathes into the places that her voice teacher told her will allow her to connect with the most authentic emotions possible, her "anus, genitals, and perineum."[9]

> Oh no. Oh no. This is very anti-climactic. I'm supposed to have a full circle moment about being Barbie. I have an inner child, a little girl who grew up in a little boy's body, in a trailer park, who wanted to be Barbie. This inner child needs to be acknowledged as the epitome of perfect plastic beauty. Let's not make her serve hors d'oeuvres. I'm walking out into the main room thinking, "Steady. Steady on your heels, Nina." I take a moment. I drop my breath into that place my voice teacher is teaching me about and think, "Just do it. Just *be* Barbie. I can make it so real. … I bless the cupcakes. They aren't just cupcakes anymore. They are pink swirls of positivity. I am breathing it into reality. I can see pink lines of energy connecting my genitals to the cupcakes. It's magical.[10]

Reflecting on Nina, as an adult who is fully aware of social reactions to her, I wonder how she deals with the pressure to maintain some sort of alignment with typical gender norms in public, even when that idea may conflict with the way she enacts the complex landscape of her own body/gender.

The hardest part of my transformation was when I was living as a woman but still looked very masculine and people would make fun of me on the street. … I realized there is a double standard for transsexuals, because if you're a beautiful transsexual, people will accept you more easily. If you "pass" you will be more accepted. You may not even be noticed. But if you don't pass … That's what really hurt me—people don't see you as human.[11]

Starting from a place of biological essentialism and determinism, Nina shape shifts her external self into an ultrafemme creation so "perfect" that it has to be fake. Reaching beyond the very notion that what is in your pants defines your gender, Arsenault's remaining genitalia, her penis, serves that very complicated role. On the one hand, it is a source of what I would interpret as shame, but on the other hand, it remains a precious artifact of her once fleshy body now made—most noticeably—of silicone. And gives her power.

J Mase III is a black/trans/queer poet and educator based in Philadephia, Pennsylvania, who is not afraid to get a little intellectual! Having had the pleasure of performing his poetry for American college campus audiences, on radio stations, in documentaries, and television programs, J Mase III has also worked with thousands of community members and service providers on issues relating to the needs of LGBTQIA people. In locations as diverse as juvenile detention centres and churches to some of the most popular poetry venues and prestigious universities in the United States, J Mase III gives voice to the LGBTQIA community in ways not always heard. An organ donor, he is the author of a chapbook titled *If I Should Die Under the Knife, Tell My Kidney I Was the Fiercest Poet Around* and creator of two annual performance events in Philadelphia called *Cupid Ain't @#$%!* and *Transfags Taking Over*.

Bibliography

Arsenault, Nina. "I W@s B*rbie." Unpublished script, 2009.

———. *The Silicone Diaries*. In *TRANS(per)FORMING Nina Arsenault*, edited by Judith Rudakoff, 191–227. Bristol: Intellect Press, 2012.

Burnett, Richard. "Interview: Nina Arsenault of the Silicone Diaries." *The Charlesbois Post*, December 9, 2010. http://charpo.blogspot.com/2010/12/interview-nina-arsenault-of-silicone.html.

Currah, Paisley. "Expecting Bodies: The Pregnant Man and Transgender Exclusion from the Employment Non-Discrimination Act." *Women's Studies Quarterly* 36, no. 3/4 (Fall–Winter, 2008): 330–6.

Diamond, Milton. "Sexual Identity and Sexual Orientation in Children with Traumatized or Ambiguous Genitalia." *The Journal of Sex Research* 34, no. 2 (1997): 199–211.

Rankin, Jim. "Sexy Transsexual Nina Arsenault on Life, Art and Her Penis." *The Star*, June 11, 2010. http://www.thestar.com/living/article/822008--sexy-transsexual-nina-arsenault-on-life-art-and-her-penisl.

Sweet, Kevin. "Silicone Diaries Explores Beauty." *The National*, CBC, December 19, 2010. http://www.cbc.ca/video/#/News/TV_Shows/The_National/1233408557/ID=1703826144.

Notes

1. Kevin Sweet, "Silicone Diaries Explores Beauty," *The National, CBC*, December 19, 2010, http://www.cbc.ca/video/#/News/TV_Shows/The_National/1233408557/ID=1703826144.

2. Paisley Currah, "Expecting Bodies: The Pregnant Man and Transgender Exclusion from the Employment Non-Discrimination Act," *Women's Studies Quarterly* 36, no. 3/4 (Fall–Winter, 2008): 330.

3. Milton Diamond, "Sexual Identity and Sexual Orientation in Children with Traumatized or Ambiguous Genitalia," *The Journal of Sex Research* 34, no. 2 (1997): 199–211.

4. Nina Arsenault, *The Silicone Diaries*, in *TRANS(per)FORMING Nina Arsenault*, ed. Judith Rudakoff (Bristol: Intellect Press, 2012), 211–214.

5. Jim Rankin, "Sexy Transsexual Nina Arsenault on Life, Art and Her Penis," *The Star*, June 11, 2010, http://www.thestar.com/living/article/822008--sexy-transsexual-nina-arsenault-on-life-art-and-her-penisl.

6. Diamond, "Sexual Identity," 201.

7. Arsenault, *The Silicone Diaries*, 208–209.

8. Richard Burnett, "Interview: Nina Arsenault of the Silicone Diaries," *The Charlesbois Post*, December 9, 2010, http://charpo.blogspot.com/2010/12/interview-nina-arsenault-of-silicone.html.

9. Nina Arsenault, "I W@s B*rbie," unpublished script, 2009, 8.

10. Ibid., 16.

11. Burnett, "Interview: Nina Arsenault," December 9, 2010.

Chapter 7

Nina Arsenault: Fast Feminist *Objet a*

Shannon Bell

And why shouldn't the Buddhist monk be an incredible, fabulously beautiful woman, the most beautiful woman in the world?[1]
Shannon Bell

In her *T-girl* column for *fab Magazine*, "Savage Vanity: Kitty has Claws,"[2] Nina Arsenault writes about her expensive pure-bred Siamese pussy, named Vanity, mercilessly attacking her face and clawing at her eyes the moment they fluttered open in the morning. This brought to mind a story that Jacques Lacan, in his lecture "On *jouissance*," tells about Picasso's parakeet.

> I can tell you a little tale, that of a parakeet that was in love with Picasso. How could one tell? From the way the parakeet nibbled the collar of his shirt and the flaps of his jacket. Indeed, the parakeet was in love with what is essential to man, namely his attire (*accoutrement*). The parakeet was like Descartes to whom men were merely clothes ... walking about. Clothes promise debauchery when one takes them off. ... To enjoy a body when there are no more clothes leaves intact the question of what makes the One, that is the question of identification. The parakeet identified with Picasso clothed. ...
>
> The habit loves the monk, as they are but one. ... What lies beneath the habit, what we call the body, is perhaps but the remainder (*reste*) I call *objet a*.[3]

Objet a is where Nina Arsenault comes in. Being *objet a* is a sublime impossibility according to Lacan, who coined the concept. But Lacan never laid eyes on a "given-to-be-seen," a subject held in the gaze of the world, such as Nina Arsenault. Nor did Lacan encounter the feminist tendency I call fast feminism. Fast because philosophy, pornography, and politics mesh in action, feminist because action is grounded in female power.

This chapter views Nina Arsenault as *objet a* and locates her as feminist precisely because she is beauty and she reveals the process and suffering involved in manifesting the perfect female given-to-be-seen. This politically negotiated position of being beautiful and revealing what is required to produce her extraordinary beauty give Arsenault a uniquely seductive *jouissance*. Jouissance, according to Lacan, is an ecstatic happening in which pleasure and suffering may transmute into the other, and the bounded body/mind and the external world are not sharply distinguished.

Objet a, the Gaze, the Screen and the Void

Objet a, an ambiguous concept, is both the object that causes desire and "the object that could satisfy jouissance."[4] "In the desire of every demand, there is but the request for *objet a*, for the object that could satisfy jouissance."[5] *Objet a* is the remainder, that which doesn't fit in the set or discourse that gave rise to it; *a* is that which eludes representation and gets us as close as we can to the real. The real is outside language and culture and resists symbolization. Lacan defines the real as "the impossible" because it is impossible to imagine, impossible to integrate into the symbolic, and impossible to attain. The real always exceeds, erupts, and undercuts the meanings of the symbolic order.

In his seminar on the Borromean knot, "Rings of String," Lacan indicates that it is the elusiveness of *objet a* that defines it: "*Objet a* is no being. *Objet a* is the void presupposed by a demand."[6] Lacan, in "Anamorphosis," collapses the real and *objet a*: "the real whose name, in our algebra, is the *objet a*."[7]

Lacan, in his 1964 seminars on vision, collectively titled "Of the Gaze as *Objet Petit a*," distinguishes between the eye's look and the gaze. According to Lacan there is the "preexistence of a gaze,"[8] a seeing that belongs to the object world that stares back at us, the subject—the "given-to-be-seen."[9] For Lacan both the I/eye and the object are looking. The gaze of the world, of the other, turns me—the subject—into a picture. "In the scopic field, the gaze is outside, I am looked at, that is to say, I am a picture."[10] The subject/viewer/ seer is the screen for the gaze of the other/object/outside world. The screen is where the eye and the gaze come together; consequently it is where identity is negotiated. The subject projects the image they desire to be seen onto one side of the screen and on the other side of the screen the image of the subject is seen by the other/object. Yet "something slips, passes, … and is always to some degree eluded"[11] in the split between the eye and the gaze. "The relation between the gaze and what one wishes to see involves a lure."[12] Why? Because "the subject is presented as other than he is, and what one shows him is not what he wishes to see."[13] Or, more succinctly, what you are seeing is not what I see you seeing because "*You never look at me from the place from which I see you*."[14] Slavo Zizek suggests that "the radical ambiguity of *objet a* in Lacan" is that it "stands simultaneously for the imaginary fantasmatic lure/screen and for that which this lure is obfuscating, for the void behind the lure."[15]

Nina Arsenault: the Given-to-be-Seen

When the given-to-be-seen is *objet a*, the fantasmatic object, one views it in the realm of fantasy. However, when *objet a* discloses what the technological process of construction entails, *objet a* offers another given-to-be-seen. The brilliance of Arsenault's construction and disclosure of self is that it produces an anamorphic gaze that strengthens her position as *objet a* in the very process of exposing its construction.

More Real than Anyone Else

NA: It's more truthful to just be hollow and present. It's actually more real. The irony is, I felt like my job as Barbie was to be more real than everyone else there [at the opening of L'Oreal Fashion Week and Barbie's official fiftieth Mattel birthday party in Toronto] and have everyone go "Oh my God, she's so fake, it's so real." The people who hired me thought I was taking the job way too seriously but I gave them nothing. I gave them vacancy.[16]

It is the simultaneity of presenting while phenomenologically meshing with the void, the emptiness of being, that situates Arsenault in the sublime position of *objet a* for the duration of her Barbie incarnation.

NA: I felt it was my job to be as empty as possible, really just to be an empty vessel so that I could just be a flat screen they could project on. In that way my performance of Barbie was impenetrable. The impenetrability of it was to let people project unto me.

SB: Do you find that people project onto you all the time?

NA: Oh yes, oh my God, yeah. Because there are so many meanings attached to the shapes in my body. There's so many meanings attached to the hip-to-waist-to breast ratio, or to the hair or to the make-up. To me it's an aesthetic practice. In my daily life I don't think about that. It also means sexual things to people. It means stupid. It means bimbo. It means self-absorbed. People have so many things they bring to it. To me it's just make-up. It's just my life.

SB: What I would call it is *techne*. The techne of self, of putting yourself together, of being in the world. It is the skill, the techne, of producing you as the perfect female on a daily basis. When I look at you, what I see is a Buddhist monk.

NA: Thank you. That ties in to something else I was going to say about the empty vessel. I felt like the most compelling way for me to become an empty vessel was to just feel the emptiness inside me, to just feel empty all through. To really go into a Zen-like place, a place where I could be so in the moment that I was no longer in the minute; where I was so in the moment that I was just sort of continuing to breathe and finding stillness, but really letting nothing in, letting nothing out. That emptiness would read as receptivity, people could project onto it, but yet it wouldn't be a weak emptiness. I can go into a really Zen place. For me that's the mannequin-type place, that emptiness, but I can roll emptiness into sexual hunger with a very subtle change of the breath. I mean sexual hunger in the same way that virile or potent is a compliment for a man.[17]

In her play "I w@s B*rbie,"[18] Nina's thoughts about doing/being Barbie exemplify the Lacanian real, the gaze, and *objet a*. She discloses her reaction when she received the request to be Barbie, "I want to say: 'Do you really want to hire someone known for having massive amounts of plastic surgery to represent a doll that's accused of fucking up the body images of millions of little girls?'"[19] It is as if in their selection of Nina as the truest likeness to Barbie, Mattel simultaneously acknowledged the impossibility of Barbie's proportions and features and recognized that with some sixty cosmetic surgeries and procedures, an exquisite eye for redesigning the flesh body, time, and money in which to do so—eight years and $200,000, aesthetic and ascetic discipline, geisha-like training, and perhaps most importantly the will to "sacrifice normal," "be plastic" and "be fabulous instead of reasonable."[20] Arsenault shows the impossible is attainable. The real always undercuts and erupts the symbolic: the closest resemblance to Barbie—the miniature mannequin of exquisite beauty whose foundation is the heteronormative values of 1950s and 1960s America[21]—is the larger-than-life fantasmatic mannequin cyborg. This mannequin cyborg's foundation is the queer values of the late 1990s and early twenty-first century, before queers became heteronormative; it is a plastic body financed not just through sex work but through excessive sex work: "Some days I saw twelve clients, with barely time enough to bathe before the next trick was traipsing to my door" writes Arsenault in her *T-girl* column "Catholic Hospital Heals Whore."[22]

In deciding to do/be Barbie, Nina confides:

> I know immediately that the only way that my beauty can be worthy of representing Barbie is if I go into The Thin Face. I'm talking about portraying an object of incredible aesthetic proportions.
>
> The Thin Face is this thing that I do. When all fat melts away from my face, the sculptural qualities of bone and silicone that I have designed are fully revealed. It's really something. After only eight hours of fasting, the eyes move forward dramatically in the face creating the larger-than-life model eye. And everything lifts.[23]

Nina knows the "crowd at Fashion Week will love The Thin Face. I'll look back at them through it. They will be looking at me looking at them looking at me."[24] Here we have the look and the gaze operating as one in which the given-to-be-seen, Nina-as-Barbie, is reflecting back the gaze of the fashion world looking at her. The lure, the screen, is The Thin Face. What The Thin Face obfuscates is emptiness. Nina reveals "behind The Thin Face I have no past and no future. I have only this moment. I'm going inside Barbie. Inside the concept of Barbie. Barbie is … still. 'Smile for us, Barbie!' 'Okay, I am beaming.'"[25] It is this light, this spark, this gleam that ignites from full presence in the moment, stillness at the core of plastic, that makes visible *objet a*.

Feminine Jouissance

At the core of *objet a* is surplus—emptiness and surplus jouissance. Not phallic jouissance, which is related to castration as lack, but other jouissance that Lacan came to call *feminine* jouissance. The beauty of other jouissance for Lacan is that it is something one can experience, but impossible to define in that it is beyond speech, language, and structure. When Lacan attempts to put a face to other jouissance he goes to the unspeakable ecstasy of Saint Teresa captured by the sculpture Lorenzo Bernini in his statue "The Ecstasy of Saint Teresa."[26] Most basically, other jouissance is oneness with the moment, world, and the gaze. Nina achieves other jouissance through a practice of emptiness and breath.

> My heart is full of love tonight. One by one, I make eye contact with each person. They see the love within me ...
> I dropped my breath into my genitals, my anus and perineum, right where my voice teacher tells me to breathe so I can have the biggest, most authentic emotions possible.
> A few people look over and go, "Oh, she's taking this Barbie thing very seriously." They literally have to turn away from the light that is shining from me. From my genitals.[27]

This emptiness in breath and breath itself is what propels *The Silicone Diaries*. It is the coupling of emptiness and breath with feminine jouissance crafted in a body self-designed for the gaze of the world, a body art object that gazes back at the world of spectators from the dual position of the "most beautiful woman in the world" and the projected images of the process of becoming "most beautiful woman in the world." The images are of surgically cut skin, bandaged face, liquid silicone entering the body. These are the underside of beauty, the cut in beauty that is not supposed to slip into the symbolic realm of the beautiful. In fact, what Nina is revealing, in showing both her technologically designed cyborg/art object body and the deconstruction and reconstruction of her human flesh body involved in this design, is the unseen. In so doing, Nina forces the spectator to look at her from precisely the place she is looking at them.

The Look of Nina Arsenault

It isn't the vivid images of the operations, procedures, and recovering face and body that trouble the gaze of the spectators. Rather, it is the magnificent dissonance, disharmony, and discrepancy between what is seen and what is behind the look of Nina Arsenault. It is Arsenault's will to power as a will to beauty, willingness to do anything it takes to be that beautiful, willingness to have underground silicone injections in the United States, surgeries in Mexico, willingness to suck enormous amounts of cock, be whatever the client's fantasy, willingness to die for beauty, and then her willingness to disclose precisely what it takes to be just that beautiful. In *The Silicone Diaries*, when silicone sister Candi threatens to cut her off from their silicone source if Nina discloses that her body is not natural, Nina says:

> I know I'll talk honestly about it when I'm all done. I will not be ashamed that I have silicone body parts, but, honestly I am not exactly sure what will happen to our bodies in ten or twenty or thirty years.

What I do know, is that we have put it all on the line for who we had to be, and that means what we had to look like.

There will be no going back.[28]

Mannequin Cyborg

Nina Arsenault designed herself to embody what she at the age of five saw as the most beautiful woman in the world: a mannequin. Nina recounts her first encounter with a mannequin.

> Her face is perfect. The arch of her eyebrows has the same shape as the Cupid's bow in her lips. The upwards swoop of the cheek bones is reflected in the upwards swoop of her almond eyes. The tip of her pointed nose. The shape of the jutting chin. It's so harmonious.
>
> I don't think this at the time.
>
> I think: "She's more beautiful than Barbie."
>
> I stare at her. Into her eyes. They seem to shimmer.
>
> "Is she real?"[29]

Yes, she is real; she is the Lacanian real, she is that which eludes, she is impossible, and she is designed and materialized as a live self-portraiture by Nina Arsenault. As Nina narrates the object of desire of her young boy self, Rodney, projected on the screen behind her are images of Nina posing with mannequins that look identical to her in size, proportion, facial structure, and comportment (for two photographs from this series, see Figures 3 and 20).[30] In two of the full-body images of three mannequins, it is difficult to see which one is alive. Then there is the image of Nina, lips almost touching her mannequin double's face, looking into the eye of the other as self, seeing self through the gaze of the object other. It is the perfect *objet a* moment: when the real cuts through and the symbolic opens. What is most uncanny about these images is that Arsenault has concretized her *objet a* and lives as it. On her website, Nina writes about the mannequin photo shoot she did:

> Since I was a child I've been mesmerized by the visual harmony that has been sculpted into the designer faces of life size mannequins.
>
> The tips of their noses reflect the shape in their jutting chins. The curves of their lips are echoed in the elegant arches of their impossibly high eyebrows, as well as the swoops of their almond eyes and the gentle bulging of their cheekbones.
>
> Moreover, their poreless plaster visages are perfectly symmetrical.
>
> Their false eyelashes are permanently attached, and their airbrushed make-up never smudges.
>
> These feminine works of art are supposed to represent women, but they are often too perfect to look like a real female.[31]

Nina, in her recent talk "Self-Portraiture, Transformation, Identity and Performance," adamantly disclosed that "at some point looking beautiful became more important than looking like a woman. It became more important than looking natural."[32] What she doesn't say is that the mannequin is a politically charged object. On her website blog entry "Mannequins at AGO's [Art Gallery of Ontario] Surreal Things," Arsenault quotes a section from the curatorial text by Ghislaine Wood:

> For the Surrealists, the mannequin embodied the contradictions of modern life. It confused the boundaries between the animate and inanimate, human and machine, male and female, sexualized and sexless, and ultimately life and death. It was simultaneously a commodity, a simulacrum, an erotic object and the embodiment of the uncanny.
>
> For Freud, the uncanniest objects were "waxwork figures, artificial dolls and automatons." In the Freudian uncanny, the mannequin also represented the suppressed primal human being emerging from the unconscious. Andre Breton saw the mannequin as the ultimate representative of what he termed "convulsive beauty."[33]

When the mannequin comes to life through technological enhancement of the flesh body and produces a mannequin cyborg, one enters the territory of posthuman *objet a*. For the first time in history, actually being the mannequin and looking out from the given-to-be-seen of a plastic/silicone body and having the gaze of the world reflect this very image back upon you, the screen, is a technological-physical possibility. But Nina doesn't merely do this, which is an identity design feat in itself; Nina does something more, way more, which both marks her as the "most beautiful woman in the world" and as a feminist, a fast feminist to be exact.

Nina's contenders for the most beautiful woman in the world are Pamela Anderson and Madonna. Anderson because "she is the ultimate silicone sex symbol of all time ... the Marilyn Monroe of the '90s."[34] Madonna because she is a shape-shifting self-portraiture in control of her aestheticized image:

> I would say I felt that way about Madonna basically since 1988. I like blonde Madonna, I like brunette Madonna, I like athletic Madonna, I like robust Madonna, I like cyborg, I think she looks like a cyborg body now. I love it. I love the puffy cheeks, the muscular body, the hair extensions, the crazy-ass skin-care that must be involved in it. I like the sort of Madonna trying to look like she's a Italian movie star. I like all the different versions of her.[35]

What sets Arsenault apart from other "most beautiful women in the world" is that a part of her beauty consists of disclosing in vivid detail the design details that constitute it, and the necessary rigorous daily maintenance regime. In "Venus/machine (2007–2009)," the final segment of *The Silicone Diaries*, Nina implies that she desired to move from the anger "about the two hours a day I need to get ready."[36] Nina explains: "I've built a perfection onto my face that needs make-up and hairstyles to complete it, or else I'm not aesthetically cohesive in my own vision."[37] In fact, Nina does transform the energy of anger, not by shortening the preparation time but through breath work and extensive exercise. And with the new endeavour, which Nina marks as "the next phase of my work with my body,"[38] Nina adds a new dimension to the mannequin cyborg: the Buddhist monk.

The Buddhist Monk

The monk evidences on stage during *The Silicone Diaries* as Nina removes her wig to expose her shaved head and the beautiful scars left by surgical cuts and suture. The gaze of the spectator is focused on that which the lure of accoutrement and enhancement has been obfuscating: the face denuded, the scars of creation. "The other who manifests herself in the face … breaks through her own plastic essence."[39] Nina's denuded face appeared on the cover *Xtra*, Canada's Gay and Lesbian Magazine. Nina identified this act of allowing her image without hair or makeup into the media sphere as "scary and a risk" for someone whose popular identity was "a persona of being fabulous."[40] Nina's exposure of her scarred shaven head doesn't diminish the power of her beauty one iota because what is driving the beauty is that which is more than accoutrement and enhancement, it is the glint, the gleam, the sparkle, the shimmer, the ecstasy of *objet a* itself. Nina finds ecstasy in the process of beauty:

I live for beauty. I have suffered for it; the suffering is sadomasochistic. The pain of it is thrilling, the endurance, the feats to achieve it have been very much a part of it. It is the act of the forbidden, the joy of the forbidden. We have this horrible schizophrenic thing in our culture, which is: women must be inhumanly beautiful and inhumanly thin. These aestheticized beings. Yet, you're not allowed to want that or to try for it.

I speak the forbidden, I speak the blasphemous: I say I have suffered for it, this suffering has been also ecstatic. Even to call it suffering is to reduce it to one thing. There's been ecstasy and joy. I enjoy going for surgeries, I like having people taking care of me, I like the anaesthetic needle going in my veins, I like the feeling of the anaesthesia, the ability to see myself one way, one day and then two weeks later having a completely new face. It's an ecstatic experience.[41]

The anger at the daily rigour of beauty gets transmuted in a deep breath practice: "One of the ways I get through the rigour is by breathing and going completely into the moment in the mirror."[42] This moment in the mirror is Nina the mannequin cyborg gazing at Nina the Buddhist monk gazing at Nina the mannequin cyborg, an anamorphic gaze in which each, which Lacan would deem the stain of the other,[43] comes together in the image of the mannequin cyborg monk. This begs a return to Arsenault's fascinating narration of her pussy, Vanity, clawing at her face. Was Vanity, true to her name, manifesting an envy of the time and attention Nina was required to spend with her face in the mirror, or was Vanity mimicking Nina by pawing her face in order to access the gaze of the Buddhist monk; was Vanity, like Picasso's parakeet, trying to get to the remainder, that which lies beneath the habit of the monk, the "no being" of emptiness she somehow recognized in Nina and mistakenly located in the face and the eyes?

Body-in-Action, Image-in-Motion

Arsenault's design and construction of self as body-in-action, image-in-motion, never fixed, ever elusive and transforming, is one of the main principles of fast feminism: not to congeal the process of doing live theory into the identitarian logic of THIS IS.[44] "Fast feminism is a feminism of affect—of intensity and movement. As feminist philosopher Luce Irigaray says: 'A woman is more at a loss when she is still than when she is moving, because when fixed in one position, she is a prisoner, open to attack in her own territory.'"[45] While Arsenault's own territory is *objet a*, she is constantly in motion as *objet a*. Arsenault states in her artist talk "Self-Portraiture, Transformation, Identity and Performance," "at each phase of my life I created a new self-portraiture and a new shape shift, a 'new me,' a new social role, a new fantasy I wanted to be, a new fantasy I had become, a new aesthetic calling, to make real. They are all me."[46] *The Silicone Diaries* closes with a new process:

> In my mind's eye, I see the next phase of my body.
> There will be the signs of aging on my body. There will be facelifts, resurfacing, the ways I honour aging with make-up.
> There will be the spiritual pursuits, the meditations, the therapy, the art-making that allows me to deal with aging.[47]

Nina Arsenault: Fast Feminist

SB: How would you describe your feminism?

NA: Every woman has the right to seek out whatever pleasure she wants. This is what feminism should be about. Being trans has given me the experience of being part of the queer community. Exposing the structure of my construction as an art object would definitely make me a postmodern artist and feminist.[48]

The excess femme and the deconstructive radical technopolitics that Arsenault deploys and discloses in her construction of self as *objet a* make her a fast feminist according to the manifesto of fast feminism that I put forth in my book *Fast Feminism*.

If fast feminism were to have a manifesto it would be:

1. Critique the world quickly.
2. Interrupt intellectual scholarship.
3. Position the body as the basis of intellectual work.
4. Write theory as art.
5. Do art as theory.
6. Do theory from nonobvious points of departure.
7. Do violence to the original context.[49]

Nina embodies and personifies the three principles of fast feminism: theory must be grounded in action, otherwise it is dead; "we are to the degree that we risk ourselves,"[50] and never write about what you don't do.

Of course *Fast Feminism* morphs its speed and action with past feminisms—postmodern feminism, postfeminism, cyberfeminism, third-wave feminism, and radical feminism.[51] Nina is a cyborg who has made the third-wave feminist assumption of independent female sexuality her *modus operandi*. She has designed and constructed the perfect female body structure and then exposed and deconstructed this very construction from inside it.

In her deconstructive narration of her very beauty, Arsenault provides a brilliant fast critique of the heterosexist assumptions at the foundation of hegemonic female beauty: to actually have the perfect mannequin female body and face requires extensive surgical procedures, a monk-like, disciplined daily routine of maintenance, a significant but not unreasonable sum of expenditure cash, and a will to beauty *uber alles in der Welt* (more than anything else in the world). In the duration of Arsenault's show, *The Silicone Diaries*, one understands precisely the phallogocentrism of the symbolic way faster and clearer than endless university lectures on gender and sexual exploitation could communicate. Nina seduces the gaze of the spectator, and in the process queers it.

Cutting Beauty and Its Critique in One

Fast Feminism's "natural" home is in queer theory. Queer gets its meaning and its politics from its oppositional relationship to hegemonic norms. To queer something is to disrupt it, to put it under scrutiny and to attempt to change it.[52] Living and performing as a self-identified queer artist isn't sufficient to queer beauty, but what is enough is the double disruption Arsenault performs; she reveals that mannequin Barbie proportions are a posthuman technological possibility and she discloses the scars of "the unreal cyborg I have constructed."[53] It is in and as the void doubly presupposed by the demand to make impossible beauty possible and the demand to disclose the scars of the attainment that Arsenault queers both beauty and its critique. In the doing Arsenault cuts beauty and its critique in one, seamlessly suturing the Buddhist monk and mannequin cyborg Barbie into the most beautiful woman in the world. A fast feminist.

Shannon Bell is a performance philosopher, who lives and writes philosophy-in-action. Her books include *Fast Feminism* (2010); *Reading, Writing and Rewriting the Prostitute Body* (1994); *Whore Carnival* (1995); *Bad Attitude/s on Trial* co-authored with Brenda Cossman, Lise Gotell and Becki Ross (1997); she is co-editor of *New Socialisms* with Robert Albritton, John R. Bell and Richard Westra (2004).

More recently Bell has been researching extremes in art, particularly bio and hybrid art.

Bell is currently working on shooting theory: videoing-imagining philosophical concept such as Heidegger's stillness, Husserl's epoché, Batiallian waste, Weil's attention, Deleuzian deterritorialization, Virilio's vision machine and accident.

Bell is an associate professor of political science at York University, Toronto, Canada. She teaches modern and postcontemporary theory, cyberpolitics, aesthetics and politics, violent philosophy, and fast feminism.

Bibliography

Arsenault, Nina. "Catholic Hospital Heals Whore." *T-girl, fab Magazine*, no. 228. http://fabmagazine.com/tgirl/archive/288.html.

———. "I W@s B*rbie," unpublished script, 2009.

———. "Mannequins at AGO's Surreal Things." *NinaArsenault.com*, September 4, 2009. http://ninaarsenault.com/category/im-passionate-about/.

———. "Savage Vanity: Kitty has Claws." *T-girl, fab Magazine*, no. 300. http://209.197.78.9/tgirl/archive/300.html.

———. "Self-Portraiture, Transformation, Identity and Performance." Lecture presented during the speaker's series of Canadian artists at York University's Visual Arts Department's "The Body: from Liminal to Virtual," Toronto, ON, February 9, 2011.

———. *The Silicone Diaries*. In *TRANS(per)FORMING Nina Arsenault*, edited by Judith Rudakoff, 191–227. Bristol: Intellect Press, 2012.

———, and Hamish Kippen. "Mannequin." *Fresh*, September 2007. http://ninaarsenault.com/2009/10/605/#more-605.

Bell, Shannon. *Fast Feminism*. New York: Autonomedia, 2010.

———, and Noam Gonick, and Dan Irving. "Why Queer? Why Now?" In *Canadian Dimension* 43, no. 4, July/August 2009: 20–21.

Lacan, Jacques. "Of the Gaze as *Objet Petit a*." In *The Four Fundamental Concepts of Psychoanalysis: The Seminar of Jacques Lacan, Book XI*, edited by Jacques-Alain Miller, translated by Bruce Fink 67–119. New York: W.W. Norton & Company, 1998.

———. *On Feminine Sexuality, the Limits of Love and Knowledge, 1972–73: Encore the Seminar Book of Jacques Lacan Book XX*, edited by Jacques-Alain Miller, translated by Bruce Fink 6–126. New York: W.W. Norton & Company, 1998.

Levinas, Emmanuel. "The Trace of the Other." In *Deconstruction in Context*, edited by Mark Taylor and translated by Alfonso Lingis, 345–359. Chicago: University of Chicago Press, 1986.

Rudakoff, Judith. *Faux Arts or Beaux Arts: Nina Arsenault and the Possibilities of the New.* "I W@s B*rbie," Toronto, ON, June 9–13, 2010. Playbill.

Zizek, Slavoj. "Objet a in Social Links." In *Jacques Lacan and the Other Side of Psychoanalysis: Reflections on Seminar XVII*, edited by Justin Clemens and Russell Grigg, 107–128. Chapel Hill, North Carolina: Duke University Press, 2006.

Notes

I wish to thank Gad Horowitz for his editorial assistance, Calvin Lincez for transcribing my interview with Nina Arsenault, Raan Matalon for reading Lacan with me with an eye to *objet a* and the gaze, and Niki D'Amore for reading Lacan with me, our gaze directed to feminine jouissance.

1. Nina Arsenault, personal interview with author, November 17, 2010.
2. Nina Arsenault, "Savage Vanity: Kitty has Claws," *T-girl, fab Magazine*, no. 300, http://209.197.78.9/tgirl/archive/300.html.
3. Jacques Lacan, "On *Jouissance*," in *On Feminine Sexuality, the Limits of Love and Knowledge, 1972–73: Encore the Seminar Book of Jacques Lacan Book XX*, ed. Jacques-Alain Miller, trans. Bruce Fink (New York: W.W. Norton & Company, 1998), 6.
4. Lacan, "Rings of String," in *On Feminine Sexuality*, 126.
5. Ibid.
6. Ibid.
7. Jacques Lacan, "Of the Gaze as *Objet Petit a*," in *The Four Fundamental Concepts of Psychoanalysis: The Seminar of Jacques Lacan, Book XI*, ed. Jacques-Alain Miller, trans. Alain Sheridan (New York: W.W. Norton & Company, 1981), 83.
8. Ibid., 72.
9. Ibid., 74.
10. Ibid., 106.
11. Ibid., 73.
12. Ibid., 104
13. Ibid.
14. Ibid., 103. Italics appear in the original.
15. Slavoj Zizek, "Objet a in Social Links," in *Jacques Lacan and the Other Side of Psychoanalysis: Reflections on Seminar XVII*, eds. Justin Clemens and Russell Grigg (Chapel Hill, North Carolina: Duke University Press, 2006), 115.
16. Arsenault, interview, November 17, 2010.
17. Ibid.
18. Nina Arsenault, "I W@s B*rbie," unpublished script, 2009. I saw Nina Arsenault performing "I W@s B*rbie" at PSi16, Performing Publics, Buddies in Bad Times Theatre, Toronto, June 9–13, 2010.
19. Ibid., 3.

20. Nina Arsenault, *The Silicone Diaries*, in *TRANS(per)FORMING Nina Arsenault*, ed. Judith Rudakoff (Bristol: Intellect Press, 2012), 217.
21. Judith Rudakoff, *Faux Arts or Beaux Arts: Nina Arsenault and the Possibilities of the New*, "I W@s B*rbie," Toronto, ON, June 9–13, 2010. Playbill.
22. Nina Arsenault, "Catholic Hospital Heals Whore," *T-girl*, *fab Magazine*, no. 228, http://fabmagazine.com/tgirl/archive/288.html.
23. Arsenault, "I W@s B*rbie," 4.
24. Ibid.
25. Ibid., 6.
26. Lacan, "God and Woman's *Jouissance*," in *On Feminine Sexuality*, 64.
27. Arsenault, "I W@s B*rbie," 9.
28. Ibid., *The Silicone Diaries*, 214.
29. Ibid., 206.
30. Nina Arsenault and Hamish Kippen, "Mannequin," *Fresh*, September 2007, http://ninaarsenault.com/2009/10/605/#more-605.
31. Ibid.
32. Nina Arsenault, "Self-Portraiture, Transformation, Identity and Performance," lecture presented during the speaker's series of Canadian artists at York University's Visual Arts Department's "The Body: From Liminal to Virtual," Toronto, ON, February 9, 2011.
33. Nina Arsenault, "Mannequins at AGO's Surreal Things," *NinaArsenault.com*, September 4, 2009, http://ninaarsenault.com/category/im-passionate-about/.
34. Arsenault, *The Silicone Diaries*, 218.
35. Arsenault, interview, November 17, 2010.
36. Arsenault, *The Silicone Diaries*, 224.
37. Ibid.
38. Ibid., 225.
39. Emmanuel Levinas, "The Trace of the Other," in *Deconstruction in Context*, ed. Mark Taylor, trans. Alfonso Lingis (Chicago: University of Chicago Press, 1986), 351.
40. Arsenault, interview, November 17, 2010.
41. Ibid.
42. Ibid.
43. Lacan, "Of the Gaze as *Objet Petit a*," 85.
44. Shannon Bell, *Fast Feminism* (New York: Autonomedia, 2010).
45. Ibid., 174. Original quotation from: Luce Irigaray, *Sexes and Genealogies*, trans. Gillian C. Gill (New York: Columbia University Press, 1993), 102.
46. Arsenault, "Self-Portraiture, Transformation, Identity and Performance."
47. Arsenault, *The Silicone Diaries*, 227.
48. Arsenault, interview, November 17, 2010.
49. Bell, *Fast Feminism*, 174.
50. Ibid., 22. Original quotation from: Georges Bataille, *On Nietzsche*, trans. Bruce Boone (New York: Paragon House, 1994), 72.
51. Bell, *Fast Feminism*, Chs.16–17. *Fast Feminism* shares the most general features of postmodern feminism, postfeminism and cyberfeminism: gender is viewed as performative; there is no

essential female/male self; grand referents and feminist ontologies are abandoned; multiple, complex and contradictory subjectivities are acknowledged; philosophy is overshadowed by politics; politics is lived as a realm of contestation, instability, and struggle, and ethics is reconfigured as a situated pragmatics. *Fast Feminism* works in accord with the deconstructive tendency of postfeminism: it dismantles the phallogocentric paradigm of gender. *Fast Feminism* shares the in-your-face sexuality of third or new wave feminism while it retains radical feminism's relentless critique of sexism.

52. Shannon Bell, Noam Gonick, and Dan Irving, "Why Queer? Why Now?," in *Canadian Dimension* 43, no. 4, July/August 2009.

53. Arsenault, *The Silicone Diaries*, 226.

Chapter 8

The Artist as Complication: Nina Arsenault and the Morality of Beauty

Alistair Newton

My body has become a site for public debate. And that is what I wanted.[1]
ORLAN

Through her sixty surgical alterations, Nina Arsenault has created a fusion of life and art dedicated to the achievement of both a personal ideal of beauty and the feminization of her body. Her artistic media include surgery, silicone, make-up, hair extensions, and fashion, but her artwork, her body and her performance of self, does not end when she crosses the fourth wall; the permanence of her surgical practice cannot be scrubbed away like a layer of makeup. Her audience is—by way of the conflation of *life* with *art*—everyone she encounters every day, onstage as well as offstage. Is there a socially damaging aspect to Arsenault's extreme quest for beauty or does she represent the apotheosis of the self-actualization of the queer body? Arsenault's art practice (*vis-à-vis* her life) exemplifies and magnifies many of the female beauty tropes that contribute to a negative body image for girls and women. Paradoxically, her transformation can also be viewed as an empowering form of self-expression, self-awareness, and self-actualization. Ultimately she walks a line between body fascism,[2] "which places a value on a person's worth on the basis of physical appearance or attributes,"[3] and the liberation of self-recreation. Through her ownership of the multiplicity of implications, and emotional, socio-political, personal, and cultural consequences inherent in her transformation, Arsenault has, in fact, transgressed and transcended a simplistic moral critique. By situating herself as a beautiful art object for public consumption, Arsenault invites an adoring gaze but also sets herself up as a site for scrutiny and debate. Further, by complicating often naive conceptions of art and life, empowerment and oppression, Arsenault engages with and challenges the complexities of being a woman, an artist, and a citizen of the world she inhabits.

Arsenault's use of her body as a medium of expression for her artistic practice is akin to the contemporary work of French artist ORLAN,[4] who engages in radical cosmetic surgical procedures as her central artistic practice. In her "Manifesto of Carnal Art," ORLAN declares "Carnal Art is self-portraiture in the classical sense, but realized through the possibility of technology. It swings between defiguration and refiguration. Its inscription in the flesh is a function of our age."[5] By way of surgical interventions, both Arsenault and ORLAN interrogate and blaspheme against the Western beauty myth by ironically engaging with its purpose, but also by acknowledging its impossibility as an ideal state in a natural world. Both artists' surgically altered appearances change the way they are related to by the general public. In effect, each carries out her life as a performance with no ends or boundaries. There are, of course, distinctions. In particular, ORLAN is focused on process while Arsenault, though process-oriented, is also interested in—some might say obsessed with—product. ORLAN writes, "Carnal Art is not interested in the plastic surgery result, but in the process of surgery, the spectacle and discourse of the modified body which has become the place of a public debate."[6] Whereas ORLAN seeks to destabilize notions of beauty through monstrous surgical alterations, Arsenault's self-produced body strives for the hyperstylized glamour of North American beauty tropes, as Arsenault states in *The Silicone Diaries*, "a magnificence usually reserved for porn stars and Vegas showgirls."[7] Though Arsenault and ORLAN may appear to be very different, they actually share one goal: Arsenault is, like ORLAN, interfering in heteronormative conceptions of gender. Further, they both share the belief that "Carnal Art opposes the conventions that exercise constraint on the human body and the work of art."[8] Freedom from the imposition of a conventional body image and its implied goal of a life of conventional quotidian reality is at the core of both women's practice.

Any attempt to deconstruct the moral implications of Nina Arsenault's artistic practice must examine her relationship to radical beauty from all angles in order to fully investigate the socio-political implications inherent in her transformation. At the opposite end of the spectrum from ORLAN's engagement with monstrosity is the idealized art of the film-maker, photographer, and Nazi propagandist Leni Riefenstahl. Arsenault is well aware of Riefenstahl's aesthetic, even comparing, in her stage play "I W@s B*rbie," the stagecraft of the Mattel Corporation's exhibition tent at Toronto Fashion week as "kind of like a digital Leni Riefenstahl film."[9] Riefenstahl, like Arsenault, is often the target of moralistic attacks on the grounds of her preoccupation with beauty. In her 1974 essay "Fascinating Fascism," Susan Sontag also invokes the Nazi film auteur and besotted beauty freak, charging Riefenstahl with perpetuating a fascist aesthetic, which is, according to Sontag, "both prurient and idealizing. A utopian aesthetics [of] physical perfection."[10] In a 1966 interview with the magazine *Cahiers du Cinéma*, Riefenstahl reasserted the apolitical stance she clung to after World War II "I am fascinated by what is beautiful, strong, healthy, what is living. I seek harmony."[11] For Sontag, Riefenstahl's entire oeuvre celebrates an icy, inhuman, physical beauty. One of Sontag's criteria for what constitutes the aesthetics of fascism is "the turning of people into things."[12] In her autobiographical solo stage play, *The Silicone Diaries*, Arsenault both admits to her obsession with a version of body fascism and owns it:

> If you cannot look like a normal woman, sacrifice being normal. I will be plastic. I will think of geisha. Stylized abstractions of beauty. Shuffling through the world. I love them. Nina, give yourself permission to be fabulous instead of reasonable. Really fucking fabulous. Every fucking day.[13]

In recreating herself into a living Barbie and then performing that role as part of a stage play, and by embracing her obsession with ideal beauty in *The Silicone Diaries* and performing that too, Arsenault embodies both the liberating aspects of Riefenstahl's Romantic notion of prettiness and Sontag's dehumanizing concept of objectification. By performing both, Arsenault queers each.

It is abundantly clear that Arsenault has no interest in presenting as a biological, natural woman. *The Silicone Diaries* invites the audience to judge her for the lengths to which she has gone in transgressing the aesthetic standard of "normal women." The piece also serves as a self-aware portent of the endgame of where the quest for beauty may ultimately lead.

The end of Arsenault's journey of self-creation is the actualization of a posthuman objectified state. Self-identifying as a cyborg rendered in silicone, Arsenault yet again transcends simplistic, conventional moral judgement. In "A Cyborg Manifesto," feminist theorist Donna Haraway points to the cyborg's ability to interrogate and destabilize homogeneous societal norms: "The cyborg is resolutely committed to partiality, irony, intimacy, and perversity."[14] By way of the surgeon's knife, Arsenault has become Haraway's cyborg woman, transgressing well past any accepted or acceptable standard of female beauty. In doing so, she has queered the very rubric by which the socio-cultural ramifications of her transformation continue to be judged as moral, immoral, or amoral. In a 2008 photograph by inkedKenny (Figure 6), we see Arsenault in the guise of the cyborg woman, a patchwork of composite parts representative of the biological and plastic elements that make up her artistic body. In the image Arsenault poses in front of a garage door, infiltrating a mundane setting with her hyperstylized performance of beauty.

In the biography for her 2010 appearance at Moses Znaimer's ideaCity Conference in Toronto,[15] Nina Arsenault is touted as "Canada's Most Famous Transgendered Person."[16] In this, as in many things, she is—to co-opt a phrase employed by the world's first transsexual superstar Christine Jorgensen—a "minority of one."[17] Radically opposed to Arsenault, Jorgensen, a former soldier who rose to fame in the early 1950s after undergoing the world's first widely reported sexual reassignment surgery, cultivated an expertly constructed, rigidly heterosexual persona throughout her years as a media darling, carefully distancing herself from the potential taint of association with the more radical elements of the mid-century's emerging queer subculture. Jorgensen strategically presented her life story as inspiring and affirming. Speaking at ideaCity in 2010, Arsenault offered the corollary position:

Something that's really sacred to me are [*sic*] empowerment narratives, stories where people become better people. Unfortunately, I think our culture is permeated with story-lines of empowerment through transformation … that's what people like, that's what people applaud, that's what people appraise; it's emulated. I find story lines of empowerment and transformation so pervasive, I find it suffocating and yet in many ways I'm the poster girl for that.[18]

At the conclusion of her lecture Arsenault summated, "my art is not created from a place that is trying to make the world a better place."[19] Sounding like Jorgensen's postmodern doppelgänger, Arsenault delivers the deathblow to the moralism that would seek to indict her as a body fascist or superficial, obsessive aesthete. Arsenault continues to follow her quest for an ecstatic form of stylized cyborg beauty. Her transsexual body, constructed through both legal and illegal and sometimes dangerous surgery, and embellished with a ritualistic beauty regimen of wigs, make-up, and fashion, has transgressed well beyond any recognizable North American standard of "real female" beauty. She has entered into a relationship with the world, whether in performance or walking to the corner store. It is both this transgression of beauty standards coupled with the way her queer body acts as an art object that has effectively managed to remove her from the moral discourse that seeks to indict her. It is at the moment when Arsenault denies the empowering nature of her life story that it becomes profoundly so.

Alistair Newton is a Toronto-based journalist, playwright, director of theatre and opera, and the founding artistic director of Ecce Homo Theatre. His previous theatrical projects include three consecutive productions for Toronto's SummerWorks Theatre Festival including *The Pastor Phelps Project: a fundamentalist cabaret* in 2008. Alistair is also the writer/director of *Leni Riefenstahl vs the 20th Century*, a piece which explores the presence of the fascist aesthetic in contemporary pop culture and was presented at the 2009 Rhubarb Festival. In 2010–11, Alistair served as apprentice director for the Ensemble Studio of the Canadian Opera Company, where he directed a production of Pergolisi's *La Serva Padrona*. In April 2011 Alistair was director/dramaturg for *Bella: The Colour of Love*, a commission for the Philadelphia International Festival of the Arts and he is currently developing *Of a Monstrous Child: a gaga musical* through a residency with Buddies in Bad Times Theatre. As a journalist, Alistair has been published in *fab Magazine* and *Xtra* on topics such as the cultural legacy of Tom of Finland and the history of the gay emancipation movement in Germany. Alistair holds a Bachelor of Fine Arts degree from the University of Victoria and is a member of the Director's Lab of Lincoln Center Theater.

Bibliography

Arsenault, Nina. "I W@s B*rbie." Unpublished script, 2009.

———. *The Silicone Diaries.* In *TRANS(per)FORMING Nina Arsenault*, edited by Judith Rudakoff, 191–227. Bristol: Intellect Press, 2012.

Haraway, Donna Jeanne. "A Cyborg Manifesto: Science, Technology, and Socialist-Feminism in the Late Twentieth Century." In *Simians, Cyborgs, and Women: The Reinvention of Nature*, 149–81. New York: Routledge, 1991.

ideaCity. "2010 Presenter Nina Arsenault." Accessed January 2011. http://www.ideacityonline.com/presenters/nina-arsenault.

———. "Presenter Video." Accessed January 2011. http://www.ideacityonline.com/video/nina-arsenault.

———. "What is ideaCity?" Accessed January 2011. http://www.ideacityonline.com/node/53.

Meyerowitz, Joanne. *How Sex Changed: A History of Transsexuality in the United States.* Cambridge: Harvard University Press, 2002.

Miglietti, Francesca Alfano. "Extraneous Bodies: Incarnations." In *Extreme Bodies: The Use and Abuse of the Body in Art*, 165–86. Milan: Skira Editore S.p.A., 2003.

ORLAN. "Manifesto of Carnal Art." Accessed January 2011. http://www.ORLAN.net/texts/.

Shaban, Neil. "Disability and the Performing Arts: There is No Fair Play." May 2000. Accessed January 2011. http://www.oocities.com/jinghiz53/DISABILITY_AND_THE_ PERFORMING_ARTS.htm (original site discontinued).

Shernoff, Michael. "Body Image, Working Out and Therapy." *The Journal of Gay & Lesbian Social Services* 14, no. 1 (2002). http://www.gaypsychotherapy.com/jglssgym.htm.

Sontag, Susan. "Fascinating Fascism." In *Under the Sign of Saturn*, 73–105. Toronto: McGraw-Hill Ryerson Ltd., 1980.

Notes

1. Francesca Alfano Miglietti, "Extraneous Bodies: Incarnations," in *Extreme Bodies: The Use and Abuse of the Body in Art* (Milan: Skira Editore S.p.A., 2003), 174.

2. For the purpose of this chapter, I am using the definition established by the actor and disabled rights activist Nabil Shaban, who claims to have coined the term "body fascist" in 1983. The term is widely used by queer theorists and can be found in a variety of sources such as Michael Shernoff, "Body Image, Working Out and Therapy," *The Journal of Gay & Lesbian Social Services* 14, no. 1 (2002), http://www.gaypsychotherapy.com/jglssgym.htm.

3. Neil Shaban, "Disability and the Performing Arts: There is No Fair Play," May 2000, accessed January 2011, http://www.oocities.com/jinghiz53/DISABILITY_AND_THE_ PERFORMING_ARTS.htm (original site discontinued).

4. ORLAN spells her name in upper case letters.

5. ORLAN, "Manifesto of Carnal Art," accessed January 2011. http://www.ORLAN.net/texts/.

6. Ibid.

7. Nina Arsenault, *The Silicone Diaries*, in *TRANS(per)FORMING Nina Arsenault*, ed. Judith Rudakoff (Bristol: Intellect Press, 2012), 217.

8. ORLAN, "Manifesto of Carnal Art," http://www.ORLAN.net/texts/.

9. Nina Arsenault, "I W@s B*rbie," unpublished script, 2009, 13.

10. Susan Sontag, "Fascinating Fascism," in *Under the Sign of Saturn* (Toronto: McGraw-Hill Ryerson Ltd., 1980), 93.

11. Ibid., 85.

12. Ibid., 91.

13. Arsenault, *The Silicone Diaries*, 217.

14. Donna Jeanne Haraway, "A Cyborg Manifesto: Science, Technology, and Socialist-Feminism in the Late Twentieth Century," in *Simians, Cyborgs, and Women: The Reinvention of Nature* (New York: Routledge, 1991), 151.

15. From the website of ideaCity: "ideaCity, also known as 'Canada's Premiere Meeting of the Minds,' is an eclectic gathering of artists, adventurers, authors, cosmologists, doctors, designers, entertainers, filmmakers, inventors, magicians, musicians, scientists and technologists." ideaCity, "What is ideaCity?" accessed January 2011, http://www.ideacityonline.com/node/53.

16. Ibid., "2010 Presenter Nina Arsenault," accessed January 2011, http://www.ideacityonline. com/presenters/nina-arsenault.
17. Joanne Meyerowitz, *How Sex Changed: A History of Transsexuality in the United States* (Cambridge: Harvard University Press, 2002).
18. Ibid., "Presenter Video," accessed January 2011, http://www.ideacityonline.com/video/ nina-arsenault.
19. Ibid.

Chapter 9

Landscape with Yukon and Unnatural Beauty

Nina Arsenault

I AM MY CONTAINER: Prologue
January 28, 2011, Toronto
Nina in voice class with three other women and her teacher

A vocalization.
Following the piano keys into my baritone.
Sounding.
In front of three bio-women.
Stretching my voice.

Shame around the male qualities in my voice.

Emotional risk.
Take it.
Go for it.

Tears.

My voice teacher tells me that all women have these parts of their voice.

The next woman screams the song.
Spectacular release.
Afterwards she says:

"YES!
I don't want to be pretty!
I don't want to wear make-up!
I just want to be a REAL woman!"

She thinks that she is helping me.
Leading by example.

How do I make her know that if I came in without my hair and make-up and femininity,
she wouldn't even be able to understand me as a woman.

The only way I get to be viewed as a woman is with the make-up, false lashes, fake hair. By being pretty.

I don't want to be fat.
I don't want to look like a mess.
I have to be an unreal woman.

Without what she understands as the symbols of oppression, I will cease to be a woman.

I will cease to be human.

I AM THE EVENT I
January 29, 2011, Toronto
Nina in the line-up at Pearson International Airport, Air Canada check-in counter

The ceiling architecture in the dawn light.
Soothing, smooth swooping lines, arching across sky.
A cathedral held together with rivets.
A slice of blue sky through the arch of angel wings.

In the line-up, I move one person closer to the check-in counter.

The uniformed security guard.

The airline hostess. The flight attendant.

I don't want to be an event here. I don't want to be discussed. I don't want to perception-manage.

I just want to get on my flight to Whitehorse.

I can feel my heart beating. Release and swoon. Like a painting of Jesus in Mexico.

Breathe. Big breath.

I will feel my feet beneath me. I will release the tension on the inside of my body and I will feel my breath drop. I will feel my back expand. I will feel the weight of my guts on my genitals.

I will move one person forward in the line-up.

In the line-up in front of me. People shift on their feet, breaking the tension that has collected in their posture.

Is it me?

I am responsible for others' calmness around me?

I will decide there is no problem. And there will be no problem.

Dropping my breath.
The architecture of the ceiling.
The ascending lines.

I move up one person closer to the desk where they will check my ticket.

Step towards security guard.

Surrender coat and expose.
No tension.

Through the gate.
Discipline, joy and ease.

My body a cross when you scan it with security wand.

Don't let anyone in.

I am above it all.
A show to protect from daggers.

I will be Barbie.

Don't let them smell fear.

The actor training.

Everything is an event.

I AM THE EVENT II
January 29, 2011, Vancouver
Vancouver International Airport, at the Gate

Waiting for the connecting flight to Whitehorse.
Three boys sitting behind me at the gate, in the waiting area.
With their father.
Speaking French.
Their tone does not suggest that they are talking about me.

Brunette wig: less conspicuous.
Looking out the window onto the tarmac, the airfield below.
Military style airport vehicles move with efficiency.
Men in uniforms.

The men behind me are laughing.
I move a seat down.
Touch the back of my hair.
Pull the hair to one side, exposing my long neck.

Flaunting.

Necessary.

Another man is looking at me from the bar area.

He "knows."

He wants to see more.
Wants to stare.
Perhaps has never seen a transsexual in person.
I'm curious to him, but also slightly disappointing.
Not everything he wants a transsexual to be.

Looking out into the airfield, I think of Howard Hughes.

That makes it easy.

REFLECTION
January 29, 2011, Whitehorse, Yukon Territory
Nina on Air North Flight 506, Seat 13A
Descending into Erik Neilson Whitehorse Airport

In the sky, outside the triple thick fibreglass window,
the light scintillates through the windswept clouds.
Moving in fast forward, digital stop motion,
over the mountains,
onto the smooth planes of snow
with jutting rocks,
smooth ice, pointed stone,
the light illuminates cracks,
and smooth, fast-moving shadows and light.

The woman next to me, approximately sixty-five years old, says
"Isn't it beautiful? God is talking to us."

Behind her sagging face,
beneath my silicone,
we are safe together.

She cannot judge me and continue to glow,
a halo of light around her head.
Nor can she stop the radiance in her eyes
to anticipate that I will judge her.

We have eye contact,
like lakes of frozen water high in the mountains,
reflecting sunlight back to the sky.

We turn back to the view from above,
and we stare in silence
at the whirling clouds,
the sky,
the snow,
the exposed jagged rock,
and glints of light.

DIVINATION
January 26, 2010, Whitehorse, Yukon Territory
Nina in Room 303, Westmark Hotel

On the TV: Roman Polanski's *Macbeth*.

The hotel has very thick walls.
Someone cleans for me,
but will be locked out
with a "Do not disturb" sign on the door handle.

The delivery man from Boston Pizza: low carb, no pizza, wings and lots of oil on a
Greek salad.

"Hello, how are you tonight?"

"Fine. Put it right there, please."

"Is it cold enough for you?
It was colder last week, but this is warm for this time of year.
I hope you have a good time here."

My mind is cunning.

Over your eye contact, the exact change prepared, plus tip.

The room.
Only me.
On the paper, words flow.

Out damned spot, out, I say.

FLOW I
January 27, 2010, Whitehorse, Yukon Territory
Nina in her dressing room at The Old Fire Hall performance venue[1]

Out the window, the Yukon River.
An ice jam collects in the river rushing behind the theatre.
The flow never stops moving.
Even at minus fifty degrees Celsius.

And when the ice piles up on top, the water flows below.
It will not freeze.

Watching from the dressing room: the creaking of the ice.

Being pulled onstage.
One steady, icy walk.
In six inch heels.
Click clack, click clack, click clack.

FLOW II
January 29, 2010, Whitehorse, Yukon Territory
Nina onstage at The Old Fire Hall performance venue

One night in Whitehorse, the gay audience hooting and hollering before I get onstage.

Onstage.

There is one lady who is displeased.
Her hands in the air, making noises like "ugh."

My show.
Not what she thought.

This isn't campy.

I talk about porn without prejudice.

She's DISPLEASED.

In the audience, and she wants me to know she's displeased.

I'm giving my show.

A sad moment in one of my stories.
A tear from my eye, but so faint against my face: just a drop of water.

The audience is laughing.
For the show they thought they were getting.

They still think I'm campy.

One man in the crowd.
His eyes twinkle.
Stillness that says, "You are not a joke."

It's real life.
A real life story.

The lady with her disapproval:
THIS ISN'T WHAT I THOUGHT I WAS GETTING AND I WANT THE WHOLE
AUDIENCE TO KNOW.

I'm giving my show.

Now, I am laughing.
At you, lady.
And my stories.

The head fuck.

Your arms go up in the air, exasperated.

The audience:
Laughing.
At you.
At me.

You're part of the show.
Your prejudice wanted plastic.
My silicone face, tear-stained.
Comic.
Tragic.

A spotlight.
Me.

You.
In semi-shadow, the focus.

When the lights go out and the show is over, you are the first to stand for me.

I bow to you.

LOOKING FOR GOD. FLESH IS DIVINE. JOY IS IN SORROW
January 30, 2010, Yukon Territory
Nina in a car, on the highway outside Whitehorse

Tanya, the theatre's general manager, and David, the theatre's artistic director, are taking me for a car ride in the mountains to see the natural beauty. Tanya is telling me a story about how settlers crossed these mountains with lumber, supplies, even carrying a piano.

When she finishes her story she notices a cross around my neck and asks me if I am religious.

I tell her I am spiritual and I'm exploring a bit of Buddhism, but it only works so much for me, so I'm also trying Catholicism.

The image of Christ on the cross.
The flesh becomes divine.
Through suffering.
Then death, to God.

David, the artistic director of the theatre says, "I don't want to believe in a God who allows so much suffering."

I say, "I have to believe the suffering is good for us. I just have to find a way into the moment as I'm suffering."

He asks, "Why?"

I say, "I don't know why. But that seems like the only option to me."

WHY DON'T YOU JUST ACCEPT YOURSELF?
Feb 1, 2010, Whitehorse, Yukon Territory
Nina in a Talk Back session after a performance of The Silicone Diaries

Audience member:
While you're here, my prayer for you is that I hope you can look into the face of an eighty-year-old First Nations woman and see beauty. See the beauty that shines from within her.

Nina:
I am not blind and my spirit is not dead. I do not see the faces of others as pure form that needs to be corrected. I've taken on this craft, this art, this artifice. It's not about your face or your body. It's what I did. It's what I do.

I AM THE EVENT III
January 29, 2010, Whitehorse, Yukon Territory
Nina onstage, in a Talk Back session after a performance of The Silicone Diaries

But what do your parents think?
The show isn't about my parents.

But you never told us if you're going to have a sex change operation?
The show isn't about that either.

But what about helping other people who are transgendered?
My play is not a public service announcement or an after-school special. I am an artist. For me, art has always been strengthening. PR statements that make good sound bytes only make things worse.

What kind of messages are you sending women?
Mixed messages. Paradox is empowering.

But are you just like me, or not?
I do not know.

You didn't make me understand what it feels like to be a transsexual.
You will never really know. Just like I can never know what it would really be like to be black.

I just think you're so beautiful and so empowered!
Thank you.

You make me want to get an exercise bike and a pair of heels and just take the world by storm.
Okay.

PERFORMANCE
February 3, 2011, Whitehorse, Yukon Territory
Nina goes shopping in Whitehorse

Downtown Whitehorse.
Walking down the street.
Sunglasses at all times.
Looking down.
Sunlight on snow.
People pass.
No one who passes sniffs fear.
Not too crowded here.

In stores, I take the initiative.
Always.
Speak fast.
Never to leave too much space for breath or silence in the interaction.

The thoughts behind the eyes.
The instant judgements people make.

I can let no one in.

To protect my heart.

To protect my performance.

I can let no one in.

Until the show begins.

REFLECTION II
February 4, 2010, Whitehorse, Yukon Territory
Nina on Air North Flight 207A, Seat 9A
Erik Neilson Whitehorse Airport, about to depart for Dawson City

No security at check-in.
Smiles.

The sixteen-seat plane to Dawson City.
Overweight First Nations flight attendant.
The hunter next to me carries a rifle onboard.

He sees my fear.

He says, "People are good here."

IT'S NOT A PERFORMANCE
February 4, 2010, Dawson City, Yukon Territory
Nina travels farther North to perform

Dawson City.
So far north the trees are stunted.
The old Klondike gold rush town.

Heritage buildings, restored saloons, and a brothel, painted fuchsia, baby blue, neon green.
Every building a façade for tourists.

Vegas in a blizzard.

In the hotel lobby.
Warm inside.
A great portrait.
A caricature of the famous town whore in oils: Klondike Kate.

"She married the mayor," says the girl at the desk.

A vision of Dolly Parton.
Mae West.
Anna Nicole Smith.

My lips, swollen in the cold.

The woman at the desk, almost bowing to me, points to the painting of Klondike Kate, "She's one of our town's greatest women in history."

She carries my luggage and says she studies the can-can.
And has to order false lashes from eBay, then delivered by air.

Is she trying to act like Mae West?

Looking into her eyes; it's not a performance.

She says, "I can't wait to see your show."

TRAGEDY
February 5, 2010, Dawson City, Yukon Territory
Nina onstage at The Old Ballroom performance venue

I will be myself in Dawson City.
For the first time, no one will know.

Stranger.

In a hundred-year-old ballroom, with eight chandeliers, walls from a Steven Klein photo shoot, and mirrors in the wings.

I surprise myself.

It isn't about attention.
It isn't about perception-management.
It isn't about being the best.
It isn't about bragging.
It isn't about crying.
It isn't about being what you want me to be.
It isn't about being what I want me to be.
It's not about fulfilling you.
It's not about my ego.

What has been done cannot be undone.

My lips fluttering.

No one will know if I stumble tonight, so far from urban civilization.

I will make the show for me tonight: no acting please.

Swoon, only reveal.
My feet on the ground, my head floating on the nuances of breath.

I will live and die here.

Beautiful.

Nina Arsenault is a transdisciplinary artist, who has worked in theatre, television, film, video art, photography, and print. Her life has been the subject of numerous national and international documentary television programs, radio interviews, and print articles. In 2005, she took control of her voice and image to write her *T-Girl* column in *fab Magazine*, a series of autobiographical stories that she later adapted into her one-woman play *The Silicone Diaries*. She is currently developing a long-form video called *Ophelia/Machine*.

Arsenault has performed *The Silicone Diaries* in major theatres across Canada. She has also appeared on the Canadian stage in such plays as Sky Gilbert's *Ladylike* and her own "I W@s B*rbie." Recently she portrayed Barbie for the Mattel Corporation at the plastic doll's official fiftieth birthday party in Toronto. Arsenault is a frequent speaker at Canadian universities in areas as diverse as sexuality studies, sociology, visual arts, theatre, and fashion communications. In 2010, she was a keynote speaker at Moses Znaimer's conference of avant-garde thinkers, ideaCity.

Arsenault is engaged in the continuing practice of photographing her body, something she has done at all points of her physical metamorphosis. She has collaborated on these photography projects with fashion photographers and pornographers including Bruce LaBruce, Peter Tamlin, Neil Mota, and inkedKenny.

She has been honoured with The Unstoppable Award from the Pride Committee of Toronto, and by Toronto's Mayor David Miller for continuing to challenge and illuminate culturally accepted notions of gender and sexuality

In June 2011, Arsenault's work was recognized by the Canadian Civil Liberties Association as having profoundly impacted human rights in Canada.

Bibliography

"Pivot Theatre Festival." *Nakai Theatre*. Accessed March 20, 2011. http://www.nakaitheatre.com/index.php/pivot-theatre-festival.

Note

1. Founded in 1979, the theatre's website, http://nakaitheatre.com, describes the artistic philosophy of the company: Nakai Theatre, based in Whitehorse, Yukon, Canada, is a non-profit professional theatre company dedicated to the development of live theatre that is relevant to northern audiences. Nakai Theatre is a member of the Professional Association of Canadian Theatres. Nakai Theatre's Pivot Festival presented Arsenault's *The Silicone Diaries*, January 26–31, 2010 and "I W@s B*rbie," January 25–29, 2011. The sections of this chapter refer, as specified by date, to events that occurred during either Arsenault's 2010 or 2011 performances.

Chapter 10

Performing the Prosthetics of Femininity: Nina Arsenault's Transsexual Body as a Living Art Object

Benjamin Gillespie

Through a process of surgical modification, Nina Arsenault has transformed her body into an art object, creating an idealized feminine image that echoes Baudrillard's conception of the hyperreal in productive and sometimes paradoxical ways. Arsenault's self-conscious construction of her body mirrors the hyperreal as a representation of "femininity" that has no original but rather is a copy of a copy "of an idea of woman. An image which has never existed in nature."[1] Through her very visibility as a transsexual, Arsenault exposes the theatrical nature of the feminine, a "transparency [that] is too good to be true."[2] Transposing the feminine image onto her male body, she is a "materialized projection" built out of her fantasy, brought forth through the "materialized transparency"[3] of silicone in the realm of the "real." By positioning her body as an art object within the representational frame of live theatre in her one-woman show *The Silicone Diaries*, Arsenault invokes the hyperreal but also subverts it: the examination of her body's construction simultaneously highlights its biological materiality and its artificiality, represented most obviously in the large amounts of silicone she has incorporated into her flesh to effect a feminine form. Furthermore, in performance Arsenault capitalizes on the theatre's inauthenticity through its most authentic element of the live body, and then undermines that body's coherence as an organic entity by revealing how she has shaped herself in the manner an artist sculpts marble. Thus, Arsenault's body collapses an easily readable binary between fleshy reality and its silicone representation, bringing Baudrillard's conception of the hyperreal down to the level of materiality in its phenomenal form. In other words, it is by presenting a transparent façade of the feminine that Arsenault ironically becomes "real." Through an act of *dissimulation*— representing the truth of femininity on her transsexual body—she exposes femininity's "reality" as simulacra.

In this chapter, I outline Baudrillard's conception of the role of simulacra in his construction of the hyperreal in order to show how Arsenault's transsexual aesthetic in *The Silicone Diaries* can be read through this theoretical paradigm. Critically analyzing both her body and the performance, I argue that Arsenault disrupts the binary between reality and its representation by bringing together fleshy and prosthetic body parts. I begin by unpacking the narrative of the performance, highlighting key moments that inform my analysis and judgement of her body as a living work of art. From there, I move forward to apply a concept of theatricality that explains the implications of her body within the representational frame of theatre as both artist and art object. I argue that her body is the central component of the show, made so through the play's narrative structure being built around her bodily transformation as a transsexual woman.

Ultimately, I show how Arsenault utilizes and subverts the structure of the hyperreal through her hyperfemininity in the materialization of her exaggerated feminine body. Indeed, she also undermines her own superficiality by exposing femininity's untruth—the very "overt visibility"[4] or transparency of artificiality—through modeling the feminine on her body. The paradox here is that while she creates a transparently inauthentic body, she also imposes illusive qualities on her male body and consequently subverts Baudrillard's thesis that all contemporary art lacks a "desire for illusion."[5] Arsenault's production, both the production of the play and the process of producing her body, encourages the audience to consider the gendered body as a simulation itself. Questioning Baudrillard's condemnation of contemporary art's transparency, I propose that it is by and through her overt visibility as a transsexual woman that Arsenault's body performs the seductiveness of the feminine form, even while she self-reflexively calls attention to its impossibility.

Theatricality and the Hyperreal

In *Simulacra and Simulation*, Baudrillard defines the hyperreal in relation to simulation. Importantly, he makes a distinction between *dissimulation* and *simulation*: dissimulating is marked by an aesthetic of pretending which "leav[es] the principle of reality intact."[6] Like the theatrical mode of representation, dissimulation creates a binary between truth and falsehood that marks the separation between the real and imaginary. As Tracy C. Davis and Thomas Postlewait consider in their introduction to *Theatricality*, Plato's essential definition of mimesis "evokes the 'factual' or real world but cannot capture it … As a counterfeit practice, twice-removed from the true or pure realm of the Real, theatre illusively (perhaps fraudulently) produces a mimesis."[7] The theatre then "imitate[s] life (or some ideal), but like a metaphor the representation is always removed from its model, falling short of it."[8] Simulation, on the other hand, is a parading of the imaginary *as* "real" and the "real" as imaginary, disrupting the binary configuration of representation. Simulation is thus opposed to representation and thus opposed to the practice of traditional live theatre. In consuming all levels of representation, simulation equates the sign with reality—"the radical negation of the sign as value"— absorbing it into the realm of the hyperreal.[9] According to Baudrillard, there is no distinction between reality and its simulacrum in the hyperreal: they are one and the same, enveloping all referents or signs that might point to the object's or subject's dissembling as such. His theory of hyperreality—literally, an excess or exaggeration of reality—is defined by "the real [being] confused with its model."[10] Baudrillard's infamous reading of Disneyland, for example, provides an effective instance of how a simulacrum is experienced as "real," and is worth quoting at length:

Disneyland exists in order to hide that it is the "real" country, all of "real" America that *is* Disneyland. Disneyland is presented as imaginary in order to make us believe that the rest is real, whereas all of Los Angeles and the America that surrounds it are no longer real, but belong to the hyperreal order and to the order of simulation. It is no longer a question of a false representation of reality (ideology) but of concealing the fact that the real is no longer real.[11]

For Baudrillard, both modern society and art are mediated through this logic of simulation to such an extent that there is no longer a factual or objective reading of the "real" precisely because it is inseparable from its simulation. The artificiality of the hyperreal has effectively become reality. As he demonstrates in "The Precession of Simulacra," reality is preceded by the model of simulation, and thus the real *is* the model, moulded out of a pre-existing image copied from an image of an image of the real without a sign or referent to ground it, or reveal the provenance of its origin. The model of the hyperreal comes before reality itself and the improvisational or simultaneous meanings attributed to this model cancel each other out, destroying the interpretive gap between the "imaginary" and the "real" or the image and its referent. Ironically, it is the very artificial pretence of *The Silicone Diaries* that disrupts Baudrillard's model of the hyperreal through its transparency as a model of reality; interestingly, Arsenault's body doubles this representational model by investing the silicone in her body with a hyperfeminine aesthetic to perform femininity with an overt pretense of inauthenticity.

The Transsexual Model of Femininity

Arsenault's parodic and exaggerated version of femininity self-consciously positions her body as a hyperreal feminine art object; however, she also subverts this potential superficiality through invocations of female verisimilitude. This is to say that Arsenault appears and lives as a woman, but then shows us how appearances can be (and are) deceiving. Arsenault's obsession with her own material production forces the hyperreal image of femininity out of the space of empty signification to form a representation of the female form, while resisting it holistically through her self-identification as a transsexual. Arsenault does not position herself objectively as a real woman, nor does she attempt to maintain an illusion of "actuality" or "fact," but instead questions her own womanly performance through emphasizing her obsession with being an overtly imitative model of femininity. Her overt transparency as a transsexual always references the origin of her body as male. In her life and in her art she draws attention to her transition; the fact that she still has a penis, for example (see Figures 16 and 30), marks her body as having a male history and provides a ground for her aesthetic enhancement. On the other hand she exaggerates her femininity, caricaturing the feminine bodies that flood the hyperreal in the fashion industry, advertising, and celebrity culture. Arsenault's "spectacular promotion"[12] of the feminine as constructed through prosthetics marks the very ideal of the feminine as artificial, as an art in itself in an age defined by the hyperreal. Worth mentioning is Baudrillard's own deployment of the term *transsexual*, which he suggests marks the transparency of the hyperreal age we live in, an age in which artistic illusion is now traded in for the "ambient pornography" of overt visibility or a "transaesthetic"[13] that permeates the visual register.

In performance, Arsenault always remains obviously and overtly in the realm of representation. Her performance posits the concept of gender as a simulacrum that stems from the hyperreal without any origin or finitude. She exposes the malleability of gender through disposing of the male parts on her body and replacing them with a material that stands in for feminine parts. In undergoing this surgical process, it is not that she has become "more real than real,"[14] as Baudrillard suggests of simulacra, but rather that she is an artistic composition built out of a very artificial model of femininity in the realm of the Real: a synthesis of parts configured that produce the exaggerated and outrageous model of femininity that she embodies and that could never be real in nature. Arsenault exposes femininity as synthesis, foregrounding her body as an artificial representation of reality, a transparently theatrical venture in itself.

(Re)Constructing the Performance

In November of 2009, I saw Arsenault's performance of *The Silicone Diaries* at Buddies in Bad Times Theatre (Buddies)[15] for the first time. The show's sold-out run and widespread positive critical response led to a remount as part of Buddies' 2010–11 mainstage season, and a subsequent Canadian tour in 2011. The production is constructed as a confessional performance in which Arsenault directly addresses the audience in a series of seven, chronologically ordered, monologues that detail important moments in her life. Arsenault begins by reflecting on her childhood, growing up as a little boy in rural Ontario. She recounts how as a child she identified intensely with femininity and beauty, worshipping hyperfeminine objects such as Barbie dolls and mannequins. Arsenault reveals that from a very young age she has wanted to realize these images corporeally, and in front of us, in her performance of the self, we see her youthful fantasy materialize. In a diary-like fashion, Arsenault recovers her past, looking back to locate the foundations for her inspiration and obsession with beauty and transformation. In the second production of the play at Buddies in 2010, videos are projected on a large screen behind her that document the surgical procedures she underwent and the physical changes she experienced through her long and continued period of transition.[16] At times grotesque, these recorded images are juxtaposed with the beautiful body—the surgically enhanced configuration of femininity or artistic composition—we see in front of us. Wearing stilettos, a transparent rubber dress that clings to her silicone-enhanced figure, a long flowing wig that covers the scars of facial reconstruction surgeries, and further adorned with elaborately designed make-up, Arsenault revels in and is empowered by the plastic and artificial amalgamation of these feminine signifiers on her body.

Feminization, as Baudrillard suggests, is a seduction of appearances, an illusion of the Real that is marked by its overt simulacra and informed by the hyperreal.[17] While her body does not *pass* as real,[18] it is through Arsenault's individual version of the feminine that she has become comfortable in her identity as a transsexual and as an artist who exists in a kind of hyperreal state. Inherently spectacular, Arsenault pivots her aesthetic on a theatrical version of the feminine through materializing feminine features on her body, and, in the performance of her body, manipulating her audience's gaze—both onstage and offstage. Recalling a meeting with rock star Tommy Lee, Arsenault narrates how she "shade[s]" other onlookers with,

> a downwards cast of my extra long lashes at the 45-degree angle … the shadiest angle possible … I crouch low, next to Tommy's chair, and shake his hand, a little *trick* I learned at the tranny strip club … combin[ing] the flattering angle of looking upwards into a man's face with the mental suggestion that you could at any moment give him a blowjob.[19]

Even outside the theatre, Arsenault performs her rehearsed femininity for onlookers, so that they might read her as spectacularly feminine and beautiful, regardless of her status as a transsexual woman:

> I don't want to be made to feel less beautiful because I was born into a male body, or because I have fake parts … synthetic hair, make-up, silicone, attitude, radiance – I don't have to be born a biological woman to have these things, and I want you to get that it is these things that give you the physiological feeling of a hard on.[20]

While she is obviously imitative in her construction, it is her investment in femininity that allows her to perform as such. As Arsenault suggests in *The Silicone Diaries*, Tommy Lee believes in her fantasy, as she seduces him with her artificiality and confidence, and by playing the part of the "ballsy, glamour-puss-type of chick" that she thinks Tommy Lee will find attractive.[21] Her plastic beauty plays on Lee's sexual attraction to silicone-enhanced women, showing how Arsenault is not any less "real" on the surface than the simulated images of women paraded in the realm of the hyperreal. In fact, she exceeds reality through mimicking these images and bringing them into a material form, showing how unrealistic they are, on the one hand, and the power and currency they hold in seducing an audience, on the other.

Framing the Artist as Art Object

In her performance of *The Silicone Diaries*, Arsenault's posing before both herself and others as a kind of mirror is emphatically invoked. First, she creates a mirror on stage by presenting her body as her ideal fantasy of feminine form, and by discussing the explicit details of her own modification. In this context the audience's gaze constructs a reflection out of which she creates an image of herself. Her shifting self-perceptions inform the narrative, including how she sees her body, the representations of feminine forms that affected her in the past (both "real" and imagined), and the experience of pondering other's reactions to her body.[22] Second, her documentation of her surgeries, projected on large screens behind her, is juxtaposed with the figure we see on stage. Arsenault is femininity in the flesh, but the graphic images of slicing, suturing, and bruising give the audience an explicit recounting of the aesthetic modification on her body, which we reflect back to her.

Pivoting the performance on the viewing of her body, Arsenault sets up the audience to objectify her as an art object to be manipulated in the same way she manipulated herself throughout her artistic process. Arsenault considers her own self-objectification, especially in her narcissistic focus on her body in the production, and explains:

> My body is the centre point of the show in how the stories are arranged in and around the turning point in my body, dealing with inner and outer beauty. There definitely is a blurring between art and life for me, in a way because I have chosen to augment my body in ways that make it non-normative. I have made aesthetic choices within my body's construction. Once you start talking about abstraction of form, you are using artistic language—and yet this is my life—this is the body I live in every day.[23]

Like her references in *The Silicone Diaries* to the artificial beauty of Pamela Anderson, Arsenault's own image is one that does not reflect nature. Arsenault is not a real woman; she is an *ideal* woman, pointing to the very impossibility of this ideal by foregrounding the pain, time, and money it has taken to become it. This mutating corporeal fantasy is recorded on and in her body by the scars from surgery and the changes effected by silicone injections. It is around this substance—silicone—that her bodily flesh has been moulded to compose her figure, a figure that is already marked by the history of the feminine form itself. As Rebecca Schneider suggests in *The Explicit Body in Performance*:

> Constructed as a natural unnatural, an unreal real, woman has existence relative only to her representation: her representation both precedes and succeeds her, she is always chasing after it. What the whirlwind of such analysis lays bare, then, is that ultimately, even "she herself" stands for her own representation – a particular woman stands beside herself, representative of the way womanhood has been represented (as a successful or failed, compliant or belligerent copy).[24]

Schneider exposes the endlessly reproduced female body—what, in Baudrillard's paradigm, is simulacra—grounding her argument in the reality of "woman" as an impossible ideal itself, marked by a never-ending whirlwind of representation that ghosts even the live body, exposed as biologically female. Her overall argument stems from the collapse of sign and signifier on the live body, which interrogates the gap between reality and its representation. Arsenault is caught in this similar whirlwind of representation with one obvious difference: the collapse of the sign and signifier of femininity is broken in the marking of herself as biologically male. However, Arsenault's implication as transsexually female (meaning that she produces the effect of female-ness) furthers Schneider's argument and the argument of this chapter: that the feminine body is an impossible ideal, and that it becomes more real in representative form than it will ever be on the body of a "Real woman."

In being transparent about the fact that her idealized feminine body can only be realized through surgical intervention, Arsenault continually foregrounds her own artificiality. As Baudrillard suggests,

> within the feminine, the very distinction between authenticity and artifice is without foundation, [which] also defines the space of simulation. Here too one cannot distinguish between reality and its models, there being no other reality than that secreted by simulative models, just as there is no other femininity than that of appearances.[25]

For Arsenault, it is her appearance as a feminine being that marks her body as such. Turning her life into an artistic concept with the goal of creating or representing her hyperfeminine fantasy into a lived somatic experience, she utilizes theatre's liveness to frame herself as both art object and artist, coming together in the performance's autobiographical narrative. As the subject of her own performance, Arsenault uses her material body as the stage on which she performs her unique version of the feminine. After all, it is her body that actively performs and represents the idea of femininity and the prosthetics that adorn her body, including her costume, hair extensions, garish make-up, etc., enhance the spectacle of her femininity. Her body-as-stage is set directly onto a literal stage, where we view its public rehearsal to recreate a continuous caricature of femininity, doubling the representative frame and turning her body into the ultimate art object.

The concept of theatricality is useful in discussing the ways Arsenault highlights the construction of her body as a continual process of reasserting and rehearsing her femininity. Josette Féral suggests that "theatricality [is] a *process* that has to do with the 'gaze' that postulates and creates a distinct, virtual space belonging to the other [whether one is an 'actor' or 'spectator'], from which fiction can emerge."[26] Theatricality, then, allows Arsenault to present the feminine image of herself she wishes the audience to see; however, rather than covering up the cracks that mark this femininity as constructed, she draws attention to them, making them a part of her overall, inherently theatrical, image and presence. Arsenault marks herself as a spectacular or theatrical object by foregrounding her representation of femininity as the subject of her performance. It is on the condition of theatricality that the audience's gaze allows Arsenault's personal psychic truth—that she is a woman—and her fantasy of feminine beauty, which she has achieved through massive amounts of plastic surgery, to come into being, making it as "real" as possible. Her fantasy is marked by the presence of silicone—what Brendan Healy, the play's director, refers to as "the literal personificatio[n] of our most profound fantasies"[27]— and it is through the transparency of silicone that the truth of femininity, in Baudrillard's conception of it, is unveiled as a theatrical act, perpetrated by the actor, and then simultaneously recognized and brought into being through the gaze of her audience.

Some might criticize Arsenault's creation of an unrealistic feminine ideal as superficial or antifeminist; however, it is *in* her hyperbolic portrayal of femininity that she questions the unattainable, artificial, and hyperfeminine images of women that exist in our culture, and which she ironically embodies. While she has exceeded the norm in producing her desired image as a female—as a hyperfeminine image, she is made up of a series of feminine ideals—there were and are parts of her body that are, for her, unmistakably masculine. In an article written for the *National Post*, Arsenault explains this exaggerated pursuit of the feminine:

> When I started having plastic surgery, I super-feminized some features to compensate for other manly traits that were outside the power of the doctor's scalpel—my broad shoulders, and the fact that I was nearly 6-feet tall. I told the doctor to make my lips as big as he could. Then go a little further. … Once I had the blessing of the surgeon's blade, I realized just how tantalizingly easy it was to enhance my appearance.[28]

Arsenault's decision to create an unreal feminine form highlights the importance of aesthetic cohesion. By constructing large lips, breasts, and hips, she minimizes what she characterizes as "manly traits," pulling attention away from unchangeable masculine features, such as her broad shoulders and tall stature. Arsenault's obviously constructed body undermines the images that have influenced her aesthetic reconstruction by highlighting how unreasonable and unrealistic they are on a human body.[29] Her fantasy is, however, maintained in the same way a work of art is kept at the level of an artistic object through the belief in and manipulation of an aesthetic to convey meaning. While that aesthetic is sometimes discovered to be inauthentic—as in the case of Lee's discovery of Arsenault's transsexuality—it is through the showcasing of that very fiction of "real femininity" that *The Silicone Diaries* so clearly elucidates the differences between hyperreality and representation, collapsing the feminine as overt simulacra and moving it into the more productive category of representation.

Conclusion

In the construction of her feminine image, Nina Arsenault grounds her superficial association with the feminine in a concrete materiality that is marked by its transparency as a representation of femininity. Most importantly, it is her visibility as artificially feminine that makes the truth of her femininity "real," exposing the reality of femininity as a representation of nothing that could be real in nature, but a "reality" produced and reproduced in the realm of the hyperreal. She interrogates femininity through the exploration of her body's overabundance of feminine signifiers that are incoherent singularly but create a coherent image when transposed onto her male body. Through the reconstruction of her body as feminine, and the placing of that body on stage in a theatrical frame, Arsenault also marks her male gender as an incoherent simulacrum, pulled out of a set of ideals that have no origin; she exposes gender as a hyperreal concept, even more so than silicone. This secret of gender origin does not represent, but rather creates a simulacrum against which all others are measured. Arsenault brilliantly discusses the grotesque untruth of one's gender in relation to one's biological sex. As discussed above, in reconstructing her body towards the achievement of heightened femininity, Arsenault objectifies her body and turns it into an artistic object. As a transsexual, Arsenault disrupts Baudrillard's notion that transparency disallows illusion and remains within the realm of the hyperreal by being overt about her body's construction, and open about her feminine artificiality, while also delving deeply into the fictive qualities of gender's truth. Her transsexuality works to ground her very unrealness through dissimulation. In not passing as a "real woman," Arsenault represents her version of "woman," becoming that ideal in her role and performance as artist.

In the final monologue of *The Silicone Diaries*, titled "Venus/machine (2007–2009)," we discover that Arsenault's complex relationship with her body, even postsurgery, remains unsettled. She states "the next phase of my work with my body [will be] to accept the me underneath all the glamour. The unreal cyborg I have constructed."[30] It is this "me" that structures the feminine as coherent underneath the silicone, grounding the material outside in a firm identity. But it is also an important realization that one's outer surface image will never match exactly one's inner feeling as male or female. As Judith Butler notes, if the prohibitive effects of a normalizing bodily surface "constitute[s] projected morphologies, then [a] reworking [of] the terms of these prohibitions suggests the possibility of variable projections, variable modes of delineating and theatricalizing body surfaces."[31] She further remarks, "[t]hese variable body surfaces or bodily egos may thus become sites of transfer to *properties that no longer belong properly to any anatomy*."[32] Surely, Arsenault's body can be seen as a pivotal site of transfer, not just for her exploration of her material "sex" as Butler might say, but also for reworking her transsexual body to deconstruct (and to reconstruct) the simulacrum of the feminine in transparently provocative ways.

Benjamin Gillespie received his MA in Theatre Studies at York University (2010), where he was the recipient of an Ontario Graduate Scholarship. Benjamin is pursuing his PhD at the City University of New York (CUNY), where his research revolves around related interests in queer theatre/theory, aesthetics, performance and body art, and modern and contemporary drama. Benjamin has presented at Performance Studies International (2010) on the work of Nina Arsenault and also published an article in *Canadian Dimension* (2010) on her work. Further publications appear in *Canadian Theatre Review*. He has assisted in editing and anthologizing articles for *Theatre and Performance in Toronto* for the acclaimed series *Critical Perspectives in Canadian Theatre*. He has presented at the Canadian Association for Theatre Research and the Association for Theatre in Higher Education (2011), and has also been published in the *Canadian Theatre Review* in 2012.

Bibliography

Arsenault, Nina. "My $150,000 Body." *The National Post*, April 22, 2006.

———. *The Silicone Diaries*. In *TRANS(per)FORMING Nina Arsenault*, edited by Judith Rudakoff, 191–227. Bristol: Intellect Press, 2012.

Baudrillard, Jean. "The Conspiracy of Art." *The Conspiracy of Art*, 25–29. New York: Semiotext(e), 2005.

———. *Seduction*. Montreal: New World Perspectives, 1990.

———. *Simulacra and Simulation*. Ann Arbor: University of Michigan Press, 1995.

Butler, Judith. *Bodies that Matter: On the Discursive Limits of Sex*. New York: Routledge, 1993.

Davis, Tracy C., and Thomas Postlewait. "Theatricality: An Introduction." In *Theatricality*, 1–39. Cambridge: Cambridge University Press, 2003.

Féral, Josette. "Theatricality: The Specificity of Theatrical Language." *SubStance* 31, no. 2/3 (2002): 94–108.

Healy, Brendan. "Untitled Director's Statement." *The Silicone Diaries*. Buddies in Bad Times Theatre, Toronto, ON, 2010. Playbill.

Schneider, Rebecca. "Logic of the Twister, Eye of the Storm." In *The Explicit Body in Performance*, 43–65. New York: Routledge, 1997.

Serano, Julia. *Whipping Girl: A Transsexual Woman on Sexism and the Scapegoating of Femininity*. Berkeley: Seal Press, 2007.

Notes

An earlier version of this chapter was presented at the Performance Studies International Conference, Toronto, ON, June 2010.

1. Nina Arsenault, *The Silicone Diaries*, in *TRANS(per)FORMING Nina Arsenault*, ed. Judith Rudakoff (Bristol: Intellect Press, 2012), 219.
2. Jean Baudrillard, "The Conspiracy of Art," *The Conspiracy of Art* (New York: Semiotext(e), 2005), 26.
3. Jean Baudrillard, *Simulacra and Simulation* (Ann Arbor: University of Michigan Press, 1995), 106.
4. Baudrillard, "The Conspiracy of Art," 25.
5. Ibid., 25. Baudrillard's controversial short essay postulates modern and contemporary art in the metaphor of an orgy: its obsession and deconstruction of the object and the image cripple the very mode of representation itself through the hyperproduction and reproduction of simulacra. He finds that hyperreal images have impaled the art world to such an extent that the very illusive qualities of pre-modern art have been lost in the lack of "desire for illusion," which "rais[es all art] to aesthetic banality."
6. Baudrillard, *Simulacra and Simulation*, 3.

7. Tracy C. Davis and Thomas Postlewait, "Theatricality: An Introduction," in *Theatricality* (Cambridge: Cambridge University Press, 2003), 4.

8. Ibid., 5.

9. Baudrillard, *Simulacra and Simulation*, 6.

10. Ibid., 29.

11. Ibid., 12–13.

12. Ibid., 38.

13. Baudrillard, "The Conspiracy of Art," 25.

14. Baudrillard, *Simulacra and Simulation*, 81.

15. Buddies in Bad Times Theatre is the largest facility-based queer theatre company in the world. Established in 1979 in Toronto, the company has been producing groundbreaking queer and alternative theatre and performance for more than thirty years. The company resides in the heart of Toronto's gay village and brings a variety of audiences to its space, boasting a rich history in Toronto's marginalized and radical theatre scene.

16. In the 2009 production, the projections were designed by Nicolas A. Greenland. In the 2010 production, the video projections were designed by R. Kelly Clipperton.

17. This idea is comprehensively developed in Jean Baudrillard, *Seduction* (Montreal: New World Perspectives, 1990), 16.

18. *Passing* generally refers to a transperson's ability to be accepted or *read* as the sex/gender that they present to others, even if that sex/gender is not concomitant with that person's biological matter. For a transgender or transsexual person, this involves remaining undetectably feminine or masculine in one's behaviour and bodily form depending on their desired sex. To be *read* is for someone to see through this presentation or for a person to fail at passing. For a more concrete definition and description of passing, see, for example, Julia Serano, *Whipping Girl: A Transsexual Woman on Sexism and the Scapegoating of Femininity* (Berkeley: Seal Press, 2007).

19. Arsenault, *The Silicone Diaries*, 219; emphasis mine.

20. Ibid., 221.

21. Ibid., 220.

22. Nina Arsenault, personal interview with author, Toronto, ON, February 21, 2010.

23. Ibid.

24. Rebecca Schneider, "Logic of the Twister, Eye of the Storm," *The Explicit Body in Performance* (New York: Routledge, 1997), 51.

25. Baudrillard, *Seduction*, 16.

26. Josette Féral, "Theatricality: The Specificity of Theatrical Language," *SubStance* 31, no. 2/3 (2002): 97.

27. Brendan Healy, "Untitled Director's Statement," *The Silicone Diaries*, Buddies in Bad Times Theatre, Toronto, ON, 2010, playbill.

28. Nina Arsenault, "My $150,000 Body," *The National Post*, April 22, 2006.

29. Arsenault's play "I W@s B*rbie" deals more explicitly with this topic, exploring issues of identity, embodiment, and feminine representation in the fashion world as well as Arsenault's identification with Barbie since childhood. The show chronicles her experience

actually playing Barbie at Toronto's Fashion Week in 2009, which was sponsored by the Mattel Corporation.

30. Arsenault, *The Silicone Diaries*, 226.
31. Judith Butler, *Bodies that Matter: On the Discursive Limits of Sex* (New York: Routledge, 1993), 64.
32. Ibid.

Chapter 11

Compelling Honesty: Searching for Authenticity in the Voice
of Nina Arsenault

Eric Armstrong

Nina Arsenault has been incrementally re-forming herself to achieve her personal conception of feminine beauty. Though this has been primarily through external and physical modifications and, arguably, most intimately through changes to her voice, Arsenault has begun with her self as raw material, and embraced change, spontaneity, and authenticity as her starting points. Arsenault's exploration of the feminine form, role, and voice has been rooted in images of the hyperfeminine evoked by the icons of the twentieth-century such as Marilyn Monroe and the iconic Barbie doll. Meanwhile, Arsenault's study of voice has led her to question the method of approaching the feminine voice without compromising her values of honesty, spontaneity, and presence. This chapter seeks to hear Arsenault's voice, to place it within the challenges of voicing her new feminine role, and to demonstrate how her voice's capacity to reveal her authentic self is made manifest in her life and performance. In order to do so, I interviewed Nina Arsenault on March 1, 2011, in person and in supplementary conversations, and also observed her on March 2, 2011 during a private lesson with her current voice teacher, Fides Krucker, at Krucker's home studio in Toronto.

Arsenault's Current Voice

Today, Nina Arsenault's voice is soft and pleasant, with a bright, forward placement and a slightly nasal twang. Though she has never had any voice training specifically geared towards those who are transitioning,[1] she has managed to embrace many of the vocal strategies recommended for transwomen: her average pitch is just below the ambiguous range (around 140 Hz, about the D above middle C), her speech is generally a little quieter than most, and she uses a bright, pingy vocal quality, while keeping the space in her mouth small so that her voice vibrates in the front. She often has a slight breathiness to her speech, which is another characteristic of feminized speech. She uses a fair amount of glottal fry,[2] especially at the end of phrases, which can disguise particularly low final notes; as this is a characteristic of younger women's voices, she is also making a vocal choice that reads as both youthful and feminine. In terms of her intonation pattern—the melody of her voice—she tends to use a fair amount of uptalk, with high-rising terminals, or ends of phrases, that is commonly encountered in many young people in North America, especially women.[3] Arsenault also uses a number of tag questions,[4] like "do you know?," which are also well-known strategies in the Male-to-Female (MtF) community.[5] Her speech is very expressive, using a broad range of pitch as females typically do, and she uses body language to emphasize her thoughts through gesture and subtle inclinations of the head.

Arsenault's alignment is a powerful reinforcement of her feminine image, and her use of her hands is subtle and detailed. For example, she often covers her mouth when she laughs, which appears both modest and coy. This habitual behaviour is due, in part, to some self-consciousness on Arsenault's part about her lips, and her facial movements. She clarified:

> Because I've done so much with my lips they do not move properly. I don't really think about how this has changed the way I speak. I had a really bad lisp after I had the work done last time though. Thankfully that went away. Laughing is the most strange, unfortunately. Any emotion that wants to spontaneously move my face around a lot tends to get stifled. I am not sure if that is the result of my face not moving naturally or from a knee-jerk response I have when my face starts moving around too much.[6]

Transgender Voice

The voice of transgendered MtF persons is an interesting paradox: they have the anatomical structure of an adult male larynx, but seek the sound of a woman. They have a biological voice that conflicts with their feminine role. As males pass through puberty, the effects of the hormone testosterone on their voices causes the larynx to become larger, the vocal folds to gain mass and length, and for the pitch of the average voice to deepen by about an octave, compared to the average female voice. Whereas a Female-to-Male transman can expect an effect on his voice from taking hormones, a transwoman who takes hormones can expect no change to her voice as the effect of testosterone is already complete. No hormone will cause the larynx to shrink.

Because of the anatomical changes of male puberty, MtF persons must experiment, first at home and then out in public, with strategies to counter the qualities that come with an enlarged larynx, as well as those qualities learned unconsciously by social conditioning to sound masculine. The physical appearance of the larynx can be changed by surgery, the so-called laryngeal shave,[7] which removes part of the thyroid cartilage and makes the Adam's apple less prominent. However, the surgery does nothing to change the sound of the speaker's voice, and other surgeries that work on the vocal folds themselves are generally frowned upon by health practitioners as being unproven and risky.

The primary quality that society perceives as sounding "feminine" is pitch. Though average male and female voices are roughly an octave apart, there is a small window of overlap between the range of high male speakers and low female speakers, a space of about 4 or 5 semi-tones, where perception labels the pitch of the voice as being ambiguous. Most MtF speakers work hard to raise their pitch into the ambiguous zone, somewhere between 150 and 185 Hz (D_3–G_3 on the piano keyboard), often consulting with a speech language pathologist on strategies for developing a voice that can "pass."

Vocal transitioning for MtF transpeople is challenging in many respects: it is technically difficult to adapt to all these vocal changes and maintain them consistently in daily use, and requires a significant amount of self-awareness in vocal quality, pitch, and intonation, all areas of voice that often go unnoticed. In adapting to feminized speech, many speakers tend to overcorrect, and choose the *most* feminized options in all areas of vocal use, creating a hyperfeminine voice that can be perceived as inauthentic. It has been argued, notably by Amanda Loy-Jung in her article "Psychogenic Voice Disorders and Gender: An Interdisciplinary Look at Prevention, Identification, and Treatment of the Voice in Disequilibrium,"[8] that this kind of hyperfeminine voice can, in a worst-case scenario, lead to vocal issues related to inefficient voice use, breathiness, vocal hypertension, hoarseness, or voice loss. As well, it can lead to emotional and interpersonal challenges such as feelings of being threatened, powerless, silenced, introverted, or experiencing a lack of confidence or passive-aggressiveness.

Arsenault's Voice Change

Arsenault began her vocal transition by exploring her voice in a rather unorthodox manner:

> The first way that I practised a feminine voice was on those phone lines that hetero singles can call into to chat and hook up. Being on the phone was a safe way to test out a new way of speaking. If I sounded male, guys would leave messages that said that in an electronic mail box. I think I tried to sound breathy, like Marilyn Monroe.[9]

The feedback Arsenault received came both from the men for whom she left messages, and from chat line employees:

> Guys would leave a message in my voice mail box saying "you're a guy." Employees of the phone-line would screen for people playing pranks, so I would get an automated message, "you are being disconnected from this service because you are male."[10]

By exploring her voice in a controlled environment, where embarrassment was limited, and feedback was direct and fairly non-confrontational, Arsenault was able to take risks with her sound and figure out what did and did not work for her. Her models were primarily others in the MtF community: "I listened to other transsexuals when I started transitioning. I listened to how they used their voices."[11] At first, she experimented with a choice that didn't ring true for her: "I learned how to affect a false voice, a softer voice that had a higher pitch. It did not convey emotion. It was really contrived."[12] Arsenault drew an important and apt distinction between *falsetto* voice and *head voice*, two modes of vocal use that she explored at this time. Her observations included that falsetto is a lighter, thinner sound created by a different kind of vibration of the vocal folds than a speaker's usual vocal register—Mickey Mouse is performed by a man using falsetto, for example—and head voice uses higher, lighter pitches in the normal vibratory cycle of the voice. "Sometimes I would flip up into a head voice and sometimes it would be a falsetto. Sometimes I'd have a really nasal voice, which I have since learned sounds gay not feminine. Unfortunately, it is the chest resonance that feels and sounds really male to me."[13] Arsenault's judgement of nasality is interesting, as some nasality comes in and out of her speech, though it doesn't read as gay to the author. *Chest resonance*, as she uses it here, is the vocal quality of most speakers, male and female, though it can cause her voice to drop into the average "median pitch," which for Arsenault would be in the masculine pitch range, below where she would feel comfortable speaking in her feminine persona.

Arsenault at Canada's National Voice Intensive

In May of 2000, Nina Arsenault travelled to Vancouver to participate in Canada's National Voice Intensive (NVI), a five-week-long workshop hosted by the University of British Columbia's Department of Theatre and Film. As a voice trainer and member of the NVI faculty,[14] my interaction with Arsenault was my first introduction to working with clients/students from the transgendered community.

Based upon the work of Kristin Linklater,[15] the NVI demands an intense investigation of the speaker's voice, her habits, and the psychological underpinnings of those habits. The first exploration of voice in the environment of the NVI was challenging for Arsenault:

The Linklater training was about getting sensation into your genitals. When the public becomes private in that way, anything that brings my genitals into the room is extremely challenging. In that system, you're constantly aware of your genitals, and talking about them, because it's part of the training.

I also felt like sometimes the teachers were [unintentionally] transphobic. There is self-examination built into the Linklater process that asks, "have you hit a block? Are you feeling insecurity around that issue?" [I felt] "I'm not being insecure, you're actually transphobic, and that's what I'm reacting to." [*gesturing at her centre*] I didn't know how to say to that point in my body, whatever it is, "just get over it, do the work and take the emotional risk."

I left the NVI with a lot of resentment. I hadn't had that many cosmetic procedures at that point, but I kind of had a vision of the way I look today. So any kind of language or teaching that was based in "that's not real" was painful. Just the word "real" for a transsexual has the same emotional weight I would expect the word "nigger" would have for a black person. "Why do I have to be real?" That's what I left the NVI thinking. "If you people are fucking real, I don't wanna be real."[16]

Authentic vs. Natural Voice

Perhaps the problem lies more deeply rooted than merely in one instructor's unintentional transphobia. Troy Dwyer, in his article "Freeing the Unnatural Voice: Dominant Gender Ideology in Western Voice and Speech Training," outlines the two competing ideologies that appear to dominate the conceptualization of gender: essentialism and constructionism. The former "maintains the belief that gender is stable, fixed and based on biology," while the latter "asserts that gender is an acquired matrix of learned behaviours (which may otherwise appear to be innate and 'natural')."[17] He suggests that, while Western voice trainers seem to embrace a constructionist point of view that gender identity is learned and to some degree performed, "most of our training idioms are intrinsically invested in identity *as essential*. Consider, for instance, the title of Kristin Linklater's enormously influential *Freeing the Natural Voice*."[18] Dwyer argues, quite eloquently, that "the field assumes that gender is a constellation of performed artifacts, while simultaneously supposing that there is such a thing as a fixed 'self' possessing a 'natural' voice."[19] Linklater voice, though seemingly based solely in the essentialist end of the continuum, does argue for "a balance of instinctual response and conscious control in mature behaviour,"[20] though the method also suggests that

> constructed secondary selves [which, she implies, may be necessary in order to function socially with success] are repeatedly asked to step aside so that the primary self may regain some lost ground. ... The student ... has difficulty accessing "truthful" action or "released" sound because of a physical or vocal habit; the more she performs her habit, the weaker her contact with her spontaneous core; the more she honours her "natural" impulses, the less the habit is displayed.[21]

Arsenault has invested heavily in her constructed, feminine self. She has worked hard to evolve a distinctive, decidedly feminine, "habit" voice that she does not want to lose. Though she is eager to find spontaneity, release, and presence, she is not interested in losing her feminine self in order to do it, and rejects the theory that voice, to be effective, must be instinctual.

> The Linklater approach, that I was getting from the Voice Intensive, was coming like dogma; it comes with that force. It offers the preconceived notion that all of us have some kind of natural, civilized part of us that is authentic. It's like saying ... "as children we all sound, we're sounding beings." Just because we did it as children doesn't mean that it's real. It's still a construction. To me, everything is a construction. I construct myself on a daily basis.[22]

Further, Arsenault asserted, "over time, particularly in 2007, I decided I didn't want to construct my voice anymore and I wanted to speak without thinking about it too much."[23] This speaks to the need for MtF speakers to find their own, unselfconscious voice over time. After years of "playing" her voice, Arsenault was ready to accept whatever sound might come without consciously and artificially *constructing* it.

I had been making the switch to pitch up for so fucking long, that it made me so fucking small, because it's not a power place, it's a place of construction. It didn't help me to pitch up. What that did was cut my breath off.[24]

By this time, many of the skills she had acquired from years of constructed feminine voice use had become integrated, and so she was able to speak with some ease. "I didn't really think too much about voice through my transition though. At stripping and escorting I had to affect a particularly feminine voice, but I always smoked dope beforehand. That allowed me to more easily do this."[25] By being more relaxed and less self-conscious when stoned, she was more able to be free with her voice. Many people learning a second language will say things like "oh, I speak French so much better when I'm drunk!" Of course, their language skill doesn't improve, but their inhibitions drop and so they actually are willing to make more mistakes in public, so they communicate much better. "I was more relaxed. The conundrum of the whole transsexual voice for me is that worrying if I sounded male always made me sound more male. When I relaxed, what came through somehow, without trying, was the sense that I am a woman."[26]

This self-consciousness/freedom continuum exists, to some degree, for all speakers, regardless of what roles we choose to play in life. However, for Arsenault, the challenge of addressing her voice's tendency to revert unexpectedly to biological limitations and well-ingrained habits continues to be bothersome. As she focused less on "constructing" her voice, some other aspects of her pre-transition voice (arguably, her "essential" voice) came to light:

I suppose, really, what I sacrificed is spontaneity. I was (and still am) afraid that if spontaneous sound comes from me then it might come out sounding male. I'm also afraid to yell or to scream. I worry that if I start laughing uncontrollably I will sound like a guy.[27]

Voice Training with Fides Krucker

Spontaneity is one aspect well addressed by the Roy Hart extended voice technique taught by Arsenault's current voice teacher, Fides Krucker. Krucker's teaching style is, in part, based upon the foundational work of Richard Armstrong and Roy Hart.[28] Within a voice lesson, Krucker and Arsenault are able to explore sounds that are often outside the repertoire of traditional voice or speech trainers. Together, they can explore laughing, crying, screaming, and other voice sounds that go beyond the daily usage of the voice. Arsenault explained, "I have shown her parts of my voice that I have shown no one else for over a decade, or perhaps ever. I trust her deeply. I know she has far fewer judgments about my voice than I do. I particularly enjoy screaming with her."[29] The safety of the studio is one of two places where Arsenault can be free with her voice. The other is when she is performing onstage:

> When I am onstage doing my show I laugh, cry, scream. I am expressing myself authentically. The audience knows they are coming to hear a transsexual speak. I feel safer onstage than off. I trust that no one will interrupt me. I trust that no one will say anything to hurt my feelings when I am onstage.[30]

Krucker's approach to the voice is a marriage of traditional *bel canto*,[31] and the Roy Hart technique as taught by Richard Armstrong. In a typical lesson, Krucker and Arsenault begin their investigation with breath sensation, noticing where in the body she experiences different kinds of breathing; Krucker's goal is a deeply rooted breath action in the pelvis and perineum, with a great release of tension. Krucker explains:

> This is what I call the "spa" in the breath cycle. It could lead to sleep or to a beautiful inertia and ease, and as much as it is seriously missing from most people's breath diets, on its own it would not be enough for us, either to create from or to guarantee our survival. …
> The release of the pelvic floor allows the diaphragm to work involuntarily and encourages "rest and digest" in the autonomic nervous system, which regulates the intestines, heart, and glands. It asks us to un-gird our loins and to trust that the world is a place that would like us to thrive. And it reinforces for us with each breath that things are "okay."[32]

In the lesson I observed,[33] Arsenault and Krucker worked with great specificity in an exploration of this kind of breathing in order for Arsenault to experience its potential to support her voice fully. At first, Arsenault was standing by the piano, and they discussed the idea of whether her breath might come from the third chakra, the so-called solar plexus, just below the sternum. They explored the breath together, with Krucker's hands on Arsenault's abdomen. Krucker also placed her hands on Arsenault's back ribs, and together they compared this kind of breath posture/alignment with one where Arsenault would have a more open lower back, allowing greater access into the lower back ribs. Krucker modelled a slight hyperextension of the lower back (lordosis), sometimes known as "swayback," and a preferred, more open position of the lower spine, which allowed for greater release in the back and lower belly. This permitted Arsenault to find a way to be in her "back-body," and Krucker then demonstrated a way of doing it volitionally and non-volitionally. As Arsenault had explored the image of the third chakra, she had only breathed into the front part of her body and not into the front and back simultaneously. Arsenault then tried out will-based and non-will-based breathing for herself; she observed that the will-based breath was higher up and tighter, while the non-will-based breath allowed for softening through the girdle, or lower-abdomen, to permit the diaphragm to be breathed into. This encouraged her taking time to feel alive through the space of the lower back ribs. Through these exercises and by exploring an effective, freer, more fully embodied breath, Arsenault was able to be more aware of the process of breathing, and its integration with sounding.[34]

They began to explore vocalization on what Krucker called a "scratchy" vocal quality with "no action, no socialization." She encouraged Arsenault to let go of the pressure in her chest, and warned that a lot of gunk (phlegm) might come up and be released. She asked Arsenault what she liked and did not like about that process: "I felt like I had sensation up inside the rectum (like a dick) on the third wave of the breath." Krucker encouraged this response, suggesting that it is not just the anal sphincter that is releasing but also the whole lower rectum and colon. She suggested that Arsenault think of being in a pre-toilet-training phase, as if in a relationship to pleasure and the release of habitual tensions. "You have the advantage of knowing about anal sex and release," confided Krucker. This experiential knowledge would be an advantage because the connection of sensation in the body, especially inside the pelvis and perineum, helps to give the speaker a greater self-awareness, which in turn reinforces the sense of authenticity of the voice and in the speaker.

The next phase in the lesson worked with the image of "oozing into a breathy/scratchy sigh, both luxurious and time-consuming, that is uncultured," what Krucker calls the *dark breath*,[35] in order to get away from the constructed or performed voice. In this mode of voicing, Arsenault released a sound that was slightly breathy, and she followed freely the quite low notes that Krucker offered up on the piano. "Stay with the swoon," insisted Krucker, with lots of movement in the sternum, so that Arsenault was breathing both low in the belly and freely with her upper ribcage. This dark breath is a deeply rooted breathing experience, directly connected to the personal experience of finding one's own authentic voice.

In contrast, Krucker talks of light voice in the upper registers, which demands that the student "look for space and light inside the tissues of her body. I ask her to open the inside of her mouth—like the yawn both wide and tall—and to keep it huge all the time."[36] Krucker believes "that the top of the voice is never truly ours to control but if it is both anchored behind the sternum and cushioned in the pelvic bowl it won't get away from us and risk becoming hysterical. The shape and the freedom of its overtones feel chaotic—like a bell ringing, a peal of laughter, the squeal of a young child, a whimper, even whining."[37] The chaotic also reinforces the authentic, as it is at the heart of feeling spontaneous. Throughout the lesson, the two women continued exploring chest resonance with breathiness. Together they moved into the midzone of the voice, with Arsenault preferring the light vocal quality, avoiding the darkness of lower pitches and deeper resonances. Krucker pointed out that there will be a way for those two qualities to cohabitate. She challenged Arsenault to work in the midrange, to try to feel lightweight and not super intelligent, to give into the sound of "airhead." As Arsenault sounded, going higher and higher, Krucker's coaching was to seek the "up," and to find space inside the mouth, through lifting the soft palate. This is at the core of the light sound that Krucker seeks.

As voicing fell off and the sounds became breathier, Krucker guided Arsenault to explore "swooning at the bottom and at the top," where Arsenault made a breathy onset and release for each sounding. Discussing this tone, Arsenault said "I know when light and dark match, because it has that woody resonance; as I go up in pitch there is a tendency to pop up into pitch. If I pop into pitch, then I can get the light/dark back; I like that quality because it is feminine, transgender." Krucker corrected Arsenault, "you're not popping up in pitch, you're popping up in resonance." She also clarified that the sound is "a kind of feminine, but also one that will tire you out and not age well because it is not rooted in release."

After working from the chest into a mix of head and chest, and finally into a full falsetto, they worked their way back down again. As they worked lower into the chest resonance, a question about the "bottom end" arose. Suggesting that they leave transgendering—and worries about pitch—aside for a moment, Krucker prompted Arsenault to work the sound with ease, to put her hand on her chest to "swoon" into the sound, and to find ever more room in the mouth, in order to marry the spacious light sound with the deeply rooted dark breath. "Part of you is working, part of you is yielding," said Krucker, and she prodded Arsenault to allow the bottom end of the sound be a "tad more diffuse," and breathier. A few notes lower and Arsenault broke off, saying, "that sounds like the man-voice!" Arsenault conceded that the bottom end of her sound could be some "sexy-ass woman," but rejected the sound she had just made. However, Krucker pointed out that the pitch that Arsenault reached was close to the average pitch of her speaking voice, which, though high for the perception of a male, is lower than what is generally accepted as the range of the feminine, and even a note or two lower than what is perceived to be the ambiguous range I delineated above that many transgendered persons seek.

As the lesson continued, Krucker continued to urge Arsenault to find the "sparkle" in the higher range by finding plenty of space, and then to map the lower, dark sound to that feeling space. Arsenault encouraged Krucker to give her "lots of feedback; I may be getting so much information that I stop knowing where I am." As they progressed, Krucker reinforced her student with plenty of positive language, saying, "Nina, this is fantastic, we're finding a mix of dark and light coming together!" The power of the dark was characterized metaphorically as "the businessman," while the brightness of the light was "the diva or queen." The "aw" sound they explored was placed "in the bubble"[38] of the upper oral space, "almost having bigger hair, partnering with the business man." The power also gave a sense of "now I'm here," which Arsenault identified as the state she seeks when performing onstage, writing, having sex, or being around theatre people. "My only choices aren't just to be fucked or to dominate. I can find self-possession, composure, and space. I've yielded into it, and then put a boundary around it." Krucker agreed, "[on stage] we have enormous potential to be safe, with the lights and the contract with the audience, and massive permission to be in those two areas."

Not fearing the chaotic sound of the notes that live between the chest and head registers, Krucker supported and encouraged Arsenault to work through the "wobbly," uncontrolled sound of the so-called break[39] and on to the falsetto sound. Together they worked to find the edge between the register and the break sound, which allowed them to pause for a moment to discuss risk-taking and finding that edge. The lesson ended with a discussion of self-possession, and the voice; Arsenault suggested that there hadn't been a lot of self-possession in the exercise, while Krucker reminded her that there hasn't been a lot of self-possession modelled in female voice role models: one sees a lot of pushing down, especially in female radio voice. Ultimately, what Arsenault has explored is challenging: to have lift and release at the same time demands great self-possession. "I don't experience, at this point in the training, creating any more of a freed up, authentic, real person, but just one more system of discipline now in my body with which I can construct: to not actually make myself more real, but to make myself more compelling."[40]

Compelling Honesty

Though she argues for being "compelling" over being "real," Arsenault does understand what being "honest" means for her, and how she experiences honesty within the context of autobiographical performance.

> The first time I did *The Silicone Diaries* at Buddies in Bad Times Theatre, being honest meant speaking the real life autobiographical text fast and loud. It meant not worrying about anything, and dropping down as much as possible, and keeping the whole thing rolling. Everything then ends on tension, everything ends on the "left," because you're being real, you're dropping everything in as deeply as possible, every concept, every phrase, every personal thing.
>
> Take, for instance, the story of what it was like to get figured out by Tommy Lee, or having the silicone injections: I'd just get as real as possible. All the layers of meaning start coming in, and that's what being "real" meant, just revealing as much as possible ... this is why I think that everything ends on the tension: every time I examined any situation, like the silicone injections, I would be examining it, and exploring that story.[41]

Her honesty in recounting and reliving moments of her life-story were compelling through this contrast of positive and negative experience, emotional and felt sense. Her experience of this compelling honesty led her to conclude that

> I felt that the voice ends on tension; it's like [the voice is] always getting cut off, or revealing something embarrassing, or something that threatened to overwhelm me in the moment. However, I felt like the second run of the show [a year later] had a container around it.[42]

Sometimes it is helpful for a performer to merely dip her toe into the emotional "lake," especially around something powerful, like the response to self-hatred rather than falling in and not being able to get out. The performer is making a choice to go to a place that is compelling, and yet she's able to stay in her intention or action, and not be overwhelmed by the emotional state. If she gets flooded spontaneously by the emotional state, then she cannot continue with her intention and action, and it may be perceived by an audience as being therapeutic, that that huge emotional release doesn't serve the story. In discussing what motivated her to hold back from the full release of emotion, Arsenault declared that "I felt that it wasn't beautiful. It did not feel beautiful. I should be performing beauty, 100%."[43]

Arsenault's concerns about authenticity, spontaneity, construction, and presence are all open for continuing examination in her practice of voice training and in her performance experiences. By constructing both strategies of performance, whereby she informs her artwork with compelling honesty constrained by the container of the production, and of persona, where she reveals herself in a truthfully blunt, unapologetic manner, wrapped in the packaging of beauty and wit, Arsenault has built structures to develop her self-awareness and safely shape the spontaneous presentation of her passionate self.

Eric Armstrong is a dialect designer for film and theatre, and an associate professor in York University's Department of Theatre, where he teaches voice, speech, dialects, and Shakespeare text to students in the Bachelor and Master of Fine Arts Acting programs. His recent professional projects in feature film and television include working with Michelle Williams, Luke Kirby, and Sarah Silverman on Sarah Polley's new film *Take This Waltz*; coaching Isabelle Fuhrman in *The Orphan*; and dialect consulting on *The Border, Covert Affairs, Unnatural History*, and *Resident Evil: Afterlife*. His recent theatre dialect designs include *The cosmonaut's last message to the woman he once loved in the former Soviet Union* for Canadian Stage, *Blasted* for Buddies in Bad Times Theatre, *Eternal Hydra* for Factory Theatre/Crow's Theatre, and *Master Harold and the Boys* for the Thousand Islands Playhouse. His publishing credits include articles and reviews for the journal of record for voice trainers, *The Voice and Speech Review*, on such diverse topics as embodying meter in Shakespeare text, the phonetics of the sound /r/, vocal coaching in film, and the role of the vocal coach at the Royal Shakespeare Company. Armstrong is co-host of the podcast *Glossonomia: conversations on the sounds of speech*, which is available on iTunes.

Bibliography

Adler, Richard. "Gender Voice Issues: Voice and Communication Therapy for Transsexual/Transgender Clients." In *Voice and Gender and Other Contemporary Issues in Professional Voice and Speech Training*, edited by Mandy Rees, 293–299. San Diego: University Readers, 2007.

Dwyer, Troy. "Freeing the Unnatural Voice: Dominant Gender Ideology in Western Voice and Speech Training." In *The Moving Voice, the Integration of Voice and Movement Studies presented by the Voice and Speech Review*, edited by Rena Cook, 331–7. San Diego: University Readers, 2009.

Krucker, Fides. "Chiaroscuro: The Bodhisattva in the Voice." *POIESIS: A Journal of the Arts & Communication* XIII (2011): 40–51.

Linklater, Kristin. *Freeing the Natural Voice: Imagery and Art in the Practice of Voice and Language*. Hollywood: Drama Publishers, 2006.

Loy-Jung, Amanda. "Psychogenic Voice Disorders and Gender: An Interdisciplinary Look at Prevention, Identification, and Treatment of the Voice in Disequilibrium." In *Voice and Gender and Other Contemporary Issues in Professional Voice and Speech Training*, edited by Mandy Rees, 320–332. San Diego: University Readers, 2007.

Notes

1. Typically supervised by Speech Language Pathologists, voice work for those undergoing transition focuses on aspects of the voice that are considered significant markers of gender, such as pitch, rate, and inflection.
2. Glottal fry is a vocal register typified by a periodic, pulsing tone, which frequently happens at the very bottom of a speaker's range with very little breath support; it often occurs at the end of sentences as a speaker is running out of breath.
3. To the older population, this may tend to make Arsenault sound like she is extremely tentative—as if she is asking a question all the time—while younger speakers are more likely to accept Arsenault's speech as commonplace, with uptalk-speakers perceived as only somewhat tentative, as well as being more sensitive to the thoughts and feelings of others.
4. Tag questions turn a statement into a question by adding a questioning fragment or "tag" at the end of the utterance.
5. Richard Adler, "Gender Voice Issues: Voice and Communication Therapy for Transsexual/ Transgender Clients," in *Voice and Gender, and Other Contemporary Issues in Professional Voice and Speech Training*, ed. Mandy Rees (San Diego: University Readers, 2007), 294.
6. Nina Arsenault, e-mail message to author, March 8, 2011.
7. Arsenault has had this surgery, but reports no effect on her voice as a result of the procedure.
8. Amanda Loy-Jung, "Psychogenic Voice Disorders and Gender: An Interdisciplinary Look at Prevention, Identification, and Treatment of the Voice in Disequilibrium," in Rees, *Voice and Gender*, 329.
9. Nina Arsenault, e-mail message to author, March 31, 2011.
10. Ibid., April 1, 2011.
11. Ibid., March 31, 2011.
12. Ibid.
13. Ibid., April 1, 2011.
14. I currently teach voice in the Acting Conservatory at York University in Toronto.
15. The NVI is run by David Smukler, Canada's foremost speaking voice teacher, who studied with Linklater. Linklater, in turn, studied with Iris Warren, who is arguably the fountainhead of this style of voice teaching.
16. Nina Arsenault, interview with author, March 1, 2011.
17. Troy Dwyer, "Freeing the Unnatural Voice: Dominant Gender Ideology in Western Voice and Speech Training," in *The Moving Voice, the Integration of Voice and Movement Studies*, ed. Rena Cook (San Diego: University Readers, 2009), 331.
18. Ibid., 333.
19. Ibid.
20. Ibid., Original quotation from: Kristin Linklater, *Freeing the Natural Voice: Imagery and Art in the Practice of Voice and Language* (Hollywood: Drama Publishers, 2006), 19.
21. Dwyer, "Freeing the Unnatural Voice," 334.
22. Arsenault, interview with author, March 1, 2001.
23. Arsenault, e-mail to author, March 31, 2011.
24. Arsenault, interview with author, March 1, 2011.

25. Ibid., March 31, 2011.
26. Ibid., April 1, 2011.
27. Ibid., March 31, 2011.
28. Richard Armstrong is a member of the Roy Hart Theatre of Malerargues, France. Roy Hart's theatrical investigations into extended voice work were based upon the theories of Alfred Wolfsohn.
29. Arsenault, e-mail message to author, April 1, 2011.
30. Ibid.
31. *Bel canto* (Italian for "beautiful singing") is the traditional mode of classical Western voice training used in operatic and sacred music.
32. Fides Krucker, "Chiaroscuro: The Bodhisattva in the Voice," *POIESIS: A Journal of the Arts & Communication* XIII (2011): 42.
33. Quotations in this section are from the March 2, 2011 voice lesson with Nina Arsenault and Fides Krucker, and are used with permission.
34. Breathing technique often doesn't have such quantifiable end results as other vocal exercises. Sometime we study breathing specifically in order to breathe more effectively.
35. *Dark breath* is a term from Roy Hart voice technique, where the breath is rooted in the lower abdomen with little to no tension, with great freedom in the upper respiratory tract.
36. Ibid., 45.
37. Ibid., 45.
38. By "bubble," Krucker means the sensation of a pocket of space in the oral tract, at the back of the mouth where lifting the soft palate can make a large, domed cavity which encourages bright, forward resonance.
39. As the voice modulates from the chest register into falsetto, the voice "changes gears" audibly with a dramatic shift known as the break. Frequently, there is a range of a few notes between chest and falsetto registers, so that the student can sound "within the break," a range of chaotic sound that is breath, unpredictable and evocative of highly emotive states.
40. Arsenault, interview with author, March 1, 2011.
41. Ibid.
42. Ibid.
43. Ibid.

Chapter 12

Live in Your Blood: A Fragmentary Response to Nina Arsenault's Holy Theatre and Spiritual Gift

Shimon Levy

Nina Arsenault embodies and enacts an intensely personalized, meticulously documented voyage through her body and her soul toward her spirit. Moreover, Arsenault's Holy Theatre of Self—which includes body, soul *and* spirit—is a profound, original, and genuine manifestation of a spiritual quest. "Your spiritual journey wants to take you through all this,"[1] she writes in her superbly candid, funny, and convincing *via dolorosa* play, *The Silicone Diaries*.

Between the obviously intentional sweet kitsch and the sad, though equally intentional, pathos of Arsenault's always theatrical presentation of her body and her life, there are not only many refreshing sparks of humour, but indeed a whole apparatus of spiritual fireworks flying back and forth between the holy and the ridiculous. In fact, there are real gifts offered to whoever is ready to accept Arsenault's half-masked, intensely made-up invitation to accept an intimate perspective on her spiritual journey.

Writing from within a land of contested territories and a landscape containing a multitude of fragmented identities, I offer a set of fragmentary responses to Arsenault, as artist and artwork. I present these from a variety of perspectives, and intend them to function as entry points to further discussion. I do this with full awareness that these entry points lead to challenging pathways on a map of uncharted terrain. I also do so while invoking the metaphor of the goddess, and Arsenault as far more than the sum of her own component parts.

An (im)possible Analogy between the Prophet Ezekiel and Nina Arsenault

Who is Ezekiel? The prophet Ezekiel is one of the first and best-known holy actors—in the theatrical sense—in Judeo-Christian tradition. In the Book of Ezekiel, rhetorically assuming God's name, he describes how he (as God) found and raised a baby girl, fed her, clad her, adorned her with the finest and best, and how she, grown into a young beautiful woman, betrayed him and whored with other gods and nations. Like other biblical prophets, Ezekiel, also a priest in the temple, is commanded by God to deliver His Word to the people of Israel in the exile of Babylon, which he does in a variety of speeches, sermons, proverbs, fables, and visions. Ezekiel, in his highly provocative and sexually explicit street theatre performances (for there was a distinct lack of other public, educational entertainment media in those days, about 2600 years ago), does not spare his audience explicit pornographic details while bitterly scolding the unfaithful Israelites: "you spread-out your legs to all passersby … you whored with the lustful sons of 'big-fleshed,' "[2] "thou hast played the whore also with the Assyrians, because thou wast unsatiable; yea, thou hast played the harlot with them, and yet couldest not be satisfied."[3] In order to humiliate the young woman even further, God adds "they give gifts to all whores: but thou givest thy gifts to all thy lovers,"[4] which relates to the assumption that this particular whore, to top her shameless unfaithfulness to the Hebrew God, was not paid for her services. In the full-length passages where the aforementioned quotes come from, the verb "to whore" is used eleven times in its different Hebrew conjugations, not to mention a few other highly sexually charged terms.

Ezekiel's street performances are exemplified in Chapter 16 of the Book of Ezekiel in a type of play that I call *The Diary of Unfaithfulness*, consisting of five main parts.[5] In this particular biblical play,[6] the most suggestive and rhetorically efficient image is blood. The prophet Ezekiel uses blood in an intentionally ambiguous, oft-repeated reference to both life and death, "when I passed by thee, and saw thee polluted in thine own blood, I said unto thee [when thou wast] in thy blood, Live; yea, I said unto thee [when thou wast] in thy blood, Live."[7] In these writings—to distill the use of the image—blood connotes life and death, both of which in Arsenault's subversive interpretation in *The Silicone Diaries* are explored, and also clearly shown in some of her photographs (see Figures 16 and 30).

Arsenault knowingly employs her body, her blood, and her intimate parts to invite people to observe her, understand her, love her, and engage with her in, but also through, her body. She declares in *The Silicone Diaries*, "[I] program myself to be exactly the fantasy they want me to be... I feel like a Goddess."[8]

Arsenault, I contend, does not actually represent the playwright/creator/Creator through Ezekiel's voice; rather, in my interpretation, she speaks, writes, shows, and vicariously represents the silent voice of the girl-prostitute character (representing the being who is unfaithful to the Hebrew God of Jerusalem) that Ezekiel dramatizes in *The Diary of Unfaithfulness*. In Ezekiel's pornographic theatrical visions, the scalded girl-prostitute is a profoundly oppressed, used, abused, and objectified, but also selfless, woman. She is, in fact, mute throughout her entire scene in the tradition of misogynist scriptures. Moreover, the woman's very image in the Book of Ezekiel in general is exploited as a typically antifeminist literary tool, perhaps a politically correct image in the prophet's eyes.

Arsenault, on the other hand, speaks back to her God, that of contemporary media, refusing—as though in biblical terms—to be a metaphor. "I'm not an object. I'm not an image,"[9] she says. Another convincing testimony for this argument is Arsenault's choice of the dedication at the beginning of the published script of *The Silicone Diaries*, a quotation from the German mystic Meister Eckhart (c.1260–1327): "When the soul wishes to experience something she throws an image of the experience out before her and enters into her own image."[10] Arsenault perceives god, spirit, and soul as manifestations of her worldly self, as ironic sets of mutable images attached to feeling and sensation.

Sacrifice, Death, and Resurrection: Nina as Goddess

The Silicone Diaries is replete with religious imagery, some instances presented more seriously than others. Since known Judeo-Christian gods are mostly either wholly males or females, and are in dire need of having worshippers in order to be worshipped, Arsenault too—a self-anointed goddess—needs to be worshipped for her painful sacrifice and for her gifts of bravery, beauty, and chosen identity.

The scene "Sex/object (1979)" describes the ripping apart of pornographic pictures of women by a group of young boys in a ritual not dissimilar to that of the Canaanite god Tamuz. Like the pictures, the biblical Tamuz is torn to pieces, only to be reborn in the spring, a narrative also repeated in Dionysian and Christian mythologies. These gods all suffer immensely, but in the end, they will resurrect. Arsenault describes the actions of the boys in "Sex/object (1979)" as follows:

The way they pose. Where do they come from? They are Goddesses. ... The leader of the boys hauls on his cigarette and slowly presses the lit smoke into her eyes. Two holes burn through her paper face. She still stares back at us. The boys laugh. It's hilarious to them. He stubs the cigarette out between her spread legs. The chemical smell of burnt magazine paper rises from her crotch into our nostrils. One boy grabs the magazine and slices, a Swiss Army knife making Xs across breasts. Slashing faces. They are turning the pages haphazardly. Ripping pictures. Breasts. Rip. Legs. Tear. Face. Burn. Chasing each other around the inside of the fort trying to steal from each other the ripped magazine pictures.[11]

Arsenault ends this highly dramatic, only partly ironic scene by saying, "that's what I will be when I grow up,"[12] identifying with the implications and retrospectively prophesying her future: she knows that her mission is to be a goddess of beauty who must face the pain of sacrificial transformation. As she declares in the final speech of *The Silicone Diaries*, her mission is "to accept that my pleasure and my sublime privilege is to suffer. And to live. With. Beauty."[13]

In "Shemale porn saved my life (1999)," speaking about her work as an Internet sex worker, she writes "I'm amazed at how much intimacy is conveyed over those fuzzy digital cameras, how much sexual intimacy I can connect with simultaneously. I feel like a goddess."[14] Rather than officiating in a Phoenician or Greek temple, Nina enacts her quest for divine identity in the virtual temple of the Internet, and now in a live show, too. She gives to all who need her, simultaneously, her body and her soul.

Can watching Nina's body alone be regarded as "spiritual"? I maintain that her explanations of how and why she does what she does are justifications that elevate her tortured, beautiful body to a higher level, and allow the viewer to transcend as well. Further in the same scene Nina's giving is focused on two individuals, warmly personalized, not at all "ritual," and profoundly human and compassionate: RadicalGuy and Bigone25. To the former she gives company and fantasy; to the latter, she gives love and life. She ends this scene relating, "seven days later in San Fran, I lay down on an operating table. The nurse tells me to breathe deeply into the gas mask. From an IV drip, I can feel the anaesthetic moving through my veins. Into the separate chambers of my heart. It's washing over me. I'm fading away. I will become myself."[15] I propose that it was the impact of Nina's gifts to others that moved through her heart, not simply the anaesthetic.

In the scene titled "I am my own self-portrait (2004)" Nina is

Looking in the mirror like every day from behind my see-through plastic vanity table ... over my right shoulder, is naked Aphrodite, the Greek goddess of love and beauty. She is a four-foot-by-three-foot painting behind me. A Renaissance masterwork. A recreation of a Renaissance masterwork of fantastical natural supernatural beauty. I remember reading that the ancient priests of Aphrodite ritually castrated themselves in honour of their goddess and worked as temple whores. I think about that ... I'm a queen. Maybe a goddess. Maybe a demon. I'm the fierce fucking tranny in that nightclub. In my mind's eye. Boyfriends. Straight guys. Tattoos. Biceps. Fucking scary guys. Nina, your spiritual journey wants to take you through all of this.[16]

Because she is still essentially a human being living in the phenomenal world, Nina is not sure, given her lifestyle, whether she identifies as a goddess or a demon. Maybe there is a lesson here in (relative) theological self-criticism: Arsenault, unlike the utter seriousness with which Greek or Hebrew gods and goddesses take themselves, embraces irony.

The final section of *The Silicone Diaries* is the most spiritually explicit in the play. In "Venus/machine (2007–2009)" Arsenault states, "I have made a deep commitment to aesthetics, to recreate my image every day."[17] Aesthetics is the content of her deity. But soon after comes yet another doubt: "All the tension makes me feel like I am posing all the time."[18] A contemporary, self-conscious, often self-doubting deity like Nina inserts anthropocentric— rather than theocentric—lines in *The Silicone Diaries*. In that, at least, she is quite different, and much more human than Ezekiel's example of an Old Testament holy voice, who never for a moment doubts Jehova's absolute deity and, consequently, His authority.

Nina, on her spiritual quest, is evolving, revolving inside, completing the circle that began with external beauty (which most gods often need in order to attract people to believe in them and then worship them), and becoming a bit more humble. Perhaps not strangely, Nina envisions herself on her exercise bicycle as a giant serpent. It was, after all, the biblical serpent who spoke the truth about the after-effects of eating from the fruit of the forbidden tree: "Ye shall not surely die."[19] Thus, as a wise trickster, a rebel, and an early theatre villain, Nina in the guise of the serpent has helped people to open their eyes. Nina now wants "to find a way to accept myself underneath all my glamour, this highly editorial, avantgarde beauty that I have constructed."[20] By comparing herself to the biblical and mythical versions of the serpent, Arsenault becomes an anthropocentric, human-oriented devil rather than a detached goddess, interested only in herself. She becomes an eye-opener, a revealer, and, ultimately, a healer.

Some Final Thoughts

Halfway between kitsch and pathos, readers and spectators are invited to believe Arsenault, to see behind the masks of gender, pierce the layers of pornography, and encounter and engage with a new goddess, who resurrected and recreated herself out of surgeries and with applied cosmetics.

Arsenault uses, sometimes ironically abuses, mythical, holy, biblical, Greek, and other religious references in *The Silicone Diaries*. Rather than presenting an absolute, denominational, authoritative tone, typical to the Old and New Testaments (as referenced above in the Book of Ezekiel), Arsenault employs a tentative, humorous, self-conscious approach, much more in line with our sensitivities to contemporary notions of the holy. I do not believe that the paradoxes implied in Arsenault's different manifestations, as identified, embodied, and enacted in *The Silicone Diaries*, which range from the biblical to the spiritual to somewhere in between, are solved. Or that they should be.

As a goddess of aesthetics, but as a consciousness-awakening serpent too, Arsenault does not need to solve or resolve these paradoxes in a discursive, logical way. She allows many of the profane–holy tensions to continue and, in fact, often seems to encourage them to co-exist. This is part of the spiritual quest of this unconventional goddess: to inhabit and project the irreverent synthesis of sacred and profane, simultaneously and in such a unique way as to create synergy out of seemingly irresolvable opposites.

By transforming her body into a highly humanistic, individualized, and perhaps even sacred whole yet still searching person, Arsenault invites her followers to see her soul through the container of her courageous and beautiful body. Like all great artists, or at least those who have a message to impart through their art, Nina Arsenault's Word *is* her body. And that body is not about art or beauty or truth, but is, in and of itself, the embodiment of those very qualities.

Shimon Levy is full professor at Tel Aviv University, where he has held the position of chair of the Theatre Department. His recent books include *The Sensitive Chaos*, focusing on the plays of Samuel Beckett (2002); *Israeli Drama* (2007) and *The Israeli Theatre Canon* (2002) exploring Hebrew drama; and *The Bible as Theatre* (2000). He is the editor of *Theatre and Holy Script* (1999), and *Do Not Chase Me Away, New Studies on the Dybbuk* (2009) and has also published numerous articles in Hebrew, English, and German. Levy has served as the dramaturg for the Habimah Theatre and the Jerusalem Khan Theatre, and has translated over 140 plays into Hebrew. He was the artistic director of the Acco Festival of Alternative Israeli Theatre and has served on various Israeli arts councils and ministry of culture committees working for the promotion of Israeli theatre. Levy has also written and directed plays for theatre and radio in Israel, Canada, and Europe.

Bibliography

Arsenault, Nina. "The Silicone Diaries," unpublished script, 2009.

———. *The Silicone Diaries*. In *TRANS(per)FORMING Nina Arsenault*, edited by Judith Rudakoff, 191–227. Bristol: Intellect Press, 2012.

Levy, Shimon. *The Bible as Theatre*. Brighton and Portland: Sussex Academic Press, 2000.

Notes

1. Nina Arsenault, *The Silicone Diaries*, in *TRANS(per)FORMING Nina Arsenault*, ed. Judith Rudakoff (Bristol: Intellect Press, 2012), 217.
2. Shimon Levy, *The Bible as Theatre* (Brighton and Portland: Sussex Academic Press, 2000), 173–202. In biblical Hebrew, "big fleshed" connotes "big phallused."
3. Eze. 16:28 (Authorized King James Version).
4. Ibid., 16:33 (AV).
5. First part: Eze. 16:1–2 (AV)—A declarative opening, The Abominations of Jerusalem. Eze. 16:3–7—A dirty baby, wallowing in blood. Eze.16:8–14—A beautifying, young girl, ready for love. Second part: Eze. 16:15–35—Crime: The whoring woman. Eze 16:15–19—Giving away God's gifts. Eze. 16:20–23—Killing the children, etc. Eze. 16:24–29—Whoring with Egyptians, Philistines, Assyrians, Babylonians. Eze. 16:30–35—The unsuccessful whore. Third part: Eze. 16:36–43—Punishment commensurate with the crime. Fourth part: Eze. 16:44–58—Crimes and punishments: Jerusalem, Sodom and Samaria. Fifth part: Eze. 16:59–63—Ashamed reconciliation.
6. For a full discussion, see Levy, *The Bible as Theatre*, 173–202.
7. Eze. 16:6 (AV).
8. Nina Arsenault, "The Silicone Diaries," unpublished script, 2009, 7–8. In certain cases such as this I use an earlier unpublished version of the text not appearing in this volume, as the examples are slightly more relevant. In particular, some quotations in the earlier text offer more emphasis on spirituality.
9. Arsenault, *The Silicone Diaries*, 2012, 226.
10. Ibid., 204. Quotation and further information found in: Eckhart, Meister, *The Complete Mystical Works of Meister Eckhart*, trans. Maurice O'C Walshe (New York: The Crossroad Publishing Company, 2010).
11. Arsenault, "The Silicone Diaries," 2009, 6.
12. Ibid.
13. Arsenault, *Silicone Diaries*, 2012, 227.
14. Arsenault, "The Silicone Diaries," 2009, 8.
15. Ibid., 9.
16. Ibid., 14.
17. Ibid., 24.
18. Ibid.
19. Gen. 3:4 (King James Version).
20. Arsenault, "The Silicone Diaries," 2009, 25.

Chapter 13

St. Nina and the Abstract Machine: Aesthetics, Ontology, Immanence

David Fancy

Aesthetics suffers from a wrenching duality. On the one hand, it designates the theory of sensibility as the form of possible experience; on the other hand, it designates the theory of art as real experience. For these two meanings to be tied together, the conditions of experience in general must become conditions of real experience.
Gilles Deleuze[1]

In what follows I'll be suggesting, *pace* Gilles Deleuze and his collaborator Felix Guattari, that an understanding of aesthetics that bridges the "wrenching duality,"[2] which Deleuze speaks of above, can be a particularly useful way of approaching Nina Arsenault's work. Indeed, it can be asserted that in Arsenault's performances and other practices, "the conditions of real experience and the structures of the work of art are united."[3] From what I will describe to be an immanentist philosophical vantage, creative acts become ontological acts—*onto-aesthetics* to use Stephen Zepke's designation[4]—in that artists engage in a process of becoming that is at the same time the process of the becoming of the world. I will explore how, in Arsenault's case, the deterritorializing move to reconfigure her body and identity away from certain biological and social givens can be seen as both an embrace of the *construction of construction* that characterizes the generativity of immanentist ontology, as well as a pursuit of decidedly nonmimetic submersion of herself into the full bloom of the transformative, surgical, and performative processes at hand. The familiar notion of the "artist as work of art" will be shown to reveal a particular intensity through these lenses, one in which Arsenault's own creative and transformational practices become onto-genetic, or, as Deleuze and Guattari suggest about ontology in general, embody a new type of reality to come.

Art/Life/Work

My work explores the reality and illusions of beauty, yet to continue with my schedule is very physically and emotionally rigorous. It demands of me a lifestyle that feels monk-like. I work out. I have writing deadlines. I do my make-up. I go to skin treatments. I am constantly training as an actor. I diet very carefully. I rehearse. I coordinate my publicity. I do my stage plays. I am planning a long form video. I am devoted to a serious artistic exploration of inner and outer beauty. There is a lot of glamour in my work, but on the other hand I live like a devoted nun to achieve it. My art is my spiritual work.[5]

It is Immanuel Kant and other subsequent thinkers in the tradition of aesthetics who have historically differentiated between what Kant describes on the one hand as the Transcendental Aesthetic, and the Critique of Aesthetic Judgment on the other.[6] While the Transcendental Aesthetic deals with issues of sensation, the possible forms of sensibility, and the ontological grounding of the world, the Critique of Aesthetic Judgment revolves around notions of the beautiful and the sublime. From this perspective, Arsenault's regular everyday sensorial experience and ongoing surgical interventions are seen to be distinct from artistic practices such as her performance creation, in that from this traditional approach to aesthetics it is only the performances that are understood to be generated specifically for "artistic" effect. And yet, aren't the realities of much of Arsenault's sensorial experience (blogged about and integrated into performances), as well her many surgeries that invoke questions about the ontological grounding of identity in the body (documented in photographs and also discussed in performances), part of her overall artistic production? And doesn't the manifestly "artistic" work of performance, video, and so forth also feed back into issues of sensation, possible forms of sensibility and of the ontological grounding of the world, those modes that Kant suggested were solely the province of the Transcendental Aesthetic? If indeed these bifurcated conceptualizations of the aesthetic are irrevocably linked for Arsenault, we need to draw on a different philosophical lineage as a means of understanding both ontology and the aesthetic in their mutually generative functioning if we are to come to terms with the broader aesthetic potentials in her work.

The use of the designation "transcendental" in the first classification above implies that there are distinct and discrete categories by which we know the sensible world that are somehow objective of, preceding and outside of our experience of, our engagement with them. Deleuze's thought, fueled in part by the conviction that the history of philosophy has for a long time been anchored in a "transcendental illusion,"[7] is, in contradistinction, marked by a strong constructivist tendency that privileges the activity of experience *qua* experience in the moments of its unfolding. From this perspective, Kantian Transcendental Idealism—part of the orthodox philosophical heritage that Deleuze and Guattari assert "has for a long time been an official, referential genre"[8]—is superseded by the notion of an objective world as a construct from subjective experience. This subjectivity, as I will discuss further below, is not limited to human subjectivity, however, saving it from solipsism or relativism. It is instead related to the transcendental *field*, characterized by its potentiality rather than fixity, "a pure a-subjective current of consciousness, an impersonal pre-reflexive consciousness, a quantitative duration of consciousness without self."[9] Deleuze calls such a notion, with only the slightest of ironic inflections, "transcendental empiricism":[10] the search for actual rather than possible conditions of all possible experience, conditions that are not pre-emptively and logically necessary as in Kant, but that are contingent upon experience as it is lived, constructed *in* the moment in which it is lived, regardless who or what is doing the "living."

This form of ongoing processual and creative production of the world is underpinned by Deleuze's understanding that the notion of "difference" has, in the orthodox philosophical tradition at least, historically been subordinated in favour of "identity," with the very concept of identity being given the responsibility of corralling difference into recognizable and understandable forms.[11] The general result of this pervasive tendency is that any aspect of difference that cannot be recuperated back into the concept of identity essentially remains unthought, occluded, "ceasing to be thought, difference dissipates into non-being."[12] The immediate implications of this kind of thinking are significant for those phenomena that remain hitherto uncategorizable or unrepresentable, and thus excluded and unfulfilled, phenomena such as transsexuals: "I have an inner child, a little girl who grew up in a little boy's body, in a trailer park, who wanted to be Barbie," says Arsenault of her early years. She continues, "this inner child needs to be acknowledged as the epitome of perfect plastic beauty, let's not make her serve cupcakes."[13]

Deleuze pursues a renewal of thought beyond the simple common sense understanding of thought's role as that which represents what is already felt to exist in a transcendental and nonconceptual form. This regeneration opens up the terrain of the new, the as-yet-unthought. The removal of negative valuation (i.e., that difference must be subordinated to identity) is accompanied by Deleuze's proposal of a renewed understanding of difference based on Nietzsche's notion of the "eternal return." The process of the eternal return evades transcendentality in that it does not depend on categories of organization outside the real for its determination, but instead is an immanent process in which differences are constantly returning from within to transform identities hitherto understood to be fixed.[14] It is in this way that identifiable phenomena, human or otherwise, are understood to be the result of a constructive process of "becoming," a perpetual process of change. Those phenomena which take responsibility for, harness, intervene in, or accelerate these kinds of change are themselves more resonant with the processes of perennial differentiation that fuel the immanent system: phenomena like Nina Arsenault.

Rhizome/Assemblage/Territory

In the centre of our trailer court, in a rectangular grass field, inside a square wooden sandbox, inside the scooped steel funnel of a spiral slide, my back is arched. Toes pointed. Throwing one arm over the lip of the slide dramatically. A flexed wrist. Shooting energy from pointed fingers. Lady-kin poses. The entire trailer park radiates outwards from the spiral slide in the asphalt roads, tightly packed with families inside aluminum-sided mobile homes. I'm slipping down the spiral slide. My pointed toe pushes into the pebbles of the sandbox. I'm breathing life into the pose. The way a child believes. Making it so real. Over and over sliding down the spiral slide.[15]

The renewed understanding of thought does not simply allow for new thinking to occur, but it also permits us to conceive of the extent to which all phenomena are constituted in the same fashion. A number of conceptual arrays from Deleuze and Guattari germane to Arsenault's life and art practice are useful here, with the first of these, the rhizome, allowing us to understand her processual coconstitution with the world around her, such as the complex kinds of relationalities in evidence in her description of the trailer park above: the spiral-sandbox-foot-slide-energy-toe composition that escapes simple explanation. In *a thousand plateaus*, when discussing the formation of their collaborative text, Deleuze and Guattari note that "in a book as in all things, there are lines of articulation or segmentarity, strata and territories; but also lines of flight, movements of deterritorialization and destratification."[16] Consonant with their post-transcendentalist thinking, they assert that to "attribute the book to a subject" is "to fabricate a beneficent God to explain geological movements."[17] This superannuated understanding of narrative attribution follows the logic of what they call an arboreal model, where the singular and authoritative connection of the root system to the branches via a sole trunk operates to provide evidence of "a noble, signifying, and subjective organic interiority."[18] However, Nature, they assert, doesn't work that way, but instead escapes the binarizing and imprisoning logic of arborescence for something more complex: "In nature, roots are taproots with a more multiple, lateral and circular system of ramification, rather than a dichotomous one. … We're tired of trees," they continue, "we should stop believing in tree roots and radicles. They've made us suffer too much."[19] It is the rhizome that offers a more accurate understanding of the world and its continuous differentiation and multiplicity of connection, as a "subterranean stem is absolutely different from roots and radicles"[20] in that it enacts perpetual connection and heterogeneity, since "any point of a rhizome can be connected to anything other, and must be."[21] A rhizomatic phenomenon, be it thought or otherwise, "ceaselessly establishes connections between semiotic chains, organizations of power, and circumstances relative to the arts, sciences, and social struggles."[22] These acts of what Deleuze and Guattari call territorialization and deterritorialization[23] eventuate a complex of processes "that is perpetually in construction or collapsing, and of a process that is perpetually prolonging itself, breaking off and starting up again,"[24] a mode of continuous variation where "rhizome lines oscillate between tree lines that segment and even stratify them, and the lines of flight and rupture that carry them away."[25] In this light, Nina's various surgeries—her deterritorializations of expectations around gender and sexuality, as well as her reterritorializations around a new but constantly changing body—are a rhizomatic and continually differentiating matrix of organic and inorganic components moving in both symbiotic and nonparallel concert in a state of perpetual emergence and becoming, leading to forever shifting discoveries of as-yet-untravelled pathways:

After all my cosmetic surgery my body feels stiff and rigid. I'm wracked with tension. I feel like I'm posing all the time. I don't think my body knew I wanted to have all these procedures. I think my body thought I was getting into car accidents over and over. I know it wasn't mentally healthy to have sex with so many men, one after another, in such a short time. I know it was fucking me up. But I was not going to be reasonable. I'm very happy I was not reasonable.[26]

Through these processes of perpetual assembly and disassembly, things form into coherences or assemblages,[27] entities that borrow "decoded fragments of all kinds"[28] from the milieu in which they exist to that extent that Deleuze and Guattari will assert that "the territory makes the assemblage"[29]: "We will call an assemblage every constellation of singularities and traits deducted from the flow—selected, organized, and stratified—in such a way as to converge (consistency) artificially and naturally; an assemblage in this sense, is a veritable invention."[30] Rather than a core organizing principle at the heart of each assemblage, what might be described as a *quality of invention* is distributed over the fragments that compose the multiplicity and have a cogenerative influence over the emergence of the territory of the assemblage. Arsenault's new body becomes understood as a convergence of components and desires, a postidentitarian complex of relations.

Assemblage theory, in contradistinction to cultural materialist analysis with its emphasis on discerning the effects of context on individuals and works of art through variations on semiotic analyses, permits us to understand that the territories under study are not to be discussed simply in their status as objects but rather in terms of the expressed qualities of slowness, speed, rupture, and so forth that compose them. In other words, all the things that an assemblage can do. Arsenault's awareness of her own complex compositional arrangement permits an understanding of moments as consisting of various relationalities and lines of affect—what Nina can do—such as when she describes herself working in a virtual porn operation:

Dirty adjectives artfully ejaculating onto the keyboard, onto the computer screen, into the digital world, into the minds of men, down to their cocks. That's what gives them a hard on.

I can hold down about eighteen erotic conversations at the same time, all on different subjects. I can keep them straight in my mind. I'm typing so fast, that I am still waiting for the guys to respond to me. When they do, I can read between the lines of what they type, and program myself to be exactly the kind of fantasy of a woman that each man wants me to be. I can make her so real. Composing myself inside the computer monitor at the same time. The way I compose myself within the frame–beautiful. Jerking off at the same time.[31]

In approaching phenomena as assemblages, interpretation becomes less about studying a fixed object or an identitarian phenomenon disconnected from what surrounds it in a categorical way (such as a human being, differentiated because of its purported monopoly on agency). Instead, interpretation shifts towards entering into a rhizomatic relationship with what's under discussion, with what is unfolding: Nina as sex-assemblage, a desire machine networked with many other screens and bodies, her hand on her phallus, their hands on theirs.

Abstract Machine/Body without Organs

I am sure I will keep working and living with the image of the mannequin. Warhol did silk screening and used repetitious images for decades. Jackson Pollock explored automatist painting and pure form over and over. I think that is why it's called an art "practice." Yeah, whether it's high art or low art or just creative expression you'll always return to what is pleasurable to you, what is obsessive to you. I can't stop that.[32]

What is it that harnesses the powers of differentiation and causes the development of new rhizomatic assemblages? Deleuze and Guattari qualify an additional form of force that occupies each assemblage, namely, the *abstract machine*. First of all, the thinkers remind us that although machines are "machinic," they are not "mechanical, in the way that a tractor is a closed mechanical system."[33] Deleuze and Guattari affirm that abstract machines "surpass any kind of mechanics,"[34] but simply comprise a series of flexible and generative articulations, or more precisely, points of interruptions of pre-existing flows of affect, intensity, desire, and so forth. Additionally, if they are to be resonant with Deleuze's immanentist ontology, abstract machines cannot be abstract "in the sense of a Platonic Idea, transcendent, universal, eternal"[35] but must operate *within* concrete assemblages. They are described as "the cutting edges of deterritorialization" that make "the territorial assemblage open onto something else, assemblages of another type, the molecular, the cosmic," in other words: "they constitute becomings."[36] Abstract machines are the "life proper to material as such, a material vitalism that doubtless exists everywhere but is ordinarily hidden or covered, rendered unrecognizable, dissociated by the hylomorphic model," with hylomorphism being that procedure that would shape matter according to the strictures imposed by an ideal model, "an operation by which the world appears as obedient and predictable representation."[37] Indeed, rather than confirming existing representations, abstract machines are that force or arrangement that both deploys the engine of differentiation that constitutes all ontological processes, while at the same time is also constituted by these same processes: "The diagrammatic or abstract machine does not function to represent, even something real, but rather constructs a real that is to come, a new type of reality."[38]

In that abstract machines are constitutive of the new, they have a special relationship with artistic production. In fact, Deleuze and Guattari provide a particularly simple equation in the form of a brief statement: "Art as abstract machine,"[39] with the first principle being that artistic production is real rather than a representation. It follows from their assertion/equation that if one is to create art, then one is creating an abstract machine. In other words, one is constructing construction itself.[40] From the Deleuzo-Guattarian vantage, the artist is then a machinist, a "cosmic artisan,"[41] who, like the abstract machine itself, affirms new ways of living while at the same time destroying the old: "There is a necessary joy in creation, art is necessarily a liberation that explodes everything."[42] To construct an abstract machine "will mean constructing a new experience indissociable from a new reality"[43] leading to a circumstance where, Deleuze writes, Kant's "two senses of the aesthetic become one, to the point where the being of the sensible reveals itself in the work of art, while at the same time the work of art appears as experimentation":[44] *onto-aesthetics.*

And what does Arsenault the artist, the machinist, make? How does she answer what Deleuze describes as the Spinozan "war cry" of "we don't even know what the body can do"?[45] Arsenault's work serves as one answer to Zepke's question, "how can we create a new body, a new sensibility adequate to a life of ontological innovation?" by providing us with models of "a work entirely experimental, inasmuch as art is a permanent research on its own conditions, and is always constructing new machines."[46] Arsenault, whose name on the social media platform Twitter is "The Nina_Machina," regularly plays with the resonance and oscillation between the mechanical—in the sense of the incursion of technology into the biological body—and the machinic, that which is open-ended, innovative, and auto-poetic. A series of photographs by inkedKenny features Arsenault in antiseptic environments that appear to be a tiled bathroom or hospital space, dressed in leather that sections and articulates her body into segments that she variously palpates with seeming curiosity and a hint of the coquette as if she were asking, poking her breast, "what does this do?" (see Figures 6 and 15). The machinic continues with "Ophelia/Machine," an evolving video project featuring "gonzo porn" (pornography that attempts to situate the viewer directly within the scene) focusing on sadomasochist sexual expression with all the parts played by herself. "Ophelia/Machine" functions by mobilizing what Deleuze describes in his works on the cinema as the two tendencies of the cinema, namely the reproductive force of the image that creates the experience of totality for the viewer, as well as the productive force of the image that leads to new machinic connections to be made with the viewer and what they are connected to. The productivity or machinism of the images is in their de-narritivizing drive towards a becoming-other that defamiliarizes industrial porn and all its symbolic and representational blockages, leading to lines of flight that cause the image to no longer serve a normalizing dynamic but instead become "primarily optical and of sound, invested by the senses."[47]

Arsenault and other machinists like her are harnessing the abstract machine to construct what Deleuze and Guattari, borrowing from Artaud, describe as a "Body without Organs" (BwO). In *a thousand plateaus*, the authors explain that strata "constitute the judgment of God" as they are "accumulations, coagulations, sedimentations, foldings."[48] Strata are that which maintain a mutable coherence over the course of the general evolution of assemblages. The term BwO refers to a different kind of substrate than the strata in that the BwO is opposed to the kinds of organization and development instantiated by the strata. Instead, the BwO is a non-formed, non-organized, deterritorialized and destratified body, with the understanding that a body is any whole, comprised by a relation of specific parts, that has the capacity to be affected by another body.[49] As a performance artist disassembling her biologically given body and reassembling something new, Arsenault is actualizing the BwO of her own body, generating via a complex assemblage of relationships with location, substance, flesh, and silicone, a new and different body, then disseminating this BwO via social media, performance, parties, and sexual encounter.

Nina Arsenault

It is important to note, however, that the BwO does not exist in contradistinction to more traditional identarian forms of bodies or subjectivity of any organism. Instead, it exists simultaneously with the strata, providing opportunities for different types of arrangements and becomings: "the BwO is always swinging between the surfaces that stratify it and the plane that sets it free."[50] In fact, assuming that the BwO can be acceded via a process of extreme destratification can therefore be dangerous to the bodies that would pursue this particular line: "If you free the BwO with too violent an action, if you blow apart the strata without taking precautions," instead of generating a new arrangement, a new assemblage, "you will be killed, plunged into a black hole, or even dragged towards catastrophe."[51] Arsenault discusses these types of dangers as she mines her own BwO:

I've heard about an underground silicone trade among transsexuals, but I've never seen it. At home, I search the Internet, and there are so many things that can go wrong with this. There is a small chance that the needle will hit an artery on the way into the body. If it does, the silicone will travel through your veins. Within moments, it will either hit your heart, your brain or your lungs. If it hits your brain first, you'll have a stroke. If it hits your heart first, you'll have a heart attack. If it hits your lungs, you'll drown. In silicone.[52]

Simulacrum

It's so seductive to believe I am the image. To give into hours of posing that my job demands. To frame myself in the computer monitor. Stomach in. Bend over. Turn to the camera. Open Mouth. Hair flip. Something devilish behind my eyes. I can read between the lines the men type to me and program myself to be exactly the fantasy they want me to be. I can make it so real.[53]

For all that she is pursuing a new body, what of the apparent contradiction in Arsenault's work: the seeming need to generate images and realities of herself that embody the most obedient and predictable forms of representation such as mannequins or Barbie? Does this not demonstrate a desire to subscribe to hylomorphism, that operation that would prescriptively mould matter into something predictable? Is this not simply a question of her being recuperated and harnessed into contemporary economies of the gaze, the connection of the Nina Arsenault machine with what Deleuze and Guattari call the *axiomatic* of capital, a force that can readily capture becomings in its striated and well-organized flows of desire, securing them into closed productive loops, ends in themselves that result in an overall state of what Deleuze and Guattari describe as "technonarcissism"?[54]

As we have seen, Arsenault's attempts to evolve herself—to embody the construction of construction of art's abstract machine—involve more than simply reducing herself to two-dimensional models. Hovering underneath the body of Nina-Barbie, for example, is her

182

penis, now become part of the BwO of the perfect Mattel doll creation, inherently troubling the hylomorphic model of Barbie by its very existence:

> As the photographers disperse, I realize my dick is coming untucked, so I skitter away to the privacy of the Schick Razor's breast cancer examination booth. I don't want Barbie walking around with a bulge in her dress. She's not supposed to have anything there.[55]

Similarly, the display of grotesque post-op images or photos of her naked hairless head and upper torso complete with visible scars also enact an assemblage in process, rather than the accomplishment of an apotheosis (see Figures 11, 19, and 25). What we see operating with the Arsenault-assemblage is a celebration of what Deleuze describes as the *simulacrum*, although one more radical in nature than the simulacrum as popularized by Baudrillard. The latter's understanding of the notion is based on the substitution of the sign of the real for the real in a hyperreality in which signs stand only for themselves, referring only to other signs.[56] In response to this world of slippage, of ultimate interchangeability of signs, and of profound indetermination, those living in postmodern societies of illusion or spectacle become actualized as the receptive subjects of the digital age, lost in signs with never a referent to hold onto. From Deleuze's perspective, however, as the world is in a state of constant becoming, the simulacrum "harbors a positive power which denies *the original and the copy, the model and the reproduction*."[57] This "triumph of the false pretender"[58] is not marked by the ascendancy of empty appearances, and is therefore to be distinguished from the Baudrillardian vision in that it does not presuppose original referents to which signs no longer have any relation. Thus, instead of a duality marked by one collapsed term, the Deleuzian model proposes a world of univocal substance. This univocity does not necessarily result in unity or identifiability, however, but as we have seen rather a seething world of difference—what will become the "plane of consistency" in Deleuze's later writing with Guattari[59]—in which there are copies for which there are no originals, repetitions in which "resemblance [and] identity subsist" but only as a result of being produced "as the external effect of the simulacrum."[60] Speaking of her encounter with the American rock star and public figure Tommy Lee, Arsenault describes the realities of the simulacrum as she harnesses and experiences it:

> A powerful feeling of fierceness is coursing through me as I walk towards a man who was married to one of the most revered sex symbols of all time. On the way over, I dare to compare myself to *the* Ms. Pamela Anderson. Kohl-ringed eyes, teased hair, enormous breast implants, and a trademark teeth-together-lips-apart lusty expression of come-hither-ness. She is a caricature of a woman. Tonight I am a caricature of her. An imitation of an imitation of an idea of a woman. An image which has never existed in nature, but singled out as the shining beauty in the room.[61]

Arsenault's accession and ascension to the state of image is, in the world of the Deleuzian simulacrum, not then simply a question of the uncritical adoption of two-dimensional images circulating in heterosexist pop culture, but is rather a celebration of the triumph of *real* illusion (in the sense that everything is constructed, everything is an illusion) over the pseudo-essential realities of a representational universe in which these representations are understood to be anchored in some transcendental reality. Nothing satisfies Arsenault more than the triumph of the illusion, as she suggests when talking about a fan of hers who has stated, "He says he has always seen through the image of my male face and perceived a most beautiful woman."[62] Part of her expression of the destratifying drive of the abstract machine is to actualize BwO in others by drawing attention to and celebrating the simulacrum, such as in her encounter with the rock star at Ultra Supper Club:

> I don't want to be made to feel less beautiful because I was born into a male body, or because I have fake parts. Everything that attracted you to me in the first place, Tommy Lee—synthetic hair, make-up, silicone, attitude, radiance—I don't have to be born a biological woman to have these things, and I want you to get that it is these things that give you the physiological feeling of a hard on.[63]

Although, as she continues, not everyone is necessarily as receptive to these insights as she might like:

> Maybe he gets it, because Tommy does this *(shaking head, shaking head again, shaking head a third time, shoulders dropping, breath dropping, then double thumbs up, smiling)* and says, "I need a cigarette."
> Then, he slips out from under me, and he's out of the VIP section.
> I steal one more glass of champagne off his table before that sea of jealous bitches can come for me, and I escape Ultra.[64]

St. Nina

> They aren't just cupcakes anymore. They are pink swirls of positivity. I am breathing it into reality. I can see pink lines of energy connecting my genitals to the cupcakes. It's magical. I hold that tray of cupcakes high, offering them from my heart, from my Barbie-like silicone breasts. I will make my own full-circle moment. I walk into that room, proud to be something bigger than I am, proud to be Barbie.[65]

Steven Zepke asserts that from the Deleuzo-Guattarian perspective, "Art will be nothing … if it is not this ongoing expression of life in the construction of living machines."[66] Zepke's emphasis on the *living* aspect of these machines reminds us that the abstract machine of art expresses the ontogenetic and perpetual process of not simply representations or signs, but the expression of its own real conditions. The artwork and the work of art become key sites where the dynamics of ontology are foregrounded, "a process by which the becoming of the world is expressed in a construction which works upon its own conditions, which operates at the level of its constitutive mechanism."[67] Nina the rhizome, Nina the assemblage, a perpetual becoming-Nina. As an artist who is exploring, as per the Spinozan war cry, what the body can do, Arsenault is creating a BwO of herself. As an art-process and embodiment of art as abstract machine she is intervening and engaging consciously in the flow of becoming. In so doing, Arsenault affirms the force that Deleuze and Guattari describe in their last work together as that which "wants to create the finite that restores the infinite."[68] Indeed, rather than referring to anything esoteric or mystical, understanding art as abstract machine—as that which engages the BwO to destratify fixities, habituations, and calcifications of sensation—ultimately permits an experience of what Deleuze calls the "local absolute," the experience of an "atheistic mysticism."[69] The assertion here is that if transcendent systems promote a mysticism that takes us away from ourselves in favour of causes beyond us (God or logos), then immanent systems remind us of our own emergence from the processes that constitute all life and matter, which surround us and of which we are a part. We become immortal not "in the way we can rise to a different realm (of God or of Platonic Ideas), but in the way we participate in eternal processes."[70] Nina's joyful and living affirmation of her own potential for differentiation and becoming result in her secular saintliness, her connection with all mystical forces that she occasionally refers to as Jesus, Buddha, Gandhi, and Michelle Obama.[71] This powerful spiritual force expresses itself as a dynamic mix of her unreasonableness and perpetual disciplined commitment to evolution and change; the eternal return of her BwO; and her intense love for the present where both the living fusion of previously differentiated aesthetic modes can be achieved and where real beauty can be accessed: "Of course, this is the next step in the journey. To surrender to the beauty of whatever the moment is. Every moment has its own beauty. That is enough. Accept the moment."[72]

David Fancy is associate professor and chair in the Department of Dramatic Arts at Brock University in St. Catharines, Ontario. He writes on issues of the body, immanence, and performance. His recent work includes a book chapter on French director Patrice Chereau in *Contemporary European Theatre Directors* (2010), another on performance, electromagnetic pollution, and zombies in a forthcoming volume titled *Performance After Identity*, and an article on "geoperformativity" in *Performance Research*. His current projects include a monograph titled *Immanence, Performance, the Body: Deleuze and the Joy of the Actor*.

Bibliography

Arsenault, Nina. "I W@s B*rbie," unpublished script, 2009.
———. "The Silicone Diaries," unpublished script, 2009.

———. *The Silicone Diaries*. In *TRANS(per)FORMING Nina Arsenault*, edited by Judith Rudakoff, 191–227. Bristol: Intellect Press, 2012.

Baudrillard, Jean. *Simulations*. Trans. Paul Foss, Paul Patton, and Philip Beitchman. New York: Semiotext(e), 2007.

Deleuze, Gilles. *Cinema 2: The Time Image*. Trans. Hugh Tomlinson and Robert Galeta. Minneapolis, University of Minnesota Press, 1989.

———. *Desert Island and Other Texts 1953–1974*. Trans. M. Taormina. New York: Semiotext(e), 2004.

———. *Difference and Repetition*. Trans. Paul Patton. New York, Columbia University Press, 1994.

———. *Empiricism and Subjectivity: An Essay on Hume's Theory of Human Nature*. New York: Columbia University Press, 2001.

———. *Expressionism in Philosophy: Spinoza*. Trans. M. Joughin. New York: Zone Books, 1992.

———. "Immanence: A Life." In *Theory, Culture and Society* 14, no. 2 (1997): 3–7.

———. *The Logic of Sense*. Trans. Mark Lester. New York: Columbia University Press, 1990.

———. *Nietzsche and Philosophy*. New York: Columbia University Press, 2006.

———. "Seminar Session on Spinoza." January 24, 1978. http://www.webdeleuze.com/php/texte.php?cle=14&groupe=Spinoza&langue=2.

———. *a thousand plateaus: capitalism and schizophrenia*. Trans. Brian Massumi. Minneapolis: University of Minnesota Press, 1987.

———. *What is Philosophy?* Trans. Hugh Tomlinson and Graham Burchell. New York: Columbia University Press, 1994.

Deleuze, Gilles, and Félix Guattari. *Kafka: Towards a Minor Literature*. Trans. Dana Polan. Minneapolis: University of Minnesota Press, 1977.

Flood, Nicholas. "Nina Arsenault Lives—Part Two—Nicholas Flood Interview." October 12, 2010. http://positivelite.com/content/blog/contributors/revolving-door/item/nina-arsenault-lives-part-two.

Kant, Immanuel. *Critique of Judgment*. Trans. James Creed Meredith. Oxford and New York: Oxford University Press, 2007.

"Nina Arsenault Moving Through the Phases of Life." *The Conversationalist* (blog), September 24, 2010. http://www.danielbaylis.ca/interview-2/interview-nina-arsenault-transitioning-through-the-phases-of-life/.

Parr, Adrian, ed. *The Deleuze Dictionary*. New York: Columbia University Press, 2005.

Zepke, Stephen. *Art as Abstract Machine: Ontology and Aesthetics in Deleuze and Guattari*. New York: Routledge, 2005.

Notes

1. Gilles Deleuze, *The Logic of Sense*, trans. Mark Lester (New York: Columbia University Press, 1990), 260.
2. Ibid.
3. Deleuze, *Logic*, 261.

4. Stephen Zepke, *Art as Abstract Machine: Ontology and Aesthetics in Deleuze and Guattari* (New York: Routledge, 2005), 4.
5. "Nina Arsenault Moving Through the Phases of Life," *The Conversationalist* (blog), September 24, 2010, http://www.danielbaylis.ca/interview-2/interview-nina-arsenault-transitioning-through-the-phases-of-life/.
6. Immanuel Kant, *Critique of Judgment*, trans. James Creed Meredith (Oxford: Oxford University Press, 2007).
7. Gilles Deleuze, *Difference and Repetition*, trans. Paul Patton (New York: Columbia University Press, 1994), 334.
8. Gilles Deleuze and Félix Guattari, *Kafka: Towards a Minor Literature*, trans. Dana Polan (Minneapolis: University of Minnesota Press, 1977), 27.
9. Gilles Deleuze, "Immanence: A Life," in *Theory, Culture and Society* 14, no. 2 (1997), 3.
10. Gilles Deleuze, *Empiricism and Subjectivity: An Essay on Hume's Theory of Human Nature* (New York: Columbia University Press, 2001).
11. Deleuze, *Difference and Repetition*, 49–271.
12. Ibid., 262.
13. Nina Arsenault, "I W@s B*rbie," unpublished script, 2009, 16.
14. Gilles Deleuze, *Nietzsche And Philosophy* (New York: Columbia University Press, 2006).
15. Nina Arsenault, "The Silicone Diaries," unpublished script, 2009, 5. In certain cases such as this I use an earlier unpublished version of the text not appearing in this volume, as the examples are slightly more relevant. Specifically, some of the previous text was more "rhizomatic" in that it was more disconnected and slightly less narrativized than the more updated text.
16. Gilles Deleuze and Félix Guattari, *a thousand plateaus: capitalism and schizophrenia,* trans. Brian Massumi (Minneapolis: University of Minnesota Press, 1987), 3.
17. Ibid.
18. Ibid., 5.
19. Ibid., 15.
20. Ibid., 6.
21. Ibid., 7.
22. Ibid.
23. Ibid., 37.
24. Ibid., 20.
25. Ibid., 506.
26. Nina Arsenault, *The Silicone Diaries, in TRANS(per)FORMING Nina Arsenault,* ed. Judith Rudakoff (Bristol: Intellect Press, 2012), 224.
27. Deleuze and Guattari, *a thousand plateaus*, 9.
28. Ibid., 504.
29. Ibid.
30. Ibid., 406.
31. Arsenault, *The Silicone Diaries,* 2012, 208.
32. Nicholas Flood, "Nina Arsenault Lives—Part Two—Nicholas Flood Interview," October 12, 2010, http://positivelite.com/content/blog/contributors/revolving-door/item/nina- arsenault-lives-part-two.

33. Deleuze and Guattari, *a thousand plateaus*, 511.
34. Ibid.
35. Ibid., 510.
36. Ibid.
37. Zepke, *Art as Abstract Machine*, 4.
38. Deleuze, *a thousand plateaus*, 142.
39. Ibid., 496.
40. I am indebted to Stephen Zepke's very useful text here, *Art as Abstract Machine: Ontology and Aesthetics in Deleuze and Guattari*.
41. Deleuze, *a thousand plateaus*, 345.
42. Gilles Deleuze, *Desert Island and Other Texts 1953–1974*, trans. M. Taormina (New York: Semiotext(e), 2004), 134.
43. Zepke, *Art as Abstract Machine*, 3.
44. Deleuze, *Difference and Repetition*, 68.
45. Gilles Deleuze, *Expressionism in Philosophy: Spinoza*, trans. M. Joughin (New York: Zone Books, 1992), 255.
46. Zepke, *Art as Abstract Machine*, 4.
47. Gilles Deleuze, *Cinema 2: The Time-Image*, trans. Hugh Tomlinson and Robert Galeta (Minneapolis: University of Minnesota Press, 1989), 4.
48. Deleuze, *a thousand plateaus*, 502.
49. This concept permits a postidentitarian understanding of the body in the same way as the concept of the rhizome does, referring not simply to arrangements in their traditional material modes of reference, but the many kinds of relations of their parts dependent on the type of body under discussion.
50. Ibid., 161.
51. Ibid.
52. Arsenault, "The Silicone Diaries," 2009, 11.
53. Ibid., 7.
54. Deleuze, *a thousand plateaus*, 22.
55. Arsenault, "I W@s B*rbie," 15.
56. Jean Baudrillard, *Simulations*, trans. Paul Foss, Paul Patton, and Philip Beitchman (New York: Semiotext(e), 2007), 4.
57. Deleuze, *Difference and Repetition*, 299.
58. Ibid., 300.
59. Ibid., 506–8.
60. Ibid., 299.
61. Arsenault, *The Silicone Diaries*, 2012, 219.
62. Ibid., "The Silicone Diaries," 2009, 9.
63. Ibid., *The Silicone Diaries*, 2012, 221.
64. Ibid.
65. Arsenault, "I W@s B*rbie," 16.
66. Zepke, *Art as Abstract Machine*, 5.
67. Ibid.

68. Gilles Deleuze and Felix Guattari, *What is Philosophy?* trans. Hugh Tomlinson and Graham Burchell (New York: Columbia University Press, 1994), 197.
69. Gilles Deleuze, "Seminar Session on Spinoza," January 24, 1978, http://www.webdeleuze.com/php/texte.php?cle=14&groupe=Spinoza&langue=2.
70. Adrian Parr, ed., *The Deleuze Dictionary* (New York: Columbia, 2005), 126.
71. Arsenault, "I W@s B*rbie," 20.
72. Arsenault, *The Silicone Diaries,* 2012, 226.

PART II

THE SILICONE DIARIES

The Silicone Diaries: Director's Note

Brendan Healy

Skin is misleading ... in life, you only have your skin. ... There is a mismatch in human relationships, because you never are what you have. ... I have the skin of an angel, but I am a jackal ... the skin of a crocodile, but I am a puppy dog ... the skin of a woman, but I am a man; I never have the skin of what I am. There is no exception to the rule, because I am never what I have.
French performance artist ORLAN paraphrasing Lacanian psychoanalyst Eugénie Lemoine Luccioni[1]

When Andy Warhol declared, "I love plastic. I want to be plastic,"[2] almost fifty years ago, he was honouring the true idol of his era. Warhol wasn't being cheeky or ironic—he was getting spiritual. A substance of powerful polymorphic properties, at the time plastic was the perfect embodiment of malleability and transformability. A sleek and shiny entity that seemed indestructible, it was a paragon of immortality. Warhol rightfully recognized that plastic was a quintessential representation of mid-twentieth-century ideals. It deserved to be worshipped.

We now live in the age of silicone. These semi-inorganic polymeric compounds are even more mutable and durable than plastic. Silicone has affected our daily lives in countless ways (hello, lube!) but perhaps its most profound impact has only begun to be felt. With this substance, we have been given the unparalleled ability to manifest our innermost desires on our external flesh. We can refashion the bodies that nature imposed on us to more closely fit our own terms. We can incarnate our own visions of perfection, become the literal personifications of our most profound fantasies; we can transform ourselves into the avatars of our deepest interiors.

Much of the discourse around plastic surgery is based on a series of assumptions. On the one hand, defenders tell us that there is a schism in the way that we experience our identities—how we look on the outside is at odds with who we believe we authentically are inside—and these surgical interventions are justified because they satisfy some apparently profound need for coherence in our identities. On the other hand, detractors argue that we live in a world where one's self-image is distorted through endless media refractions, and these surgeries are turning us into reproductions of mediated versions of reality that have nothing to do with the real.

Coherence. Real.

Words that come out of a conception of identity that is constant and stable.

Like Warhol, Nina Arsenault (herself, in some ways, a Warholian creation) understands silicone. She has used this substance to raise the pursuit of the "real fake" to metaphysical levels. In doing so, she destabilizes the coherence and authenticity of identity. Like silicone itself, Nina creates a new paradigm of mutable identity: one that will not stick, that is likely to change, inconstant, variable. And magnificent. In performance, she is a silicone goddess and you are in her white temple. In her presence, you can no longer tell where the artificial ends and the real begins, what is sacred and what is profane, what is constant and what is changing. And when the goddess reveals her impossible corporeality, the imaginary merges with the physical to create the ideal that is art.

Brendan Healy is the artistic director of Buddies in Bad Times Theatre. Located in Toronto, Canada, Buddies is the largest and longest-running facility-based queer theatre company in the world.

Originally from Montreal, Healy began his career as an actor, appearing most notably in celebrated Canadian director Peter Hinton's production of *girls!girls!girls!*, presented at the 2001 Festival TransAmériques (Montreal). It was at that festival that Healy met Richard Maxwell, whose company, the New York City Players, is considered to be one of the most influential alternative theatre companies currently operating in Manhattan. That meeting led Healy to New York, where he interned with Mr. Maxwell and subsequently decided to dedicate himself exclusively to directing.

Since relocating to Toronto, Healy has established himself as a central figure in the city's independent theatre scene and his work has been presented across the country. A graduate of the directing program at the National Theatre School of Canada (Montreal), he has also trained extensively with one of the pioneers of the American avant-garde Anne Bogart and the SITI Company. He has taught and directed at Concordia University (Montreal), at the National Theatre School, and is a frequent guest lecturer at several Canadian universities and theatre training institutions.

Bibliography

Bockris, Victor, and Gerard Malanga. *Up-Tight: The Velvet Underground Story*. London: Omnibus Press, 2002.

The Irish Critic. "Feminism and Representation: An Interview with ORLAN." April 29, 2009. Accessed February 10 2011. http://theirishcritic.com/new-york-theatre/feminism-and-representation-an-interview-with-ORLAN.

Notes

These director's notes were included, in a slightly different version, in the program for the 2010 Buddies in Bad Times production of *The Silicone Diaries*.

1. *The Irish Critic*, "Feminism and Representation: An Interview with ORLAN," April 29, 2009, accessed February 10 2011, http://theirishcritic.com/new-york-theatre/feminism-and-representation-an-interview-with-ORLAN.

2. Victor Bockris and Gerard Malanga, *Up-Tight: The Velvet Underground Story* (London: Omnibus Press, 2002), 66.

The Silicone Diaries

Nina Arsenault

An earlier version of *The Silicone Diaries* was workshopped and performed at The Saint John Theatre Company, Saint John, New Brunswick in August 2008. *The Silicone Diaries* premiered at Buddies in Bad Times Theatre, Toronto, Ontario in November 2009 and was remounted in a slightly different version in November 2010.

Created and performed by Nina Arsenault*
Director: Brendan Healy
Dramaturg: Judith Rudakoff
Stage Manager: Laura Baxter (2009), Sandy Plunkett* (2010)
Production Design: Trevor Schwellnus
Video Design: Nick Greenspan (2009), R. Kelly Clipperton (2010)
Sound Design: Richard Feren

*Member of Canadian Actors' Equity Association

Dedication

To my parents for the complexity of their never ending love and support.

Acknowledgements

This performance text has developed with the support of the following companies and artists: Mitchel Raphael, *fab Magazine*, Andrea Nemeth, Anthony Collins, The Saint John Theatre Company (Theatre on the Edge Fest), Stephen Tobias, Port City Rainbow Pride, The Mahogany Manor, Sky Gilbert (Free Jane!), Brendan Healy, Judith Rudakoff, John Grundy, Nicholas Flood, J. Paul Halferty, Buddies in Bad Times Theatre, David Oiye, Erika Hennebury, Northbound Leather, Fides Krucker, Trevor Schwellnus, Nicolas A. Greenland, Shawn Hitchins, Richard Feren, R. Kelly Clipperton.

When the soul wishes to experience something she throws an image of the experience out before her and enters into her own image.
Meister Eckhart

The Silicone Diaries

Sex/object (1979)

Shemale porn saved my soul (1999)

My boy-holes vanished (2001)

I am my own self-portrait (2004)

Me 'n' Tommy Lee (2006)

The patron saint of plastic surgery (2001–2006)

Venus/machine (2007–2009)

At the beginning of each section, either a photograph of Nina's face as it appeared in the corresponding year or a video of that year's related activities is projected.

Playwright's Note

The stage, scene and personal directions included are minimal. Each new production of this performance text should embody and reflect the time, place, mood and reality of the moment.

The names—other than those of public figures—and defining characteristics of the real people I talk about have been changed to protect them, but none of us are innocent.

Sex/object (1979)

I am shopping with Mom at the discount department store, Zellers, in our home town, Beamsville, Ontario, when I lay my five-year-old eyes on one of the most beautiful women I have ever seen. She is surrounded by bins of support bras and baggy panties, standing in the centre of the Zeller's "Lingerie" department. She is lit by fluorescent tube lights. In their unforgiving glare, she is painted flawlessly. Cloaked in the white noise humming from these lights, she is frozen in time. Her neck is extended gracefully. A serene, regal expression on her face. Eyes wide open and empty. Shoppers circle her, and, unselfconsciously, they stare at her beauty as they pass. One woman even curtsies to rub the fabric at the bottom of her slip, as if an aura of glamour could be stroked from her. A Zellers employee approaches the beauty from behind and slips the straps of her satin nightie from her shoulders. As it flutters to the floor, bare breasts are exposed with no nipples.

I say, "A life-sized doll!"

My mom says, "They're called mannequins, Rodney."

I hate that she has the word "man" in her name.

Her face is perfect. The arch of her eyebrows has the same shape as the Cupid's bow in her lips. The upwards swoop of the cheek bones is reflected in the upwards swoop of her almond eyes. The tip of her pointed nose. The shape of the jutting chin. It's so harmonious.

I don't think this at the time.

I think: "She's more beautiful than Barbie."

I stare at her. Into her eyes. They seem to shimmer.

"Is she real?"

* * *

In the centre of the Golden Horseshoe Trailer Court, where we live, there is a large grassy field. In the centre of the large grassy field is a square wooden sandbox. In the centre of the square wooden sandbox is a spiral steel slide. The entire Golden Horseshoe Trailer Park radiates outwards from the spiral slide in asphalt roads, tightly packed with aluminum-sided mobile homes. Inside the scooped steel funnel of the slide, my five-year-old back is arched. My five-year-old leg is pointed. My wrist is thrown dramatically over the lip of the slide, shooting energy into the trailer park.

I'm imitating the mannequin poses. Breathing life into them. The way a child would believe. Sliding down the spiral steel slide until my feet touch the pebbles of the sandbox.

* * *

Behind our trailer park, there's a place where a forest and a swamp meet. The older boys, boys that I'm not supposed to be hanging out with, pubescent boys who swear, who already smoke, have a fort there. It is an overturned fiberglass shell that might once have been a piece of someone's trailer. It has little holes in it in the same places trailers have windows.

I follow them there one day, careful not to touch the sides of the door on the way in. Pieces of the fiberglass will come off onto my skin. I'll itch all day. Inside, there are three boys kneeling on the damp earth in a semicircle, pressed against the far wall of the clubhouse. There is a lit cigarette lighter. Underneath that flickering flame, the boys are looking at girlie magazines.

I've heard of girlie magazine before, but I have never seen them.

The leader of the pack of boys is turning the pages so gingerly, like he barely dares to touch the paper. The boys are talking about which woman is the most beautiful.

The pictures are not of women. They are Goddesses. They have the biggest hair I have ever seen. They have smouldering darkness around their eyes. Fingers rest on exposed round breasts. They are hazy 1970s portraits. I can't see what's between their legs. The pictures are magic. They are looking back at us, and they can see into every nook and cranny inside the overturned fiberglass shell, and inside me, too.

The leader of the pack of boys, maybe thinking the same thing, hauls on his lit cigarette. (*making a hissing sound*) Sssh. Sssh. Two holes burnt in the paper face of a centrefold who stares back at us.

The fumes of the magazine paper rise into our nostrils and fill the clubhouse. The boys think that is hilarious. They are now turning the pages quite unceremoniously. The edges of faces, breasts and legs are being crumpled. One of the boys has a Swiss Army knife. It has a corkscrew on it. He's slicing X's across breasts. Down a bum crack. Through a lustfully waiting mouth. The boys' excitement is turning into something that looks a lot like anger. They are chasing each other around the inside of the fort trying to steal the magazine from each other. Laughing. Tearing the pictures. Now, in the daylight, they are chasing each other around the outside of the overturned fiberglass shell, trying to own the pictures. I can hear their yells coming through the holes in the fort. It sounds like this. (*yelling, moving her hand up and down in front of her mouth.*) Inside I scream, too. The high pitched scream of a five-year-old boy's voice, screaming like a screen siren being torn apart in a movie by a giant shark.

I walk back into the daylight. The boys are running back to the Golden Horseshoe Trailer Court like little warriors. There are tiny bits of crumpled, glossy, paper, naked women's bodies, blowing on the breeze through the swamp. Into water. Wet. Blurry.

I would not touch that paper.

I have never had this much breath inside my body before. There is so much air inside me.

I don't know how I know it. Or why I know it.

But I know that this is exactly what I will be when I grow up.

Shemale porn saved my soul (1999)

I was nervous to walk up the long narrow staircase at 619 Yonge Street, which leads to Videosecrets, which is neither video nor a secret. It is the home base of an Internet porn website that caters in part to men that like transsexuals. Shemales. That's how the porn industry markets transsexuals. Someone decided "shemales" sounded sexier. The men who like us are generally straight, but they find the image of a woman with a penis very special and exciting.

I'm nervous to work here, because people say I won't make it as a transsexual. I am too masculine-looking. They say I will never find a job, or a lover. That I will always be a social outcast. But I am here to make money so I can have as much plastic surgery as possible, to look as much like a woman as I can.

I can either do that or ...

That's the only option.

I go up the stairs.

In the office, one of the other webcam models rushes by me, crying, hysterical. "Her best client died from cancer today," the manager says.

I was like, "Why the hell would a working girl cry for a guy who she's only ever met through a computer monitor, x-rated chat and a webcam?"

The manager says, "He was getting so weak his nurse used to have to type to her."

Then, my manager leads me by the hand into a large nightclub space, which is sectioned off with office dividers into cubicles. In each booth there is a webcam girl, a computer, stacks of porn. Mine has this beat-up, old, green couch.

I am convinced that I will have to be the sleaziest girl that works here to make up for the fact that I am the least feminine transsexual girl here. But that's okay. That will be my angle. I will be sleazy.

I quickly discover that I have more words than the other girls. I have two graduate degrees. A typing speed of sixty words a minute. All of those academic essays prepping my sticky fingers. Dirty adjectives artfully ejaculating onto the keyboard, onto the computer screen, into the digital world, into the minds of men, down to their cocks. That's what gives them a hard on.

I can hold down about eighteen erotic conversations at the same time, all on different subjects. I can keep them straight in my mind. I'm typing so fast, that I am still waiting for the guys to respond to me. When they do, I can read between the lines of what they type, and program myself to be exactly the kind of fantasy of a woman that each man wants me to be. I can make her so real. Composing myself inside the computer monitor at the same time. The way I compose myself within the frame—beautiful. Jerking off at the same time.

I learned how to maintain a hard on for eight hours at a time.

I did that for my femininity.

I'm fucking sexy when I work here, because I believe that the fake image on the screen is me. I have the digital camera set to wash me out. Everyone does that a bit. I'm art-porn: eyes, nostrils, lips in a close-up. The image of me on the computer monitor is something so much softer than me, so much more feminine. A cartoon line drawing of myself. A Warhol silkscreen of myself that masturbates.

Someone named RadicalGuy, a net-surfer from Phoenix, Arizona, is lurking in my shows every day. A lurker pays their money minute by minute, watches what I type, watches what other people type, watches the shows, but they don't type anything themselves. Otherwise my shifts are filled with chat about cum shots, hand jobs, blowjobs, fucking, group fucking, threesomes, cum facials, golden showers, brown showers, shemale gang bangs, shemale *bukkakes*, fuck my face, fuck my ass, fuck my wife. Every graphic shemale fantasy is allowed to be talked about. Everything except bestiality, rape and children.

Eight hour shifts. Nearly every day I work. Over a year. It's amazing how much intimacy is conveyed over those fuzzy, digital cameras. How much intimacy I'm locked into and managing simultaneously. It's quite a rush.

One day, a regular customer to the site types to me "SOMETHING MORE REALISTIC PLEASE."

I know he's demanding it because he's using capital letters.

He's paying good money for this. He wants to see what he wants to see. He's doesn't want to see an abstracted, line-drawing of a chick with a dick. He wants to see a realistic-looking, image of a chick with a dick.

I'm looking at myself in the computer monitor. That's me. I'm sexy because that's me. It's like looking into the mirror, but it's so hard to know what's really in the mirror. But I think all of us have our own personal version of sexiness going on underneath the manipulation. So I am going to take the emotional risk to reset the camera so it's just my smiling face on the screen, unaltered by digitization.

And I do.

There is a phallic column, a list of all the men watching at the time. Their sleazy login names. It is retracting. Shrinking. Very quickly. I am realizing what is fake and what is real. Very upsetting. I'm almost about to start crying in my own pornographic show, with no effects to wash away the tears.

The regular customer types, "SOMETHING MORE REALISTIC PLEASE."

I know he is demanding it, because he is using capital letters.

He's paying good money for this and he wants to see a realistic-looking chick with a dick.

I'm trying to reset the camera displays to the place where I look good. Just one button to revert them to the factory specs. Very sophisticated to get to the place where I look good.

RadicalGuy, my net-surfer from Phoenix, Arizona, my lurker, has that asshole reported to my manager, and booted from the site.

After that, RadicalGuy and I become very good friends, over private chat. While I simultaneously do my sex show and the stream of sexual chat scrolls down the screen, I open up to him, privately.

Instant intimacy. I will never meet him. I tell him how hard it is being a woman inside a man's body who looks so male, still. I tell him how difficult it is to go out in public when people reflect back to me an image of myself, that I am puzzling, grotesque, that I am out during the day and everything. "Good for you, girl."

One day I type to him, "How can you watch me every day, RadicalGuy?"

"My wife left me, and mom and dad died all within six months. I haven't left my house since. Shut in. Thirty-one years."

I am happy to be his only friend. He will have to keep paying. That's the way the business is. I am saving every dollar I make for plastic surgeries.

The only person who gives me as much money as RadicalGuy is Bigone25. Bigone25 is a doctor and the vice-president of a major American health insurance company. He says he could book airline tickets through the company he works for, and no one would know. He wants to fly me to Vegas for a "paid vacation." I don't want to go to Vegas. I want to go to San Francisco. There is a surgeon there who specializes in feminizing transsexual women's faces. I want to coincide the vacation with a consultation. So that isn't working out yet with Bigone.

Then, RadicalGuy tells me he's having chest pains, very serious chest pains, and he begins missing my shows. He tried ordering heart medication from online stores that operate out of Thailand, but when it arrived, he was afraid to take it. Too scared to leave his home for the doctor's office or the ER, he types, "You'll probably be the only one to miss me."

I agree to spend a four-day weekend in Vegas with Bigone25, because Bigone25 agrees to drive up to Phoenix, Arizona and pay a house call to RadicalGuy.

And because I think, "Go to Vegas. Why not?"

When I get to the airport, Bigone25 turns out to be a forty-five-year-old man with pop bottle thick glasses, a comb-over, wedding ring, overweight and a fake hip. He makes fun of other people all the time. That's how he keeps the conversation rolling. I don't mind being around him though, because around him, I feel sexy.

But so I don't really have to have sex with him, I tire him out with trips up and down the Las Vegas strip, in the desert sun, on that fake hip. Shopping at The Venetian. The virtual reality experience at the Star Trek Exhibit. The roller coaster ride on top of the New York, New York Hotel. I have to do it all.

Then, at dinner, I cry, "I'm sorry. I can't have sex with you because I don't look enough like a woman yet. I can't take my clothes off in front of people in real life."

They were manipulative tears, but they were real tears.

Bigone25 sees right through that. He still agrees to drive up to Phoenix to pay a house call on RadicalGuy, and he gives me First Class airfare so I can see the cosmetic surgeon in San Francisco.

Then, I have to fly home.

Bigone25 calls from Phoenix to say that RadicalGuy had to get knocked out with a sedative so they could get him out of the house. They were going to take him for emergency heart surgery. Bigone set that up right away with his medical connections. The doctor was giving RadicalGuy a 50 percent chance of survival. Then, Bigone had to fly home.

We hear nothing for months.

Then, during one of my sex shows, RadicalGuy logs in. "I'm at the Courtyard Marriott in Toronto."

When I finish work, I rush to meet him.

I knock on the door.

RadicalGuy answers the door. He is a tiny frail man with nearly translucent skin, a real life version of Mr. Burns from *The Simpsons*. His voice is a whisper, "I had to see you face-to-face, in the real world."

Since his heart surgery, he is learning to go out in public. He has a new lease on life. He says that before the anaesthetist put him under, the doctor said, "I want you to imagine the most beautiful thing you have ever seen, because this could be your very last thought." RadicalGuy says he thought of my face, the time I showed it, unaltered by digitization.

"Honey, that's the most beautiful fucking thing in the world to you? In one week I'm having a thirteen-hour reconstruction. I'm changing everything."

Seven days later in San Francisco, I lay down on an operating table. The nurse puts the gas mask to my face. I wonder, "What do you say to God if you die during plastic surgery? Which you paid for by jerking off online. And by manipulating Bigone25. Kind of."

About to fade into blackness, I think of what I mean to RadicalGuy.

We'll keep in touch. Letters in the mail. Gifts. Christmas cards.

In your mind, my male face will remain.

Beautiful.

My boy holes vanished (2001)

I'm on a six-hour drive to and through the suburbs of Detroit. In my passenger seat is one of the most beautiful and convincing transsexual girls I've ever met. Her name is Candi. I barely know her. We are in Detroit looking for Simone's house. Candi has heard about Simone at these transsexual beauty pageants she goes down to in the States. Candi doesn't have a car, and can't drive, so she asks me if I'll drive her. I know she knows I'll agree because she looks just like a real woman. She reminds me of this quite often. In our community, that means she's the alpha, and I should just be happy to be around her, to be in the presence of such realness.

I agree.

We find the address and park. We knock on a screen door. We're greeted by a beautiful woman with big bouncing breasts and an hourglass figure. Her body is so feminine, I don't realize Simone is a transsexual.

She says, "Come on in, bitches." Behind her back, Candi and I are freaking out. Simone has hips. Curves like a woman. Like a drawing of a woman. I didn't think we could ever have that. There's no plastic surgery to give us that.

Simone leads us to her bedroom. Candi's been very icy the whole car ride down, but now she's exuberant. She bounces onto Simone's bed, pulls off her top, pulls off her PVC bra, and exposes her hormone titties: a B-cup. Really cute.

Simone goes to the closet, grabs a two litre pop bottle, and pours some liquid into a glass. It's not a soft drink. It's clear. It has a thicker consistency and no bubbles. Simone goes into the nightstand and pulls out a syringe. She screws it onto an orange-coloured turkey baster canister. With one hand she pinches Candi's breast, and with the other she is pulling the contents of the glass, the silicone, into the syringe. She is injecting it directly into Candi's body. Candi's breathing Lamaze style. *(breathing)* A second syringe. *(breathing)* A third syringe. *(breathing)*

"It's getting kinda tight in there," says Candi.

Simone says, "Just one more, then, bitch, you're gonna look so fishy."

Fishy. That's what American trannies say when they mean you look like a biological female. That's something we say amongst ourselves. We mean it as a compliment. It means she looks real.

It's like this: "She's … she's … she's fishy." Work.

Candi's breasts look perfectly natural. The effect is not like a breast implant, which you can usually tell. Once inside the body, Simone can sculpt the silicone into almost any shape Candi wants. Less on top. More on the bottom. Scar tissue is going to form to hold everything into place within the next twenty-four hours.

Simone turns to me and says, "Do you want any?"

I think, "Simone is not a doctor. She's not even a nurse."

She claims to be trained by a nurse on how to do this.

I believe her. She's abrasive but she's not a liar.

She says, "It's *medical* grade silicone, bitch. It's safe. My boyfriend steals it from Dow Corning."

They roll their eyes at me when I don't want any.

At home, I search the Internet, and there are so many things that can go wrong with this. There is a small chance that the needle will hit an artery on the way into the body. If it does, the silicone will travel through your veins. Within moments, it will either hit your heart, your brain or your lungs. If it hits your brain first, you'll have a stroke. If it hits your heart first, you'll have a heart attack. If it hits your lungs, you'll drown. In silicone.

There is a photo online of a girl who's been shot up with an industrial grade of silicone, not medical grade like Simone claims to have. But how do you know for sure? It's a black market trade. The industrial stuff is like bathroom caulking. Within months, it gets hard and lumpy inside women's bodies. The woman in the pictures had to have her entire breasts amputated including the nipples. The line of scarring is a sideways "S" across her chest. There are stories of girls who've pumped mineral oil into their hips, thinking it was silicone. Mineral oil is too light, too slippery. The body can't hold it in place. It leaks down their legs, collecting in globules. It's not encased in an implant. It's enmeshed in the organic tissue. There is no real way to get it out.

I say to Candi, "Let me have Simone's number. I want to ask her some questions."

Candi says, "Girl, if you get on the phone and start asking Simone questions, she's going to cut me off." We're with our Japanese girl-friend. I won't say her name because she is sex-changed and no one knows about her. Our Japanese girl-friend says, "It doesn't matter. I have to have it. Even if it means just a few years of looking like I want to look like." Our Japanese girl-friend had a procedure where doctors shot lasers at her vocal cords to give her a high-pitched, almost cartoon-like voice, that is very beautiful and extremely feminine.

I keep driving Candi to Detroit for more silicone, because she's realer than me, and I do what she says. Each session, her breasts get a little bigger. You have to do it in increments. Fuck that bitch. The whole car ride home she's looking down her own shirt, saying, "Gorgeous! Girl, this bitch really knows what she's doing."

I tell her that I could love breast implants. As a transsexual woman, I could learn to believe that breast implants are my breasts, but having no hips makes me feel so manly when I look in the mirror, every day. She's very encouraging for me to get pumped with a little bit of silicone.

I could just put the minimum amount of silicone there so I could live with myself. So I could look at myself.

I do nothing.

For six months.

I want to see what will happen to Candi.

She is flawless. Two perfectly shaped D-cup breasts on a tiny frame. God damn it, bitch. Those are fishy.

Me, Candi and our Japanese girl-friend rent a motel room near the border. Simone doesn't want to do it at home anymore just in case the cops are watching. When we get down there Candi doesn't chip in for the room or gas. She says her job is to contact Simone. She has the number. That is her contribution, and she guards the cell phone so we can't steal the number from her.

When Simone arrives at the hotel, our Japanese girl-friend is going to go first. Even though she already looks exactly like a female, she is injecting the silicone into her cheeks and lips. She believes that true beauty is fake and too perfect and slightly inhuman. For 200 dollars, a few drops of silicone, she is morphing before our eyes into a new person, one who kind of looks like a beautiful living Japanimation.

Which is what she wants.

Candi is looking at our Japanese girl-friend like she's crazy. Candi won't say anything though, because today and every time we come down here, Candi will get her breasts pumped for free, because she has brought two new paying clients to Simone. Also, Candi is winning transsexual beauty pageants in the States now. In the transsexual world, she is one of the legendary beauties of our generation. Simone wants to tell people that Candi is her creation, and use her as a walking advertisement for the sale of silicone realness to transsexuals.

It's my turn to go next. I lay down on the bed.

Candi holds my hand for support. She says, "Listen to me, Miss Thing, it's going to hurt for a moment. Then it's going to look beautiful for a very long time. Do you understand?"

Yes, I do.

The needle only stings a bit going in, but when the silicone is flooding into my hips I can feel the muscle being stretched. Almost torn.

(breathing Lamaze style) Candi? Candi!

I look back. My boy-holes––that's what we call the little indentations men have between their hips and ass–are disappearing. *(breathing with greater vigour)*

Eighteen syringes on each side. That's the maximum Simone would pump in the first session.

My Japanese girl-friend is holding the bottle of silicone up to the light. She says, "It's clear. It's sparkly. We love it."

Simone is molding me. She tells me to stay on my stomach for twenty-four hours while everything gets locked into place. "I know you wanna be all fishy, but stand up to pee for a couple of days, bitch, or else you'll have a toilet seat ring pressed into your ass. I ain't coming back to pump that out."

We say goodbye to Simone, knowing we've just done something dangerous together, something illegal, something beautiful.

"Bye, Simone. We're silicone sisters, girl!"

"Yeah, bye, bitches."

She leaves with thousands of dollars from me.

We'll see her again.

After she goes, we talk about what it's going to like when other transsexuals see what we've done. Candi tells us we have to deny everything. She wants to tell everyone she's just lucky enough from hormones and nature to have these two perfectly shaped, double-D breasts.

Then, we see that the silicone wants to leak back out the injection holes. It's under so much pressure. We know this is going to happen. We've done our research. So our Japanese girl-friend goes to our kit. She grabs the super glue, the cotton balls and the bandages. She dabs a little bit of super glue on each of the cotton balls. She puts that over each of the injection holes. She puts a bandage over each one to hold it on. I say, "Honey, don't let any of the silicone escape."

Then, Candi says, "Girl, if either of you two talks about the silicone, I'll cut you off."

She crosses the room, tucks her cell phone under her pillow, rolls over and pretends to sleep. I look over at my Japanese friend. We make eye contact. We are thinking the same thing: she's not really sleeping. She can't look us in the eyes after she said that about the silicone.

I am wide awake. I'm lying in the hotel bed next to Candi, pretending to sleep. I know I'll talk honestly about it when I'm all done. I will not be ashamed that I have silicone body parts, but, honestly I am not exactly sure what will happen to our bodies in ten or twenty or thirty years.

What I do know is that we have put it all on the line for who we had to be, and that means what we had to look like.

There will be no going back.

I am my own self-portrait (2004)

I am just looking in the mirror one day, like I do every day. In my reflection, I see a three-pound weave. I've been weaving my hair for about six months. People say, "Don't do that. Don't do that. You won't look like a real woman if you do that. You'll look like a drag queen if you do that."

But when I got this weave, it made me feel my breath drop. That same feeling you get in a car accident, the drop in your stomach, except I was not in a car accident, I was walking away from the burning car wreckage in a highly stylized, Technicolor, music video.

That's what it feels like to have all of this hair on my head. I am never going back to my real hair.

Today, I am calm as I sit at my hypermodern, see-through, plastic vanity table. Over my left shoulder is naked Aphrodite, the Greek goddess of love and beauty. She is a three-foot-by-four-foot painting of a Renaissance masterwork, an imitation of a Renaissance masterwork of natural beauty, supernatural beauty, which I've hung worshipfully in the centre of my tiny bachelorette apartment. No doubt it is painted by a man. I like to remember that the ancient priests of Aphrodite ritually castrated themselves in honour of their goddess, and worked as temple whores.

I'm just looking at myself in the mirror, like I do every day. Different angles. Inspections. This is the most my face will ever look like a natural woman. I fool some people, some of the time. For a moment. In good lighting. A few parts look plastic. Tastefully plastic. Respectably plastic. Plastic like a TV anchorwoman looks plastic. But the jaw line, the brow bone, the nostril size, the cheek-to-chin ratio, the down-turned nose …

It's not enough.

It has to be enough. You have to accept yourself. You have to accept your body. Just be proud. Be a proud transgendered woman.

I'm reaching for my professional aesthetics tweezers. I've had them imported from Iceland. They are capable of getting even the tiniest, finest, white, invisible hairs. I'm not only interested in the perfect shape of the perfect brow. I'm interested in the annihilation of the presence of even the most invisible hairs. I turn to the window so the sunlight can glint off the hair shafts. When I'm about to pluck, if I think of pain I think of geishas. Trained from a young age for beauty. If I have a hair on my upper lip, I think of African women and lip disks. I know nothing about them, but, my Goddess, the sacrifice.

Next on my face is a layer of moisture. Crème de la Mer, which apparently is made from a six-month-long process, developed by a NASA scientist where ions are shots through collagen and seaweed. Work! I like that marketing. My skin tone is soft. The estrogen is working.

Next on my face, foundation in little dabs. Smoothing that out. My face looks flat, like a doll, a clay doll, so I add colour to it. Three different tones of blush: a melba, a red and a pink. Paler cheek highlights.

I draw a dark line where my red lip meets white skin. Inside that line, I like to do another paler line. Inside that, I put lots of lip gloss. People say, "Don't do that. Don't do that. You won't look like a real woman if you do that. You'll look like a drag queen."

I'm just looking in the mirror, like I do every day. This is the most I will ever look like a normal, natural woman.

It's not enough.

It has to be enough. The quest has to end eventually. One has to be reasonable, right? Reasonable. Reasonable enough to accept this life.

In the mirror, I am drawing the black liquid liner over my eye, like I do every day. At the corner of the eye, a flick that gets bigger all the time.

I'm just looking in the mirror, when Mom calls to say "Nina, Dad and I saw this documentary on TV last night, and there were these two transsexuals. Well, the one, she had her make-up and hair done very tasteful. Just like a real woman. And, well, the other one, well, she looked like a whore."

The eyelash glue was drying on two 66 millimeter false lashes that I had imported from Japan. They are made by a Japanese master who has made nothing but false lashes for the last 80 years.

My mom says, "Nina, when you do your make-up to go out, tell me, you don't do your make-up like a whore, do you?"

"Mom, yes, I do. A very high-priced, beautiful one. Mom, I can't have this conversation right now."

I have another call coming through. A long distance call. Coming from Mexico.

I'm looking at myself in the mirror as I'm changing phone lines. In my reflection, Aphrodite is bursting from my head.

I pick up the phone and say, "Hello? Oh, hey, Nancy. How ya doin', Mami? Listen, when I come down to Mexico for my "orchi," I want Dr. Arias to do some other stuff as well."

"Orchi" is a name we use for the surgical castration of our testicles. It's technically called an orchiectomy. To get through the gruesomeness of it, to get through the pain, we give it a cute name. We call it "orchi". I'm nervous that after my "orchi" I'll be unlike anyone I've ever known, a woman with a dick but no balls, but by removing my body's testosterone-producing parts, I will be doing everything possible to have the most beautiful skin I can achieve.

I say into the phone, "Yeah, Nancy, when I come down to Mexico for my 'orchi,' I want Dr. Arias to do some other stuff as well."

I just catch my reflection in the mirror. Thoughts are going through my head. Thoughts that go through my head all the time. Just do it. Be empowered. Go down to Mexico where the doctors will do stuff to your body that they won't do up here. You don't want to look at your face for the inspection of male flaws. You don't want to be cute. You don't want to be passable. You want to be beautiful. You want lights. You want photo shoots. You want hot, fucking, smutty, porn sex that looks like a video shoot.

On an interior screen in my mind's eye, I'm visualizing. I believe in the power of visualization. I see an image of me so clearly. The way the light is hitting me. Just right.

On the dance floor of a nightclub. I'm an angel. Maybe I'm a demon. I don't know. I'm going to be the fiercest tranny at the nightclub.

I'm visualizing straight guys. Tattoos. Biceps. Fucking scary guys. Nina, your spiritual journey wants to take you through all of this. If you don't get it, you will be stuck at this layer of development.

Aphrodite above your head. That is a sign. If you cannot look like a normal woman, sacrifice being normal. I will be plastic. I will think of geisha. Stylized abstractions of beauty. Shuffling through the world. I love them. Nina, give yourself permission to be fabulous instead of reasonable. Really fucking fabulous. Every fucking day.

"Nancy, I've thought it over calmly. I want Dr. Arias to give me not a woman's nose. I want a nose like a Barbie doll, girl. Pull the eyebrows tight. Underline that. Extreme Extreme. Extreme. Jaw shaving. I want to put silicone in my face when I get down there, girl. I want you to handle that personally, so it's done properly. Yes, more in the hips and ass, too. You get it. Make me plastic. Make me beautiful. Thank you, Nancy."

After I get off that phone call, I'm just looking at myself in the mirror, looking at my over-the-top, unreal weave. It is giving me permission to go to Mexico and to get artistic with my body.

Me 'n' Tommy Lee (2006)

One night, before heading to Ultra Supper Club, I pop an Ativan. Ativan's a mild tranquilizer, less than a Valium. It takes away my anxiety, but also some inhibitions wash away too. I give into a primal urge to tease my hair up with a magnificence usually reserved for porn stars and Vegas showgirls. I paint my eyeliner so intricately.

What a gorgeous pill.

As I glide into Ultra Supper Club, the restaurant manager, Neil, leads me by the hand, passing a line-up of over-the-top, skeleton-thin, silicone-enhanced women. Lots of extensions. Lots of rocker chicks.

Neil says, "Ugh! All wannabe star-fuckers. Here for the biggest-dicked rocker in the world."

He sweeps me to a seat on one side of the restaurant, directly facing, on the other side of the restaurant, what looks to me like former Motley Crue drummer and reality TV star, Tommy Lee. Tommy is seated behind a twinkling, translucent curtain. That curtain gives him a sparkling aura. Or maybe that's my drugs. Or maybe that's celebrity.

Neil pulls out my chair and compliments the shimmery grey slacks that I am wearing— they are skin-tight to my hips and ass—and a low-riding, latex, black tube top that hangs off the top of my new boob job, very swollen at the time. Neil says, "Darling, tonight, your ensemble could be a classed-up version of Pamela Anderson's wardrobe from the movie *Barb Wire*." Right then, I know that Tommy Lee is real, because that's the punch line of Neil's joke: Tommy Lee used to be married to Pam, and I take the reference to Ms. Anderson as a compliment. She is the ultimate silicone sex symbol of all time, and I'd say she was the Marilyn Monroe of the '90s.

Neil offers me sparkling water.

High, I reply, "Sparkling wine would be lovely. Thank you very much."

The Ativan mingles with the champagne. All of a sudden, I am happy. In fact, I am radiating a child-like, innocent joy and confidence that only a careful combination of dissociative drugs can give you. I know that I've created quite a stir, that all eyes in the restaurant are locking onto me, but I have Ativan-reinforced self-esteem. Nothing gets through that. Because I'm not wrapped up in my own self consciousness, I can see, upon closer inspection, that most of the women here purposefully trying to catch Tommy's attention are poorly painted and half-dressed, with all the class of off-duty Hooters waitresses. I usually don't let myself judge people like that, but the Ativan has really lowered my inhibitions. I drink in their stares with a smile, and chase them down with another glass of champagne.

I'm radiant. My inner calmness is a light that is filling a room full of women posing nervously, and I'm visualizing on my interior screen, in my mind's eye, that Tommy Lee can't take his eyes off me. Even though I never look over at him. Not even once. Believing it so easily. The way a child believes. It's already happened, the way I am seeing it.

A man comes to the table, saying he's Tommy's associate, and tells me that the rock star wants to meet.

I say, "I'm in the middle of dinner," referring to untouched salmon and grilled vegetables, having a little bit more champagne. I am not a disposable, fart-catching bimbo for a rock star who's claimed to have had slept with "a *lot* more than a thousand women." That's one of his Wikipedia quotes! He's slept with "a *lot* more than a thousand women." "*Lot*" is in italics.

But after his man leaves, I think, Tommy Lee has an employee pick up his chicks. It's fabulous. He never has to face rejection.

The employee didn't even know I'm a transsexual. Maybe just having enough confidence to feel that I belong, drug-induced or not, makes me belong. I'm thinking about the power of that, the entire time visualizing on the interior screen in my mind's eye that my rejection of Tommy Lee has made me all the more attractive to him. Before I know it, his representative is at my table again, saying, "No, no, no, no, no, no, no. Tommy *really* wants to meet you. He thinks that you are fabulous."

I think, Nina, you cannot cut yourself off from everything life has to offer just because you're afraid people will reject you for being a transsexual. Besides, it's a huge ego boost to be hand-picked out of a pack of posing, real women. Many of whom are very beautiful, upon second glance, despite what I consider very incorrect, low-class, trashy fashion. But I get it. Straight men often find low-class women very enticing for a night.

I stand.

The women scoff at me. It's like I can see their thoughts on their faces.

"Why her?"

"That fake plastic bitch?"

"That's a man!"

I shade these Tommy Lee-rejects with a downwards cast of my extra long lashes at the forty-five-degree angle, which everyone knows is the shadiest angle possible, and by flipping my head to the side, knowing that the four bags of fake twenty-eight-inch-long hair extensions look positively pornographic as they cascade through the air to bounce off my glowing, tanning-cream-bronzed shoulder. I see the moment as if I am outside myself. As if I am watching a slow motion snippet from a movie. I'm the star of the movie now.

A powerful feeling of fierceness is coursing through me as I walk towards a man who was married to one of the most revered sex symbols of all time. On the way over, I dare to compare myself to *the* Ms. Pamela Anderson. Kohl-ringed eyes, teased hair, enormous breast implants, and a trademark teeth-together-lips-apart lusty expression of come-hither-ness. She is a caricature of a woman. Tonight I am a caricature of her. An imitation of an imitation of an idea of a woman. An image which has never existed in nature, but singled out as the shining beauty in the room.

I can't believe this is happening to me. I'm the person who was always told she would never be accepted as a woman.

I'm slipping behind the glimmering, semi-opaque drapes that divide the common dining area from the celebrity VIP section where Tommy Lee and his entourage are seated. I think, "I'm fierce enough to do it. I can make Tommy Lee fall for me." I will drop a powerful feeling of belonging deep inside of me, and he will see how truly fabulous I really am.

I approach boldly. I crouch low, next to Tommy's chair, and shake his hand, a little trick I learned at the tranny strip club where I work. It combines the flattering angle of looking upwards into the man's face with the mental suggestion that you could at any moment give him a blowjob, right there in front of everybody. I like to offset the sleaze factor of this position by smiling sweetly, and by looking up into the scintillating light of an overhead, dangling chandelier, knowing that it will make my make-up sparkle at just the right angle.

Yes, I think all these thoughts around a man I want to seduce.

Tommy says, "Whhoooooaaaaa. You are extraordinarily beautiful."

Ex-tra-or-din-ar-i-ly. It's a seven-syllable word. My beauty inspires Tommy Lee to use a seven-syllable word.

He looks better in person than on TV. I don't want to think he's Botoxing. I'm seeing everything through the haze of a champagne-Ativan cocktail. He looks just like one of my ex-boyfriends. We're making a bit of small talk. Fuck, we're getting along so well. My confidence amplifies my sex appeal by a factor of ten.

Now, Tommy is looking at me with a look in his eye that says, "Wait a minute. Is she …? Is that …? Is …?"

I drop in a powerful feeling of complete and total belonging and maintain eye contact. It smoothes the whole moment over.

He asks me if I want to do drinks.

I say, "Yeah, let's do shots of tequila."

They're at the table like *that*, 'cause when you're Tommy Lee, that's how fast your tequila gets to the table.

I throw mine back.

Tommy chokes on his: "Ghack!"

He says he's been drinking since 7 a.m. about fifteen hours ago now. I'm a little bit disappointed that a guy who has apparently snorted his own band mate's piss can't throw back a shot of Cuervo. I'm also disappointed to see him eating something like that looks like a deconstructed serving of pâté, decorated with a delicate array of Asian greenery. Hardly what I consider rock star food.

I guess a lot of us have a public image out there that does not encapsulate the complexity of who we really are. But I still say, "You're a fucking pussy!"

Tommy says, "Someone get this girl a chair."

Members of his entourage are looking around the VIP section for a chair.

I am not going to act star-struck. I will portray a ballsy, glamour-puss-type of chick, the kind of chick who talks fast and parties hard: exactly the kind of fantasy of a woman I imagine Tommy Lee could fall for. I will make her so real.

When an extra chair can't be found, Tommy invites me to share his. There's not enough room on that chair for Tommy and for my hips and ass.

I can't believe how well things are going between us. It's hard to remember that your actions have consequences when you're this excited, when you're drinking, when you're popping dissociative pills … and I do something I never do.

I ease myself onto the unwitting lap—I don't know what he knew—of Tommy Lee. On the surface I'm totally cool because of the Ativan. Inside, inside, inside … I'm freaking out.

He asks me what I do for a living.

"I'm an exotic dancer." I don't mention that it's a strip club for trannies.

He wraps his arms around me in a tight embrace. He gives me a double "thumbs up" and goes, "Aaaaaaaaiiiiiieeeeeeeee!"

He pulls me into him, and he pushes up into me. The base of Tommy's dick. There's so much dick down there. I can feel it. I can feel all that dick. I'm drunk on male attention when I'm sitting on that much dick.

Time seems to stop.

On the interior screen, in my mind's eye, a life with me and Tommy Lee is flashing by. First we go back to his hotel room and we fuck like animals all night long, recording everything on his camcorder. The footage leaks to online celebrity blog sites like *perezhilton.com* and *TMZ.com*. Two days later, on *Entertainment Tonight*, Mary Hart's eyes are filling with tears of joy as Tommy defends the film and declares, "I love her." They have paparazzi night-vision video footage of Tommy and me, in and out of L.A. nightclubs. Pamela Anderson is on his one arm. I'm on the other. The soundtrack is Tommy's old hit *Girls, Girls, Girls*. No one thinks it's ironic. When they slow the footage down, you can see right into my eyes. You can see what I'm thinking. I'm thinking, "I love you, Tommy. Because you love me. I love what that must mean about my beauty."

It's getting harder to believe in this fantasy.

Back at Ultra Supper Club, I can see a member of Tommy's entourage mouthing the words, "That's a guy! That's a fucking guy!" The guy beside him is going, "How did we let this happen? How did this happen?" Each man whispers to the next. The news is travelling around the table. A countdown is ticking in my head. Ten, nine, eight, seven seconds until he finds out I have a dick, six, five, four. As each second goes by I shrink a little bit. Three, two, one.

When the news is whispered into Tommy's ear, he looks every part of me up and down. Feet, knees, hips, waist, tits, shoulders, Adam's apple, hair, and he stares directly into my face for what feels like an eternity. I don't know what to do, so I do this. *(gesturing a flower blossoming from her face with her hands)* A light-hearted gesture that I am hoping will suggest, in the softest possible way, "Surprise."

Tommy goes, "Woooaaaaaaaaaaaaaah! You really *are* beautiful …"

I don't know if the subtext at the end of his sentence is "… for a man" or if he just likes the way I worked the whole encounter.

That brings me completely back together on his lap. I don't want to be made to feel less beautiful because I was born into a male body, or because I have fake parts. Everything that attracted you to me in the first place, Tommy Lee—synthetic hair, make-up, silicone, attitude, radiance—I don't have to be born a biological woman to have these things, and I want you to get that it is these things that give you the physiological feeling of a hard on.

Maybe he gets it, because Tommy does this *(shaking head, shaking head again, shaking head a third time, shoulders dropping, breath dropping, then double thumbs up, smiling)* and says, "I need a cigarette."

Then, he slips out from under me, and he's out of the VIP section.

I steal one more glass of champagne off his table before that sea of jealous bitches can come for me, and I escape Ultra.

The patron saint of plastic surgery (2001–2006)

Nancy Bianca Valentino meets me at the airport when I go down to Mexico for my first breast enhancement and rib reshaping in 2001. Nancy is the chain-smoking, Puerto Rican transsexual who connects North American transsexuals with safe, affordable surgical procedures in Guadalajara. It's much cheaper there. The first time I see her she is wearing a shimmery fuchsia and chartreuse asymmetrical, one-sleeved, batwing top—really major— Dolce and Gabbana jeans, cheetah-print heels and glittery jewelry everywhere. Slicked back peroxided hair. Nancy looks like a woman. The most surgically altered woman I have ever seen in my life. Nancy makes the Jacksons look conservative. The bridge of that nose is so razor sharp, it looks like you could grate cheese off it. A customized chin implant so pointed that I wonder "Do you ever poke yourself with that thing?" And her tautly pulled, face-lifted face reveals none of the love she has in her heart for those she helps. I heard a rumour before

I got down here that Nancy was sixty years old. I can't believe it. That face is so tight. But when she turns to walk me to the car waiting in the airport parking lot, she clomps on her cheetah-print heels like a woman much older than her face betrays.

She takes me directly from the airport to the operating theatre. She introduces me to the gorgeous Dr. Arias. He's a brilliant plastic surgeon, but he only speaks Spanish. Nancy translates my surgical needs to Dr. Arias.

By the way, Dr. Arias looks like a Latin soap star on steroids. I say, "Honey, just tell him to turn me into whatever he likes to fuck. That's what I want to be." She gets the nuances of that.

We're hitting it off right away. She stays as I wait to be put under in the operating room. I think that's because it's scary when I'm down here alone with everyone talking a language I don't understand. An anaesthetic IV needle is going into my arm. I look over. Nancy is at the side of the room scrubbing down, putting on latex surgical gloves. Her face does not move, but her eyes are alive and dancing. She turns and looks at me over her shoulder and says, "Mami, I like to give Arias notes during the operation. I'm the one who knows where to file the bones down. I know where to take the cartilage out. Mami, I don't play. Give me a girl, and I'll scrape the man right off her face."

From the operating table I say, "Work, Mami."

Finally someone who's not going to play with my procedures.

After the operation, Nancy is there to cook and care for me in a modest Mexican apartment where all of the doctor's transsexual patients recover together. We all sleep in the same room. One of the other girls asks, "So what do y'all do for a living? How did y'all afford your surgeries?"

"Oh, honey, don't give that show. You're a whore, too, darlin'. I can smell it on ya'. We all are."

Nancy pulls a painting of The Virgin of Guadalupe—the Holy Madonna, Mexico's version of her—off the wall to show us how the Mother of God's silhouette has been inscribed onto the clay wall with a water stain behind the image in the same shape as the painting . My first thought is, all those folds of fabric and that radiance reduced to a line drawing look like a big shining vagina on the wall.

Nancy says, "This proves the Holy Madonna watches over us whores as we heal."

In the room are statues, idols of Catholic martyrs that Nancy has placed between the beds. At their bases are offerings of money, decaying fruit and this incense that I love but the other girls can't stand. The rumour amidst the girls is that Nancy has lost her sense of smell due to all of her nose jobs.

That rumour might be true, because one day Nancy goes out and gets us a pillow case full of marijuana. All the girls are taking these powerful hormone shots you can get in Mexico to make our breasts bigger. Everyone is getting very moody, though. We're getting into a lot of arguments. Dr. Arias worries that if we aren't having good experiences, we'll go back to North America and talk shit, and the money won't keep rolling in.

We lie around smoking Mexican marijuana—doctors' orders. The girl next to me has bandages over her nose. My breasts are bound. Nancy tells us how she made her nose smaller, made it smaller again, made it smaller a third time, scooped it out like a ski jump, put an implant in there to make it more pointed, made the nostrils into little triangles, like Janet Jackson. It could change season to season, depending on what Mexican actress she was obsessed with.

I love Nancy. She's regal, like a queen, and she validates every desire that she has.

She gets whatever surgical procedures she wants for free because she brings so many surgery-hungry girls to Guadalajara. She also stays awake during cosmetic surgery. Arias will work on her nose under local anaesthetic, put it all back into place, put a hand mirror in her hand and she will give him directions mid-procedure.

One night, I wake up in the middle of the night. I see Nancy in the moonlight praying to her beloved martyrs, head bowed. Her back is to me, but I know she is crying. Tiny tremors are rolling down her spine. A Marlboro cigarette in her hand burns to a stub without her taking a single haul on it.

In the morning I say, "What's wrong, Mami?" She confides to me that she didn't like her silicone injections in her hips. The guy who was pumping her kept telling her, "You don't look like a woman yet. That's not feminine enough." That fucked with her head because she trusted him. It's very easy for a woman to look in the mirror and not know what is exactly there, especially when it is changing. When she saw a photograph of herself though, she realized he'd pumped two square blocks of silicone on her hips.

She lived with that for years until she found another doctor down in Mexico (not Arias, someone else). He knew how to open her up here, here and here *(referring to the side of the hip, under the buttocks and mid-thigh)*. He went in and scraped out the silicone from inside her muscles and fatty tissue. He brought the entire volume down, but that left her entire hips and ass dimpled and rippled with scar tissue. Nancy couldn't stand that. When she pumped out the ripples, the person who sold her the liquid silicone mixed it with water to make it look like he was giving her twice as much silicone for half as much money. The watered-down concoction looked like two massive boils that covered her entire hips and buttocks. It was horrific to look at, and I'm sure quite painful for her when she sat down. North American doctors refused to even try to help her. In Mexico they couldn't agree on what she should do.

Obviously, it wounds her a little bit every time she helps another transsexual attain gorgeous cosmetic results. Some girls were leaving Dr. Arias' operating theatre looking like beauty queens. He's a genius, and she's tortured by her own disfigurements. Praying to martyrs in the moonlight.

Years later, in 2006, I go back down for my final surgical refinements: a millimeter here, a millimeter there. A millimeter here. A millimeter there. Subtle changes that will create a big overall effect. Nancy is giving Arias notes during the procedure. She knows how to do it.

As I wake, she is by the bed and says, "Mami, I'm very pleased for how beautiful you will become. When I think of where you started …" *(as Nancy, bowing slightly)*.

She also tells me that she's started repairing the damage her body has sustained. She's found a woman doctor who is tapping out the silicone-water boil from her hips similar to how a how a tree is tapped of maple syrup. It is experimental, but it is working. They will have to do it in increments. The problem is that the anaesthetist is having trouble reviving her after surgery. Maybe because she's been under so many times.

They told her if she went under again she might not come up. "Mami, they're not playing."

When Dr. Arias or anyone else refuses to work on her anymore, Nancy gives her free surgeries to these transsexual girls who are working in a brothel giving blowjobs for *pesos* a night to survive as transsexuals in Guadalajara. These girls would never have been able to afford surgery. Nancy makes sure they get their breasts done so they can feel more like women. They can also earn more money now.

Back in Toronto, I get a phone call from Chicago. I assume it's Nancy, 'cause she lives there part-time.

It's this other girl, who says that Nancy died due to complications of surgery that she had been warned about, but which she felt she could not live without.

I say, "She will always be remembered. She helped hundreds, maybe thousands, of girls who just wanted to be comfortable with the bodies that nature gave them."

Then, the girl on the other end of the line says, "Well, we all knew Nancy was a plastic surgery addict."

I get off the phone.

I think about that.

Some girls just want to be comfortable, and once they get started, some girls want to be as beautiful as they can be. Nancy and I have shared a passion for beauty and femininity that is far greater than that.

To reduce a full, fabulous life to a single word, "addict", is wrong.

I get down on the floor of my apartment.

I promise that I will do everything I can to stay mentally healthy.

I pray that the spirit of Nancy Bianca Valentino has moved to a place without her wounded physical body.

I hope you have found the peace that you so absolutely deserve, Mami.

Venus/machine (2007–2009)

After all my cosmetic surgery my body feels stiff and rigid. I'm wracked with tension. I feel like I'm posing all the time. I don't think my body knew I wanted to have all these procedures. I think my body thought I was getting into car accidents over and over. I know it wasn't mentally healthy to have sex with so many men, one after another, in such a short time. I know it was fucking me up. But I was not going to be reasonable. I'm very happy I was not reasonable. I'm also very angry about the two hours a day I need to get ready. I've built a perfection onto my face that needs make-up and hairstyles to complete it, or else I'm not aesthetically cohesive in my own vision.

At this point in my life, I buy an exercise bike because I think this will be the next phase of my work with my body. I will keep all of this fresh and young. I've never exercised before because I always associated sports with masculinity, and I've always been very thin.

One day, I pop a caffeine pill. Five minutes after I am on the bike, I can feel my breath release from my sternum. I can feel the air moving into my back ribs. It's like I can feel the air touching the bones. It's like there's two little Cupid's wings back there. Every time I pedal, they flap. That brings more breath into my body. Ten minutes after I'm on the hill cycle, the angel wings have grown to my entire arm span. I don't know. Maybe they're demon wings. Every time they unfold outwards, they pull my ribs with them. That brings more breath into me. Twenty-five minutes into the workout, there is stuff happening in this part of my body *(referring to pelvis area, hips, genitals)* that I have never felt before. I can feel my pulse in my fingertips. I can feel the blood rushing through my veins. I can hear my heart beating in my temples. I can feel my heart pounding against my left breast implant.

Of course. This is the next phase of my work with my body. To get out of my head. To get out of the idea that I am an image to be posed from the outside. I will get inside the sensations on the inside.

Too many anxieties? Get on the bike.

Insecure? Get on the bike.

Hunting for male approval? Get on the bike.

Get on the bike. Get on the bike. Get on the bike. Get on the bike. Get on the bike. Get on the bike. Get on the bike.

It becomes my mantra.

I name the bike. Beelzebub. Every day I will get up on it and ride out my demons. It has two horns that come up—handlebars. I like to think I am grabbing the devil by the horns.

My therapist loves this. She is a Buddhist. She tells me that she believes that in the moments of pain and suffering in our lives, that the breath wants to constrict, and if we let that happen we can lock the pain right into our muscle tissue, into the fat, into the bones. She says we have to breathe through these moments to unlock the pain.

I say, "Of course, this is the next phase of my work with my body. To breathe through the trauma I have put inside my body."

I get back up on the bike.

I notice very quickly that music takes on an entirely new dimension on the bike. I hear things in the songs I have never heard before. They make me feel things I have never felt before. Sometimes unpleasant things. I can feel that the breath wants to constrict in this moment, but it can't. I'm struggling to get over the next hill cycle. This physiologically just keeps the breath open.

Now I am intentionally working with this technique. Putting on music that upsets me and breathing through. Breathing through the pain. I can heal myself.

I don't work out with my wigs on, obviously. My real hair is in cornrows. That's how I secure my wigs. I put bobby pins through the cornrows and through the wigs. Nothing shakes that off. But because I am working out so much, the cornrows are nappy from the sweat. They are dreadlocks braided on my skull. I can't even look at that. They are so aesthetically offensive to my sensibilities.

I cut them off. I have no choice. I shave my head.

(removing wigs, dropping them onto the floor)

The woman in the mirror looks like no woman I have ever seen before.

This will be the next phase of my work with my body. To accept the me underneath all the glamour. The unreal cyborg I have constructed.

I get back up on the bike, because I know the positive feelings that come from working out, the endorphins that go through me, with repetition will attach to the image in the full length mirror in front of me. I will reprogram myself to love myself. I will learn to love the scars that have constructed my face. I will accept them the way some women have learned to accept their wrinkles.

I get on the bike every day.

One day, I work out harder than I ever have before. My breath is deep down low inside me. On the pelvic floor. I can feel the breath caressing the genitals. Oh, it feels so good. I am dancing on top the bike as much as I am pedaling on top the bike. Oh, yes, it feels so good. Oh fuck, it feels so fucking good. I am breathing more deeply than I ever have before.

There is a tiny pocket of pink flesh inside me where my vagina should have been. The area is throbbing with energy.

I'm not an object. I'm not an image. There's a woman in here. There's a human animal inside this body.

I'm making eye contact with the woman in the mirror. Beneath the mask of my face she has the eyes of a snake.

I get back on the bike.

One day, I work out so long, so hard, that I reach a state of such inner calmness that I have pedaled past all of my chaotic thoughts this day. I have no fears for the future. No worries from the past. I am just in a room with four walls under the painting of Aphrodite. My wigs are on the floor, tangled and distressed from nightclubbing the night before. From the smoke and sweat. This usually annoys me, but they are beautiful.

Of course, this is the next step in the journey. To surrender to the beauty of whatever the moment is. Every moment has its own beauty. That is enough. Accept the moment.

I keep pedaling.

One day, I am looking in the mirror. I wondered how much the bike was changing my body. I never know how much I can trust the mirror, but there is no denying it anymore. Because I don't have testosterone, I didn't gain muscle but I have become noticeably thinner. My stomach is flat. The human parts of me are gaunt and the silicone parts of me have stayed pumped. My arms and legs are almost anorexic-like.

This will be the most I will ever look like a mannequin.

I accept this moment. I think of geisha. Trained from a young age for beauty. I love them. I am them.

I get back onto the bike.

One day, I work out to such a point of exhaustion on the bike that I allow myself to go into the moment, into sensation, into only what I am seeing and hearing around me. I have reached a place of almost no rational thought. I touch a Zen-like place of just breath moving through me. I release the weight of my head, allow it to drop. My room is dark. Lit only with candles and the vibrating blue display of my computer as it plays electronic music.

Underneath me, the shadow of the bike becomes a horned demon I am straddling. The demon's face is a glowing red face that stares back at me with changing computerized digits and schematics of moving dots that reconfigure into new formulations.

I stretch through my back and neck. I don't feel myself pedaling anymore. I recline inside the exhaustion of the workout. I can go on forever.

I look into the mirror, and my body is the body of a giant serpent. I see the serpent in a spiral. I see the breath moving through the spiral. Glittering scales. The skin shedding off the snake.

It unfolds.

In my mind's eye, I see the next phase of my body.

There will be the signs of aging on my body. There will be facelifts, resurfacing, the ways I honour aging with make-up.

There will be the spiritual pursuits, the meditations, the therapy, the art-making that allows me to deal with aging.

It will make my life better. It will make me a better person.

The next phase is to be reasonable.

To be rational.

To accept the moment as it is happening.

To accept that my pleasure and my sublime privilege is to suffer.

And to live.

With. Beauty.

The End

PART III

THE PHOTOGRAPHS

Image Credits

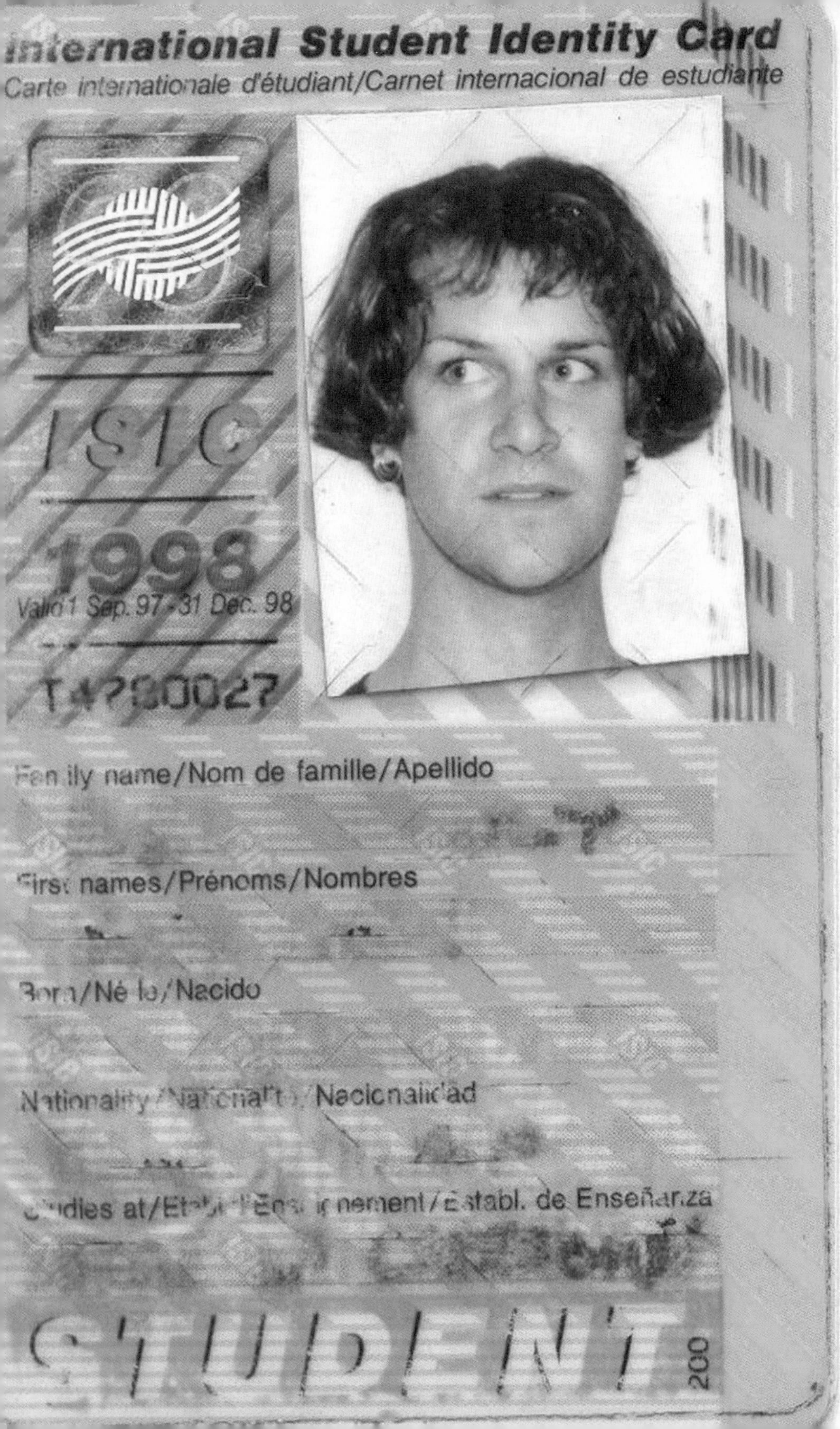
International Student Identity Card
Carte internationale d'étudiant/Carnet internacional de estudiante

ISIC

1998
Valid 1 Sep. 97 - 31 Dec. 98

T4780027

Family name/Nom de famille/Apellido

First names/Prénoms/Nombres

Born/Né le/Nacido

Nationality/Nationalité/Nacionalidad

Studies at/Etabl. d'Enseignement/Establ. de Enseñanza

STUDENT

200

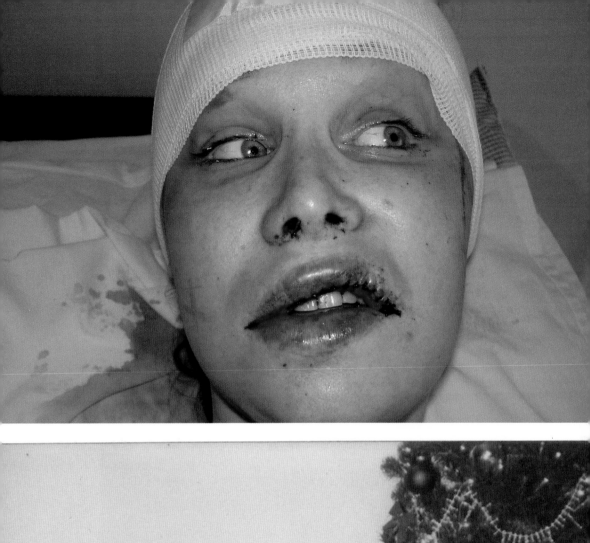

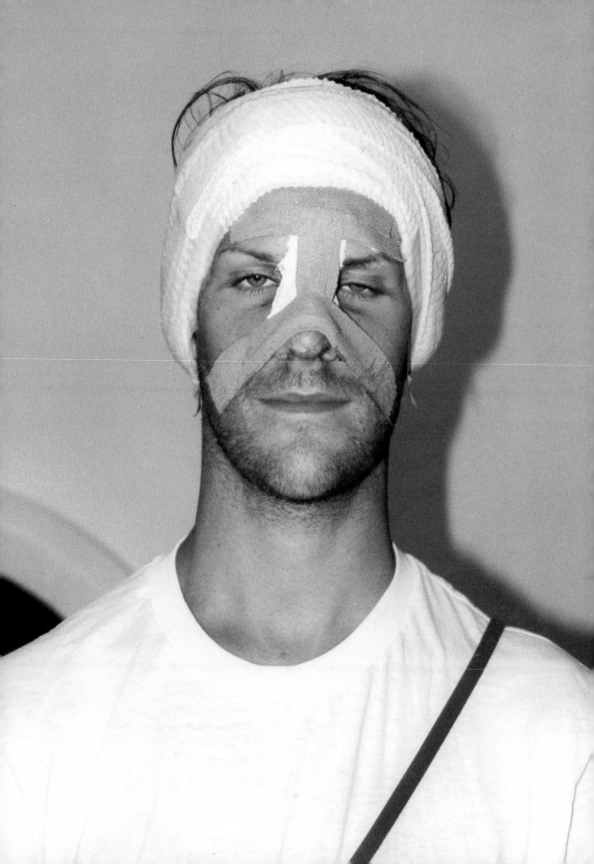

→ full nude shot → the last one
before anything permanent was
changed

in dialogue

↑

should / [feet / body] all give as different things
hands / give and take
neuralgic

chewing → breed into two groups
lower / louder exercise
w / a genie → groove spine
13

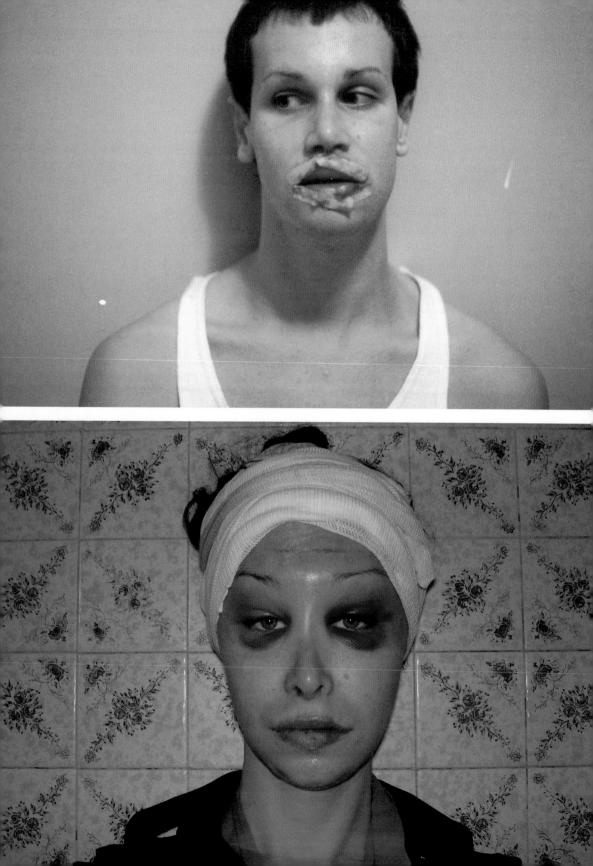

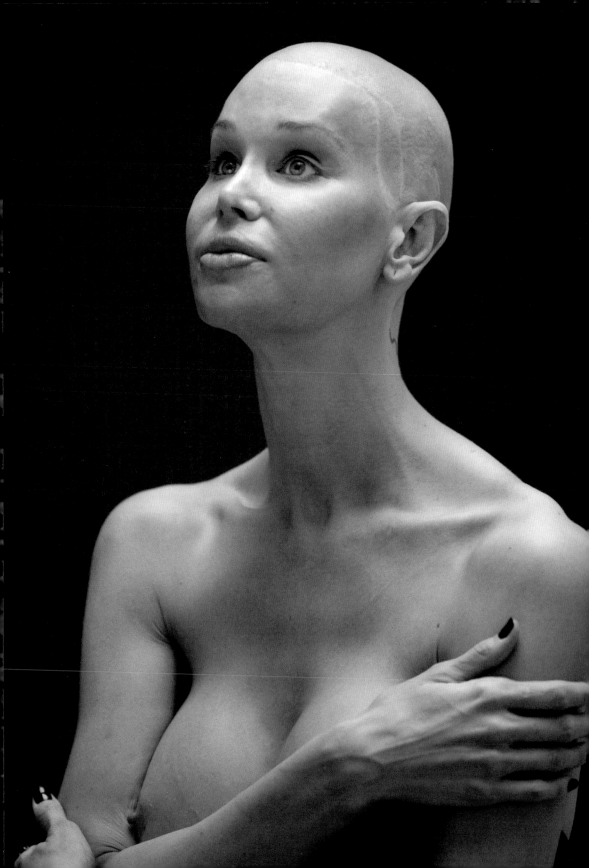

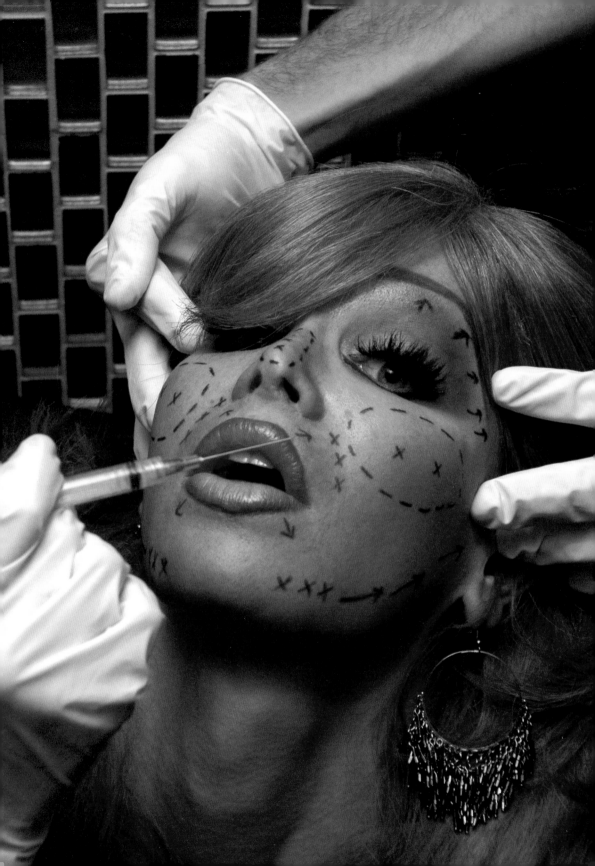